INTRODUCTION TO THE BEVERAGE SPECIALIST CERTIFICATE

MW01092889

The Society of Wine Educators' Beverage Specialist Certificate is an entry-level program designed for students and professionals in the hospitality and culinary fields, as well as individuals looking to enter the wine, spirits, culinary, or hospitality industries. The program provides a broad base of product knowledge in the most commercially relevant beverages including wine, spirits, beer, sake, cider, coffee, and tea. The Beverage Specialist Certificate represents the Society of Wine Educators' recognition that the holder has attained working knowledge about beverage products and the beverage industry, equivalent to a first-line supervisor or manager.

The Beverage Specialist Certificate is offered as a self-paced, self-study program. The course registration fee includes access to the Online Beverage Specialist Certificate Course for one full year as well as access to the final online exam. The final exam consists of 80 multiple-choice questions; a minimum score of 75% (the equivalent of 60 correct questions) is required to pass. Successful completion of the online exam will earn candidates the Beverage Specialist Certificate.

For more information about the Beverage Specialist Certificate program, please visit the website of the Society of Wine Educators at http://www.societyofwineeducators.org/.

© 2017 The Society of Wine Educators

All rights reserved. No part of this publication may be reproduced or utilized in any form or by any means, electronic or mechanical, including photocopying and recording, or by any information storage and retrieval system, without permission in writing from the publisher.

This publication is intended to provide accurate information about the subject matter covered; however, facts and figures regarding numbers of appellations, relative rankings of countries, and legalities are all liable to change over time. Please contact the Society of Wine Educators if you have any questions or comments about the contents of this guide.

BEVERAGE SPECIALIST CERTIFICATE

An Educational
Resource Published
by the Society of
Wine Educators

SOCIETY
of WINE
EDUCATORS

BEVERAGE
SPECIALIST
CERTIFICATE

STUDY GUIDE

ABOUT THE SOCIETY OF WINE EDUCATORS

The Society of Wine Educators (SWE) is a membership-based nonprofit organization focused on providing wine and spirits education along with the conferral of several certifications. The Society is internationally recognized and its programs are highly regarded for both their quality and relevance to the industry.

The mission of the Society of Wine Educators is to set the standard for quality and responsible wine and spirits education and professional certification. SWE is unique among other educational programs in the wine and spirits field due to its diverse programs. Each year, the Society presents an annual conference with over fifty educational sessions and significant opportunities for professional interaction. Education and networking are further enhanced through symposiums, the Society's newsletter, and robust social media efforts.

In addition to the Beverage Specialist Certificate, SWE offers four, higher-level, professional credentials for those seeking to certify their wine and spirits knowledge. These include the Certified Specialist of Wine (CSW), the Certified Specialist of Spirits (CSS), the Certified Wine Educator (CWE), and the Certified Spirits Educator (CSE).

SWE members include the following types of individuals:

- Educators offering classes and tastings
- Instructors in public and private colleges, universities, and hospitality schools
- Importers, distributors, and producers
- Retailers, restaurateurs, and hoteliers
- Industry consultants
- Sommeliers, wine stewards, bartenders, and mixologists
- Culinary and hospitality school students
- Wine and spirits industry media professionals
- Wine and spirits enthusiasts

For more information about the Society's educational and membership programs, please contact us.

Society of Wine Educators
1612 K Street NW, Suite 700
Washington, DC 20006, USA
Telephone: (202) 408-8777
Fax: (202) 408-8677
Website: www.societyofwineeducators.org

TABLE OF CONTENTS

SOCIETY
of WINE
EDUCATORS

COFFEE

Coffee is a brewed beverage derived from the roasted seeds (we call them beans) of a tropical berry plant. Coffee beans are the world's second most valuable traded commodity, following petroleum oil. Coffee exports account for more than half of the foreign exchange of many developing countries. The coffee industry and all its facets employ hundreds of millions of people around the world. The top three countries producing green (unroasted) coffee beans are Brazil, Vietnam, and Colombia. Other leading producers include Indonesia, Ethiopia, Honduras, India, Uganda, and Mexico.

This chapter outlines coffee in the marketplace, the history of coffee, different types of coffee, and how variations in production affect the flavor of the final product.

COFFEE IN THE MARKETPLACE

More than half of all Americans over the age of eighteen drink some form of coffee every day—that's 150 million people—and thirty million of those drink specialty drinks, such as espresso-based coffees. Statistically, one cup of coffee is consumed in the United States each day per American adult, but among coffee drinkers, the average is 2.02 cups a day. This certainly sounds like a solid level of coffee consumption, but the United States does not even make the list of top ten countries in terms of coffee consumption.

The top three coffee-consuming countries in the world are all located in northern Europe. They are, in order, Finland (in the number one spot, at 3.43 cups per person per day), Sweden (number two, at 3.31 cups per person per day) and The Netherlands (number three, at 3.13 cups per person per day). These top three countries are followed by Germany, Norway, Denmark, Belgium, Brazil, Tunisia, and Slovenia respectively. The United States lands at number eleven on the list.

CAFFEINE

One reason for coffee's broad appeal is that it has a mild stimulating effect—thus its widespread use as an early morning "eye-opener" or a mid-afternoon "pick-me-up." The stimulating effect is due to caffeine. Caffeine is present in many types of tea, cola-type drinks, chocolate, and many energy drinks, but coffee is the world's primary source of caffeine.

Technically speaking, caffeine is a central nervous system stimulant and the world's most widely consumed psychoactive drug. While this sounds unnerving, caffeine is legal and unregulated in nearly all parts of the world. In its pure form, caffeine is a bitter, white, organic compound. The effects of caffeine are due to its ability to block the reception of certain naturally-occurring chemicals that cause drowsiness, and its ability to stimulate portions of the autonomic nervous system. Some people experience insomnia or other forms of sleep disturbance if caffeine is consumed late in the afternoon or evening; others experience little or no sleep disturbance.

Caffeine, used in moderation by adults, is generally regarded as safe. Moderate intake is defined by the Mayo Clinic as up to 400 milligrams (mg) a day for adults. The use of caffeine by adolescents is less clearly defined and is not universally advised; however, Mayo Clinic guidelines state that adolescents should be limited to no more 100 milligrams (mg) a day.

Table 1.1: Caffeine in Common Beverages

Below are approximate caffeine levels for some common beverages.
Note: The level of caffeine in coffees and teas may vary widely depending on the variety, origin, brewing process, and other factors.

Type of Beverage	Size	Caffeine
Coffee, brewed	8 ounces (237 ml)	95–200 mg
Decaffeinated coffee, brewed	8 ounces (237 ml)	2–6 mg
Espresso	1 ounce (30 ml)	47–75 mg
Decaffeinated espresso	1 ounce (30 ml)	0–10 mg
Coffee, instant	8 ounces (237 ml)	27–173 mg
Decaffeinated coffee, instant	8 ounces (237 ml)	2–5 mg
Black tea, brewed	8 ounces (237 ml)	14–70 mg
Decaffeinated black tea, brewed	8 ounces (237 ml)	0–12 mg
Green tea, brewed	8 ounces (237 ml)	24–45 mg
Iced tea, brewed	8 ounces (237 ml)	14–70 mg
Iced tea, instant	8 ounces (237 ml)	11–47 mg
Iced tea, ready-to-drink	8 ounces (237 ml)	5–40 mg
Cola-type soda	12 ounces (355 ml)	23–39 mg
Diet cola-type soda	12 ounces (355 ml)	23–47 mg
Root beer-type soda	12 ounces (355 ml)	0–18 mg
Lemon-lime-type soda	12 ounces (355 ml)	0–55 mg
Energy drink	8 ounces (237 ml)	70–100 mg
Energy shot	2 ounces (60 ml)	200–207 mg

Source: http://www.mayoclinic.org/healthy-lifestyle/

As with all stimulants, caffeine has both positive and potentially negative health effects. Among its positive effects, caffeine may have a moderate preventative effect against some diseases, including Parkinson's disease. On the negative side, extended use of caffeine may produce a mild dependence resulting in withdrawal-like symptoms such as headache or irritability if an individual suddenly stops the intake of coffee (or other source of caffeine). Other ill effects—which are usually seen if daily intake rises above the "moderate" level—include irritability, stomach upset, and muscle tremors. There is also evidence that the intake of caffeine may have more serious, negative health effects—such as increased blood pressure. As in all things, one should consult the advice of a physician if there are questions about the use of caffeine.

THE HISTORY OF COFFEE

We may never know for sure when or where coffee was first discovered, but a colorful legend from the ancient coffee forests of the Ethiopian plateau is the tale most often told. As the story goes, a goat herder named Kaldi noticed his goats became giddy after eating berries from a certain bush. The goats were so giddy they stayed up all night, showing very little interest in rest or sleep. Kaldi relayed this observation to the Abbot of the local monastery. The Abbot prepared a drink with the berries, and he found he was able to stay alert and focused throughout his long hours of evening prayer. Soon, the knowledge of the energizing berries spread throughout the monastery. Eventually, the news moved east and the consumption and appreciation of coffee reached the Arabian Peninsula. From there, it would begin its journey across the world.

Coffee cultivation and trade began on the Arabian Peninsula. By the 15th century, coffee was being grown in the Yemeni district of Arabia. Soon thereafter, the Yemeni town of Mocca became particularly well-known for its distinct and aromatic roasted coffee beverages.

By the next century, coffee was popular in Persia, Egypt, Syria, and Turkey. Coffee was prepared and enjoyed in homes, and was beginning to be offered in public coffee houses—known as *qahveh khaneh*— appearing in the Middle and Near East. Coffee houses quickly became popular for all kinds of social activity and for keeping up with the latest news and local information—so much so that coffee houses soon became known as "schools of the wise."

Figure 1.1: Traditional Turkish coffee making

With thousands of people from all over the world making annual pilgrimages to the holy city of Mecca (located in present-day Saudi Arabia), it was not long before knowledge of the "wine of Araby" began to spread. Soon, Europeans had heard of this mysterious black beverage, and in 1615, Venetian merchants brought coffee to Italy from Istanbul. It didn't take long for coffee to become popular across the European continent.

Some people reacted to this new beverage with suspicion or fear. In some cases, the local clergy condemned coffee as the "bitter invention of Satan." The controversy became so ingrained that Pope Clement VIII was asked to intervene. He agreed to do so, and upon tasting coffee for the first time, found it delightful, and deserving of papal approval.

As they had in the East, coffee houses began to spring up in London and were soon emulated across England, Austria, France, Germany, and Holland. These coffee houses were soon hubs of social activity and communication. They were often called "penny universities," because for one penny (the price of a cup of coffee) one could learn the news of the day.

By the mid-1600's, coffee came to the New World by way of New Amsterdam (later known as New York). As in previous locations, coffee houses began to appear in the New World. However, the population— dominated by English colonists—still preferred tea. This all changed on December 16, 1773, when the colonists staged a revolt against a heavy tax on tea imposed by King George III. This event, known as the Boston Tea Party, forever changed the American preference from tea to coffee.

In the meantime, coffee plantations were spreading throughout the world. By the 1700s, the first European coffee plantation was established on the Dutch island of Java. Not long after, the Dutch introduced coffee to their South American colony of Surinam, and from there it spread to French Guyana, Colombia, and ultimately to Brazil—currently the largest producer of coffee.

In 1720, a French naval officer acquired a single coffee plant in Paris and brought it—at great peril— back to his post in Martinique. Once planted, this single coffee plant thrived and is today credited with the propagation of over eighteen million coffee plants on the island of Martinique and throughout the Caribbean.

Travelers, traders, and colonists continued to spread the culture, consumption, and cultivation of coffee worldwide. Coffee was soon grown on large plantations and small plots, in tropical forests, and high in the mountains. By the end of the 18th century, coffee had become one of the world's most valuable commodities.

THE CULTIVATION OF COFFEE

Coffee is cultivated in a tropical climate band that circles the earth between the Tropic of Cancer and the Tropic of Capricorn. While different coffee varieties require slightly different conditions, in general, coffee plants need plentiful rainfall interspersed with dry periods and consistently warm temperatures.

The coffee plant itself has dark, waxy, green leaves and powerfully aromatic, white flowers that grow along the length of each branch. As the growing season progresses, these flowers are replaced by oval-shaped berries (often called "cherries") containing seeds—the coffee beans.

Figure 1.2: Coffee flowers

Most coffee cherries have two seeds that develop with flat facing sides. In rare cases, about 5% of the time, only one of the two seeds is fertilized, and a single seed develops into an oval- or pea-shaped bean. These unique beans are known as "peaberries" and are considered by some coffee aficionados to have a more concentrated flavor. This is yet to be proven; however, it has been observed that peaberries roast more evenly due to the rounded shape of the bean.

Coffee plants can grow to about 30 feet (9 m) in height unless they are pruned—and most trees are, in order to make them accessible for hand harvesting. Peak harvest times in the Northern Hemisphere fall between December and March; in the Southern Hemisphere, the harvest typically occurs sometime between May and September. Some coffee-producing countries (Kenya, for example) experience two harvests a year; of these, one will be the main crop and one will be a smaller, secondary crop known as the "fly-crop."

Although there are close to one hundred distinct species in the *Coffea* genus, only two of these are widely grown for coffee beans: *Coffea arabica (Arabica)* and *Coffea canephora (Robusta)*. Arabica is considered to produce the highest-quality beans and therefore the superior beverage. Over 60% of the world's coffee harvest and the great majority of high-quality specialty coffee is Arabica. Robusta coffee makes up about 35% of the global coffee harvest. Robusta coffee is primarily used—in small portions—in coffee blends, and comprises the majority of lower-grade commodity coffee products. Each species has different growing requirements and produces coffee with distinctive characteristics.

Arabica coffee is sought after for its acidity, complexity, aromatic quality, and fresh, delicate taste. Arabica is more difficult to grow than Robusta, requiring an even climate and higher altitudes, which often means challenging mountainous terrain for growers and harvesters. Arabica is also susceptible to pests and diseases and has a lower yield than Robusta, at 1,500 to 3,000 kilograms per hectare (1,340–2,680 pounds per acre), versus 2,300 to 4,000 kilograms per hectare (2,050–3,570 pounds per acre) for Robusta. The relative difficulty of growing Arabica and its superior bean quality means it typically has a higher price.

Robusta is more tolerant of climatic extremes and can be grown at lower altitudes than Arabica, making it possible to harvest by machine. It has a higher yield and can have caffeine levels as much as 50% higher than Arabica beans. Robusta coffee is known for its robust flavor and body and is often included in blends to give them a rounder mouthfeel. In addition, it is often added to espresso blends to improve the *crema*, the desirable layer of foam on top of brewed espresso.

Figure 1.3: Ripe Arabica coffee cherries

HARVESTING COFFEE

Coffee cherries turn bright red when ripe, but not all cherries on a single plant will ripen at once. This uneven maturation may extend the work of the harvest over several months. Workers can harvest from 100 to 200 pounds of coffee cherries each day, which yields twenty to forty pounds of green coffee beans.

Depending on the terrain and the type of coffee being farmed (high quality versus commercial quality); one of following three methods is used:

- Selective picking: This is a handpicking process whereby individual cherries are selected as they ripen. This may be accomplished entirely by hand or may be done with a comb that is used to "rake" the tree, shaking loose the ripe cherries. Unripe cherries are left on the plant for future picking. Selective picking requires multiple passes through the field to harvest the cherries as they ripen, and is therefore used for high-quality beans that can be priced to support this labor-intensive picking method.
- Strip picking: In strip picking, all cherries, both ripe and unripe, are stripped by hand from each branch and collected in sheets beneath the plant. This process is somewhat less laborious than selective picking—requiring only one trip through the field. Unripe and overripe cherries are later separated from the ripe ones.
- Mechanical harvesting: Machines can be used for harvesting coffee beans only where the terrain allows. The coffee harvester is similar in concept to a grape harvester. The machine straddles the plant and agitates it, causing ripe and unripe

cherries to drop into a collection tray. The berries are sorted after picking. Mechanical harvesting is most often used in Brazil, where the landscape is relatively flat and the coffee plantations are immense.

At the completion of each day's harvest, the coffee cherries are transported to the processing plant. Processing should begin as soon as possible to avoid spoilage or contamination of the fruit.

Figure 1.4: The harvest of Arabica beans

PROCESSING COFFEE

After the harvest, the coffee cherries must be processed. Processing includes separating the beans from the pulp, drying the beans, and preparing them for roasting. When the cherries are picked, a thin coating known as the silver skin surrounds the seeds. Outside the silver skin is a parchment-like layer known as the endocarp. The endocarp is surrounded by a slick layer of mucilage called the parenchyma. The endocarp and the mucilage must be removed prior to export.

There are three principal methods used to process coffee: the dry method, the wet method, and the pulped natural method (also known as the semi-washed method). The particular method used to process the coffee cherries depends upon location, local resources, and the quality of the beans. The processing method used has a large impact on the flavor and quality of the resulting coffee beans.

Dry method: The dry method is the easiest and least expensive, but it cannot be used in humid regions or areas where it is likely to rain during the drying period. Almost all Robusta coffees are processed this way, as well as most of Brazil's and Ethiopia's Arabica crop. Dry method processing results in full-bodied coffees that are smooth and rich. The three basic steps are cleaning, drying, and hulling.

- Cleaning: In this stage, ripe cherries are separated from unripe cherries, dirt, sticks, and debris. This can be done by winnowing, using a large sieve, or by a flotation method in which the cherries are placed in water and the ripe cherries sink to the bottom, leaving debris and green cherries floating at the water's surface.
- Drying: The ripe cherries are then spread out in the sun, either on large concrete patios or on tables with netting or wire mesh to allow circulation around the cherries. If a patio is used, the cherries must be raked frequently to ensure even drying and avoid the formation of mildew. In the case of tables, the cherries are turned by hand. The cherries are often covered at night and during rain to keep them dry. The goal is to reduce the moisture content of the cherries from 50% at harvest to 12.5% maximum, and often as low as 11%. Depending on the climate and weather, this process may take as long as four weeks. The process can be sped up by transferring the cherries into drying machines. Drying is essential in preserving the beans. Insufficiently dried cherries may invite bacteria. On the other hand, over-drying is equally undesirable because it makes the beans brittle and creates the potential for broken beans.
- Hulling: In dry-processed coffee, hulling removes the entire dried outer coating of the coffee beans, including the parchment. After hulling, the beans are bagged, stored in warehouses, and readied for export.

Wet method: Coffee processed by the wet, or washed method is considered higher quality because the process better preserves the sensory qualities of the bean. This method is used for almost all Arabica coffees (with the exception of those grown in Brazil) and results in a pure-tasting coffee with bright, fruity flavors that retain acidity. The steps are as follows:

- Cleaning: This step is essentially the same as in the dry method.

- Pulping: In wet method processing, the pulp is removed from the cherries by machine before drying. The skin and pulp are removed leaving the mucilage (parenchyma), parchment, and silver skin layers still surrounding the beans. The beans are next separated by weight as they pass through water channels. The lighter beans float to the top, while the heavier, ripe beans sink to the bottom.
- Fermentation: After separation, the beans are transported to large, water-filled tanks where the fermentation process takes place. This is not an alcoholic fermentation but rather an enzymatic process that breaks down the mucilage layer so it can be washed away. Depending on a combination of factors—the condition of the beans, the weather, and the altitude—this step will take twelve to forty-eight hours to dissolve the mucilage completely. When this stage is complete, the beans feel rough to the touch. After the beans are rinsed, they are ready for the next step.
- Drying: After fermentation, the beans are dried in the sun using the same raking or stirring techniques used in the dry processing method. After drying, wet-processed coffee is referred to as "parchment coffee." At this point, it may be bagged and stored in warehouses.
- Hulling: At some point before export, the parchment coffee will be hulled. In wet-processed coffee, hulling machinery removes the parchment layer from the processed coffee beans.

Figure 1.5: Arabica beans in the fermentation stage of wet processing

Pulped natural method: The pulped natural method, also called the semi-wet method, is a variation on the wet method where the beans are not fermented. Instead, the mucilage is removed by machine. This method combines some of the most desirable sensory traits of the wet and dry methods resulting in coffee with body and sweetness while retaining some acidity.

SORTING AND GRADING

In high-quality coffee production, workers inspect the coffee to remove over-fermented, broken, insect-damaged, or otherwise defective beans. The remaining beans are sorted and graded according to size, density and color. Sorting by size is carried out using screens of different gauges. Sorting by density involves a machine using calibrated air pressure to blow less-dense beans from among the heavier, denser ones. Color sorting may be done by hand, or by computerized machine. The dried beans may also be polished to remove any remaining silver skin, although this is considered optional.

At this point, the beans are referred to as "green coffee"—processed but unroasted coffee beans. Green coffee is typically bagged in jute or burlap and warehoused until ready for export and roasting.

COFFEE ROASTING

To roast coffee, the green beans are heated to between 350°F and 500°F (177°C and 260°C) for eight to fifteen minutes. During this time, the beans lose moisture and undergo physical and chemical changes that transform the green coffee into the variously-hued, brown beans familiar to coffee lovers. Roasting coffee softens the beans, transforms the aromatics, and does much to create the flavor profile of the finished coffee.

Coffee beans are typically roasted inside a heated drum that rotates slowly, keeping the beans moving throughout the process to avoid burning. For the first six or seven minutes after the raw beans are released into the drum, they absorb heat and shrivel, releasing their moisture. As they reach 220°F (105°C), they begin to change color from light green to yellow-tan. As they reach 370° (188°C), the beans swell in size and further change color as a result of caramelization (the oxidation of the beans' sugars) and the Maillard reaction (a chemical reaction that occurs between amino acids and sugars in dry heat). These chemical changes create new aromatic compounds that contribute to the flavor complexity of the finished coffee.

When the beans approach an internal temperature of around 400°F (205°C), they begin to release a highly

fragrant oil called *caffeol* (coffee oil). At this time, a heat-induced chemical decomposition process called *pyrolysis* begins—marked by the darkening color of the beans.

Soon thereafter, closer to an internal temperature of 420°F (216°C), the beans split, making a popping sound caused by the rupture of the bean as trapped heat and steam escape. Depending on the desired level of the roast, the beans go through one or two of these stages known as the "first crack" and the "second crack." At the first crack, the bean swells and turns light brown. At this stage, light roast coffees' roasting process is complete. Medium and dark roast coffees will continue to heat until they reach an internal temperature approaching 450°F (232°C), when the second crack occurs. At this point, the beans appear medium-to-dark brown and begin to develop an oily sheen.

Figure 1.6: Darkly roasted coffee beans in a modern roaster

It is up to the roaster to determine the ideal roast. Under-roasted beans may show green, vegetal aromas and create a watery, overly acidic, brewed coffee. As the beans darken, their acidity decreases and sugars caramelize, creating brewed coffee with lower acidity and fuller body. However, at a certain point, the beans begin to turn bitter and charred. As with any such art, it is a balancing act; the roaster's goal being to maximize the complexity of the coffee's flavor without masking the subtleties inherent to the bean's variety and place of origin. After roasting, the beans are immediately cooled. After being cooled, the beans need to "rest," from one day for lighter roasts, to a week for darker roasts. As they rest, they continue to release the carbon dioxide remaining in the beans. For this reason, packaging with one-way valves that allow the egress of carbon dioxide without allowing air inside is often used to preserve roasted coffee before use.

Despite widespread practices, freshly roasted coffee is best used within three months. Purists may claim the ideal usage time is much shorter—a few days or a week. Due to this fact, coffee roasting is generally performed by importing countries to allow the roasted beans to reach the consumer as quickly as possible.

COFFEE ROASTS

The final character of a batch of roasted coffee beans depends on several factors including the variety of the coffee beans, country or region of origin, and degree of the roast. In general, it's believed that subtle nuances inherent in a bean due to its region of origin are best expressed in lighter roasts. The darker the roast the more dominant the flavors derived from the roasting process become—to the point where they overpower most regional characteristics.

Coffee roasts are typically divided into three basic categories: light roasts, medium roasts, and dark roasts. The names given to different levels of roasts and individual coffee styles are quite subjective and can vary from country to country and region to region. In general, the basic categories of coffee roasts can be described as follows:

Light Roasts: Light roast coffees are generally roasted until just before or just after the first crack. Light roast coffee appears light-to-medium brown with no oily sheen on the outside of the beans. Light-roast coffee beverages tend to be lighter in body, higher in acidity, and show flavors of toasted grain but no charred or roasted flavors. Regional characteristics are better retained in light-roasted coffee as opposed to darker roasts and, as such, many roasters specializing in single-origin coffee prefer light roasts. Common aromas include malty, floral, herbal, citrus, and hay. Terms used to describe variations of light roast coffee include the following:
- Cinnamon Roast (roasted to before the first crack)
- New England Roast (roasted to before the first crack)
- City Roast (roasted to just after the first crack)

Medium Roasts: Medium roast coffees are typically roasted until just before the second crack. Medium roast coffee appears medium-brown with some oil beginning to show on the beans. They tend to be slightly less acidic, but with more complexity and body than light roast coffees. Taste components include a bit of both sweetness and bitterness, and typical aromas include chocolate, ripe berries, and caramel. Medium to medium-plus roasts are sometimes used for espresso. Terms used to describe variations of medium roast coffee include the following:
- Breakfast Roast
- American Roast
- Full City Roast
- Vienna Roast (often considered medium-dark)
- Continental Roast (often considered medium-dark)

Dark Roasts: Dark roast coffees are typically roasted until just after the second crack. Dark roast beans have a dark brown-to-black color and an oily sheen. Dark roast coffees lose the subtle "place of origin" flavors, but take on more flavors from the roasting process itself. Dark roast coffees are somewhat spicy, somewhat bitter, and not at all sweet. Dark roast coffees are ideal for beverages made with milk and sugar, and are sometimes used for espresso. Typical aromas include smoke, toasted nuts, char, carbon, caramel, chocolate, or burnt sugar. Terms used to describe variations of dark roast coffee include the following:
- Italian Roast
- French Roast
- Spanish Roast
- New Orleans Roast
- High Roast

Grades of Coffee Roasting

Figure 1.7: Color representation of various levels of coffee roasts

STORING COFFEE

Coffee should be stored in an airtight container in a cool, dark, dry place. If coffee is received in a non-airtight container (as may be the case with either retail or bulk purchases), it is best to transfer the beans into airtight containers for storage. Coffee beans can look beautiful stored in a glass jar on a shelf or kitchen counter, but light can compromise the flavor components of the beans, so an opaque container is preferred. A cool spot is also important, so it is best to avoid a shelf or storage area next to cooking equipment or in direct sunlight.

If at all possible, coffee should be stored as whole beans and ground only as needed. Contact with air, moisture, and heat have a negative effect on coffee freshness. Whole beans offer less vulnerability, via surface area, to the atmosphere. Ground coffee, on the other hand, will lose its freshness in a matter of days.

The use of the freezer for long-term storage of coffee is open to debate. Some experts argue that beans retain their freshness over long periods of time stored in the freezer (with the caveat that the beans are very well-wrapped and airtight to avoid absorbing moisture). Other experts believe that the absorption of off-flavors is inevitable with prolonged freezing or even refrigeration.

THE GRIND

The grind is one of the most important facets of making a good cup of coffee—yet it is often the most overlooked. The level (coarse to fine), uniformity, and freshness of the grind will have a great impact on the overall quality of the finished beverage.

The level of extraction achieved in making a cup of coffee will vary by the length of time the coffee solids are in contact with the water as well as the level of the grind. As such, coarser grinds are used in brewing methods with longer immersion times (such as French press or percolation), and shorter brew times, such as those used in making espresso, require finer grinds. In either case, an uneven grind can cause "channels" to form in the coffee grounds, which will cause a portion of the coffee to be over-extracted and other areas to be somewhat untouched—leading to bitter, bad-tasting coffee. The proper grind for a specific coffee beverage varies based on the method of brewing, so it is wise to choose your coffee machine before investing in a coffee grinder. Keep in mind; some commercial coffee machines have built-in grinders.

There are two basic types of stand-alone grinders: blade grinders and burr grinders. Blade grinders (coffee mills) are generally inexpensive and work similar to a blender with one whirling blade. Blade grinders are easy to use and maintain, but tend to wear out quickly and may produce an uneven grind. Burr grinders, with gear-like blades that grind against each other, are considered superior and can produce consistent, even grinds with versatility and precision. The downside is that burr grinders are expensive, and take some skill and practice to switch out and maintain the blades and adjust the level of the grind.

The basic grind levels for coffee and their appropriate uses are as follows:
- Coarse grind: Coarse grind coffee has easily visible "chunks" and is often described as resembling the texture of potting soil. Coarse grind coffee is useful for cold brew coffee, or for use with a percolator.
- Medium-coarse grind: Medium-coarse grind is slightly finer than coarse grind, but still visibly chunky. Medium-coarse grind coffee is often used in French press and other types of immersion brewers, or for cupping.
- Medium grind: Medium grind coffee is sometimes described as being the size of coarse sand or kosher salt. Medium grinds are often used with auto drip makers with flat-bottom filters.
- Medium-fine grind: Medium-fine grind coffee is often used in pour-over (filter cone) brewing.
- Fine grind: Fine grind coffee appears smooth, and may resemble the texture of sugar or salt. Fine grind coffee is used for espresso.
- Very fine grind: Very fine grind coffee has a powdery texture almost like flour, and is most often used in Turkish coffee.

Figure 1.8: Much depends upon the level of the grind

BREWING COFFEE

There are two main methods of brewing coffee: immersion (ground coffee is immersed in water for a period of time) and pour-over (water is poured over and through the ground coffee). Other more specialized methods certainly exist, and two of these—espresso and cold brew—are discussed later in this chapter.

Of these methods, there is no "best" or "right" way to produce coffee. Each method offers something different in terms of flavor, body, ease of operation, time required, and necessary equipment. When making a decision for a particular coffee program, consider cost, taste, service style, and convenience. Whatever the chosen method, best practices for brewing coffee are intended to give the customer the absolute best cup of coffee possible. Some of the basic procedures to ensure a quality cup of coffee are listed below:

- Filtered or spring water is best for coffee as tap water may impart off-flavors to the finished product, and distilled water's lack of mineral content can make coffee taste flat.
- The water should be just slightly "off-boil". A temperature range of 195°F to 205°F (91°C to 96°C) is considered ideal.
- As previously discussed, the level (fineness) of the grind used depends on the method of preparing the coffee.
- The temperature of a freshly-brewed cup of coffee is typically close to 180°F (82°C), but its flavors are likely to show best at 140°F (60°C).

- Coffee should not be pre-made, heated on a burner, or left to idle on a hot plate; these practices cause water to evaporate from the coffee and results in a burnt flavor. The preferred method to keep coffee warm and flavorful (for up to thirty minutes) is to pour the freshly-brewed coffee into an insulated carafe.
- Proper cleaning of coffee-making equipment can have a surprising effect on beverage quality. Coffee oils accumulate on machine parts and quickly become rancid, making coffee taste sour or metallic.

Best practices specific to each brewing method are discussed in the sections that follow.

POUR-OVER BREWING

The pour-over process, as its name states, involves hot water passing through the ground coffee at a steady rate. This process uses medium-fine grind coffee, because the water does not stay in contact with the coffee for very long. The pour-over method has several advantages: it produces what most people consider to be a classic cup of coffee, it gives the operator a high degree of control over the finished product, and it is ideal for single-cup or small batch brewing—which allows a restaurant to provide customers with the freshest possible product. In addition, this method is fairly easy to perfect and inexpensive in terms of equipment needed.

The pour-over brewing method requires a brew chamber and a filter. Most equipment designed to produce single servings or small amounts of coffee use a paper filter. Paper filters trap many of the coffee's insoluble oils, producing a beverage of lighter texture and good clarity. Metal filters, often used in auto-drip coffee makers, retain the coffee oils and sediment, producing a fuller-bodied cup of coffee with richer flavors. (Note that while not required, it is often possible to use a paper filter inside the metal filter of a commercial coffee machine.)

A sample procedure for single-serving pour-over coffee brewing is as follows:
- Bring a kettle of water to the boil.
- Place a filter in the brew chamber (coffee filter holder) and arrange it over a cup or other container.

Figure 1.9: The pour over brewing method

- Place a measure of freshly-ground, medium-fine grind coffee in the filter. Make sure the coffee is evenly distributed. The ideal proportion of coffee to water will vary, however, two tablespoons of coffee (0.38 ounces [10.6 grams]) to six ounces (177 ml) of water is an often-quoted ratio.
- Once the water is boiling, remove the kettle from the heat, and allow the water to cool to the ideal temperature of 195°F to 205°F (91°C to 96°C).
- Begin the process by pouring just enough water over the grounds to wet them evenly. This step allows a final "de-gassing" or "bloom" of the coffee grounds, and you may notice that a few bubbles appear in the grounds—this is a good sign. (Recall that fresh coffee beans release carbon dioxide gas.)
- After thirty seconds have passed, carefully pour the rest of the water through the grounds at a slow, steady pace. Ideally, this step should take two to three minutes—avoid pouring so quickly that the grounds form a "pool" or start to float.
- Once the water has dripped through, the coffee is ready to enjoy!

The auto-drip method is actually a machine-made variation on the pour-over method. This is the most common brewing method used in American offices and homes. The auto-drip method is so ubiquitous in the United States that it is often associated with bland, poor-quality coffee, but this does not have to be the case. Even with the use of large-scale coffee makers, the operator has control over many aspects of the process. These may include the quality of the water, the freshness of the beans, the level of the grind, the ratio of coffee to water, the brew temperature, and the brew time.

If approached with care, the auto-drip method can be used to produce consistent, quality coffee in large batches. However, there is one serious caveat to the quality of machine-brewed coffee: most coffee machines come equipped with a hot plate that, as mentioned in previous sections, will quickly have a negative impact on the quality of the coffee. Do your customers, co-workers, and friends a favor by turning the hot plate off (or, better yet, disconnecting it) and use insulated carafes instead.

IMMERSION BREWING

For the immersion brewing method, medium-to-coarsely ground coffee beans are fully immersed in hot water for a short period of time. This process produces rich, full-bodied coffee full of flavors and oils (and quite possibly some sediment). The French press is perhaps the most widely known and used immersion-brewing device. It is ideal for making small amounts, single serving to several cups, of freshly-brewed coffee.

A sample immersion brewing procedure using a 4-cup French press is as follows:
- Bring a kettle of water to the boil.
- Preheat the press and plunger by pouring the hot water into the container, adding the plunger, and allowing it to rest for thirty seconds. Before continuing, drain the container.
- Add five tablespoons (27 grams) of coffee to the container. (This example is based on a typical ratio of fifteen parts water to one part coffee or roughly three tablespoons ground coffee for every cup of water). Give the container a gentle shake in order to level out the coffee.
- After the water has cooled to 195°F to 205°F (91°C to 96°C), pour just enough water into the container to barely submerge all of the coffee. Using a wooden spoon or chopstick, gently stir the coffee to ensure that all of the grounds are wet.
- After thirty seconds, pour in the rest of the water to a total of 1 ¾ cups (400 g/415 ml).
- Push the plunger down just far enough to submerge the grounds.
- Set the timer and allow the coffee to steep for two to four minutes.
- After sufficient time has elapsed, lower the plunger to the base of the carafe and immediately pour the coffee into a cup or insulated carafe to avoid over-extraction.

Besides the French press, other systems such as the Aero Press and Café Solo may be used for immersion brewing.

COLD BREW

Despite the name, cold brew is essentially an immersion method of brewing coffee in room-temperature water. Cold brewing will take from twelve to twenty-four hours to complete and requires a coarse grind. Cold brewing results in a cup of coffee that is smooth, concentrated, and decidedly low in acid. While a home-version of cold brew might be made with standard home kitchen equipment, specialized cold brewing equipment is available and appropriate for commercial use. Typical cold brewing steps are outlined below:

- Use four ounces of coarse ground coffee and four cups of water (of course, the ratio may vary).
- To begin, place the coffee into a container and pour one cup of water over the grounds.
- Wait five minutes and add the remaining three cups of water by slowly pouring in a circular motion.
- Use a wooden spoon or similar implement to press down on the top of the mixture in order to ensure that all of the grounds are wet.
- Cover and allow the coffee to steep for twelve to twenty-four hours.
- To finish the cold brew, line a fine mesh sieve or a cone with a standard coffee filter, and work in batches to filter the coffee. Repeat the filtering process if necessary.
- Transfer the coffee to a clean container and store either on the counter (but out of the sun) or in the refrigerator, for up to five days.

Keep in mind, cold brew coffee is concentrated, so it is often served diluted with either water or milk. Iced coffee aficionados swear by the superiority of cold brew coffee.

ESPRESSO

Espresso is a strong, rich coffee prepared according to its own method, made-to-order, and served by the "shot." This might seem a bit confusing, as the term "espresso" is often used to refer to a certain type of coffee bean or a certain style of coffee roast. However, used properly, the term refers to a specific type of coffee beverage defined by its production method, just like the terms "French press" and "pour-over."

Figure 1.10: The French press

A shot of espresso requires the use of specialized equipment along with finely ground, tightly packed coffee grounds. An espresso machine provides hot water under high pressure (roughly 135 psi), shortening the extraction time. The entire process should take less than thirty seconds and produces a coffee beverage with a high level of dissolved solids and emulsified oils. This yields intense coffee flavor, rich body, a robust-yet-balanced taste profile, and a distinctive layer of caramel-colored foam (crema) on top.

Many variables go into the formula for the "perfect" espresso. Every barista probably has his or her preferred technique—so much so that there may never be a true consensus on the matter. However, it can be agreed that the most important element is the espresso machine itself and the recommendations of its manufacturer. While variations will inevitably exist, a good starting formula is as follows: to produce a one ounce shot of espresso, begin with six to eight grams of medium or dark roast coffee ground fine and evenly. Next, the coffee is pressed ("tamped") into the espresso machine's portafilter, which is then locked into the espresso machine. Whether you pull a lever or push a button, the machine starts with pressurized water—typically heated to 185°F to 205°F (85°C to 96°C)—flowing through the coffee grounds, and the espresso flows into a demitasse cup placed below the filter.

Figure 1.11: Espresso

ESPRESSO-BASED BEVERAGES

While many people insist that the best way to drink espresso is an unadulterated shot, the popularity of espresso based drinks, made with an endless variety of milk and flavorings, cannot be denied. Some of the most well-known and popular espresso drinks are listed below. However, please keep in mind that different countries, cultures, and even neighborhoods may adopt their own version of a particular beverage.

- Americano: a double shot of espresso diluted with a dash of hot water; the espresso is pulled atop the hot water to ensure the consistency of the crema
- Caffe Corretto: espresso "corrected" with a measure of liqueur, grappa, or other brandy
- Cappuccino: equal parts espresso and foamy steamed milk, served in a standard cup; it is often said that cappuccino is 1/3 steamed milk, 1/3 espresso, and 1/3 foam
- Cortado: foamed milk and espresso; ½ espresso, ½ foamy milk; served in a gibraltar glass
- Espresso Romano: a shot of espresso with a slice of lemon served on the side
- Flat White: steamed milk and espresso in a ratio of 1/3 espresso and 2/3 steamed milk topped with a very thin layer of foam; served in a six to eight ounce cup (also known as an "Australian latte")

- Latte: steamed milk and espresso with a thin layer of foam served in a standard cup; 1/3 espresso and 2/3 steamed milk
- Lungo: "long" espresso made with twice the typical amount of water in order to make a somewhat weaker, 2 to 3 ounce espresso; served in a standard cup
- Macchiato: a shot of espresso served with a dollop of frothed milk in a demitasse cup. Macchiato means "stained" (as in "stained milk") and refers to the fact that the steamed milk is put into the cup first, and the espresso is pulled atop the milk
- Mocha: espresso, milk, and cocoa (hot chocolate) typically served in a ratio of 1/3 espresso, 1/3 cocoa, and 1/3 frothed milk; the cocoa goes in the cup first with the espresso pulled on top; whipped cream topping is often requested
- Resentin: more of a tradition than a true beverage, a "little rinser" is a dash of grappa served after a shot of espresso in order to "rinse out" the cup
- Ristretto: espresso "restricted," made with only half of the typical amount of water in order to produce a much stronger espresso; served in a demitasse cup

While not technically a beverage, any discussion of espresso should include mention of the *affogato*. An affogato (Italian for *drowned*) is an espresso-based dessert typically consisting of a scoop (or two) of vanilla gelato with a shot of espresso poured over the top.

Figure 1.12: Affogato

DECAFFEINATED COFFEE

Despite the fact that most coffee drinkers appreciate the energizing effects of caffeine, nearly 10% of all coffee sold (and consumed) is decaffeinated. It should be noted, however, that "decaffeinated" does not mean the coffee contains no caffeine; rather, according to the USDA, the term "caffeine-free" or "decaffeinated" means that 97% of the caffeine has been removed from the beans. This means that an eight-ounce cup of brewed decaffeinated coffee may contain up to six mg of caffeine.

Decaffeination is carried out on green (unroasted) coffee beans in a special industrial plant. The process begins with steaming or soaking the beans in water to open the cell structure and begin the release of water-soluble caffeine. Inevitably, this process also allows oils and flavor constituents to render from the beans, altering the flavor of the final coffee. The challenge, then, is to remove the caffeine while leaving the other chemicals as undisturbed as possible.

To this end, several different methods are used to decaffeinate coffee. They may be roughly categorized into two camps: solvent-based (those that use chemicals) and non-solvent based (those that do not). Nearly 70% of decaffeinated coffee is made using a solvent-based process.

Solvent-based decaffeination procedures use chemicals such as methylene chloride or ethyl acetate to remove the caffeine from beans. In the direct solvent process, green coffee beans are steamed for about thirty minutes to open the pores, and are then rinsed with solvent-laced water for about ten hours in order to extract the caffeine, and then the beans are steamed again to remove any traces of solvent. In a variation known as the indirect solvent process, green coffee beans are soaked in hot water for several hours to remove the caffeine as well as the other flavor elements and oils. The beans are then separated from the water, and the beans are steamed to remove any chemical residue. The caffeine-and-flavor laden liquid is then heated, which allows the solvent chemicals and the caffeine to evaporate away. The green coffee beans are then re-introduced to the water (and its remaining flavors and oils), which allows them to re-absorb most of the flavor components of the original coffee.

Chemical-free (non-solvent) decaffeination was pioneered by the Swiss in the 1930s. The resulting "Swiss Water Process" became commercially available in the 1980s through the Swiss Water Decaffeinated Coffee Company based in British Colombia. The Swiss Water Decaffeinated Coffee Company currently produces the only certified organic and certified kosher decaffeinated coffees in the world.

The Swiss Water Process begins by soaking green coffee beans in hot water in order to extract the caffeine. The water is then passed through a charcoal filter that catches the larger caffeine molecules while allowing the smaller-sized oil and flavor molecules to remain. Next, the soaked, flavorless, caffeine-free beans and the caffeine-charged water are both discarded. A new batch of green coffee beans is then soaked in the caffeine-free but flavor-laden water, allowing the caffeine (but not the flavors or oils) of the new coffee beans to dissolve into the flavorful water. Coffee processed using this method may be up to 99.9% caffeine-free and will be labeled with the term "Swiss Water Decaffeinated Coffee."

A recent innovation in decaffeination, developed at Germany's Max Planck Institute, involves the use of carbon dioxide. This process begins by soaking green coffee beans in water within an enclosed stainless steel tank. Compressed carbon dioxide is then pumped into the tank, which dissolves the caffeine while leaving most of the coffee oils and flavors behind. The caffeine-laden carbon dioxide is then transferred into another container and de-pressurized. This method promises to become a commercially-viable option for processing large volumes of coffee without the use of chemicals.

In addition to the obvious loss of some flavor components, decaffeinated coffee beans also pose a challenge to coffee roasters. The unroasted-yet-decaffeinated beans have a brown, rather than green, appearance, making it difficult to judge the progress of the roasting process. Decaffeinated beans also have low moisture content, causing them to roast faster and, in some cases, unevenly. As such, decaffeinated coffee beans are generally best suited to light and medium roasts.

Figure 1.13: Cupping

CUPPING

The systematic tasting of coffee is known as *cupping*, and professional coffee tasters are often called *cuppers*. Cupping is used to evaluate the aromas, flavors, and overall quality of coffees. As with wine and other beverages, coffee has some universal characteristics that the consumer may notice and appreciate, including aroma, tastes, flavors, and mouthfeel.

Aroma, which is usually the first component to be evaluated, is arguably the most important attribute of coffee. Coffee aromas may range from fruity and sweet, to roasted, earthy, caramel, or spicy—depending on bean origin, roast level, and brewing technique.

Next, the coffee is evaluated by taste. The coffee attributes perceived on the palate include the following:

- Acidity: Acidity is a desirable characteristic that adds brightness to a coffee. It is especially present in Kenyan and Central American coffees, and is promoted by wet processing. Acidity is also thought to be more prevalent in coffees grown at high altitude. The perception of acidity also depends on the degree of roasting (darker roasting decreases acidity) and the brewing method.
- Body: Body (sometimes referred to as texture or mouthfeel) is the weight or thickness of the coffee on the palate. Darker roasts have a fuller body, as do Robusta coffees.
- Bitterness: Bitterness, in small-to-moderate amounts, is a desirable characteristic that adds to the complexity and flavor of coffee. Bitterness is closely tied to the dissolved solids in coffee, which in turn are affected mostly by roast, grind and brewing technique. Robusta coffees tend to have more bitterness than Arabica.
- Flavors: Flavors may range from the obvious "mocha" or coffee flavor to spicy, nutty, chocolate, and a range of other flavors.
- Finish: The finish or aftertaste is as important in coffee as in wine. A lingering finish is often a sign of a superior brew.

Table 1.2 lists some of the more common terms used to describe the characteristics of coffee.

Table 1.2: Coffee Cupping Terms

Aromas	Tastes and Flavors	Mouthfeel
Fruity	Sweet	Smooth
Citrus	Acidic	Rich
Floral	Bitter	Buttery
Caramel	Delicate	Creamy
Resin	Rich	Velvety
Chocolate/cocoa	Intense	Watery
Spicy	Pungent	Oily
Peppery	Flat	Dry
Nutty	Green	Astringent
Malt	Fruity	Gritty
Vanilla	Balanced	Rough
Earthy/leathery	Exotic	
Toast	Chocolate	
Roasted	Spicy	
Smoke	Nutty	

SINGLE-ORIGIN COFFEES

Most commercially-available coffee is a blend of different bean varieties, grown in different locations. These blends are created and produced by individual roasters and commercial brands in order to fill the need for a well-rounded product with general consumer appeal. By contrast, *single-origin coffees* are similar in significance to place-specific, varietal wines—they come from a single coffee variety and a specific place-of-origin intended to showcase flavor characteristics of the variety and growing conditions of the region.

Single-origin coffees are often appreciated for the traceability of their origins and their unique flavors. However, it should be kept in mind that a single estate or farm may occupy many square miles and that single-origin coffees are often defined merely by country of origin (many of which are geographically huge). In addition, some coffee producers believe that milling and roasting should be part of the definition of *single-origin*, but as of yet there is no industry-wide standard for the use of the term in these regards. Almost all single-origin coffees are made using Arabica beans.

As is the case with wines, some coffees are defined by country or region while some use more specific parameters. The term *single farm* or *single estate* may mean that the coffee is sourced from one farm, a group of farms that use a common mill, or from a single co-operative. To truly experience the characteristics of coffee from a single location, one should look for a *micro-lot* coffee labeled with specific information such as the name of a single field on a specific farm, a range of altitudes, a specific day of harvest, specific sub-variety, or other such details.

THE POLITICS OF COFFEE

Many agricultural products sourced in developing countries have, in the past, been traded in such a way that has not proven beneficial to all parties involved. As such, programs and policies associated with ensuring fair labor standards, sustainable farming practices, and parity in international trade have become widespread in parts of the coffee industry. In many instances, these social policy programs have proven successful and are becoming known among and important to coffee buyers and consumers.

Fair trade coffee is traded based on a minimum price guaranteed to the farmer, which helps to keep unscrupulous middlemen out of transactions, provide a living wage to workers, and stabilize a potentially volatile market. Fair trade standards also prohibit child labor and forced labor. In the United States, Fair Trade Certification is granted by the non-profit organization Fair Trade USA; similar organizations control fair trade standards and certification in other parts of the world. In addition to coffee, the fair

trade movement now includes products such as tea, chocolate, spices, and some types of fruit.

Certified organic coffees are those that have been produced without the use of most synthetic substances such as pesticides, herbicides, and fertilizers. In the United States, the U.S. Department of Agriculture sets the standards that must be met for a product to be labeled as "organic." Many other countries have government-defined organic certification as well. In the United States, a coffee may be labeled "organic" if at least ninety-five percent of the beans have been grown under verified organic conditions.

Figure 1.14: Coffee Plantation in India

A type of farming, now referred to as "shade-grown coffee," is the only way coffee was cultivated until new, full-sun coffee varieties were developed in the 1980s. Shade-grown coffee refers to the farming of naturally-occurring varieties of coffee shrubs, cultivated under at least a partial canopy of shade trees. Full-sun coffee plants produce higher yields for farmers and have allowed for the creation of huge coffee plantations. In some cases, these plantations threaten the natural habitat, increase soil erosion, and have decimated migratory bird species.

There is currently no third-party certification available for shade-grown coffee. However, the Smithsonian Migratory Bird Center (SMBC) of the United States has created the Bird Friendly Certification. Bird Friendly standards are very strict in all matters pertaining to sustainability and the environment. To qualify for Bird Friendly Certification, coffee growers must meet organic standards, abide by recommendations for the diversity and size of the trees that make up the canopy, and maintain a minimum of forty percent shade coverage.

TEA

After water, tea is the most consumed beverage in the world. In its earliest and simplest form, tea came from the leaves of the *Camellia sinensis* plant. These leaves are used to create the more traditional range of tea beverages and include white, green, oolong (also spelled wulong), black, and dark teas. Varieties of *Camellia sinensis* are grown on a major commercial scale in Asia, Africa, and South America.

Herbs and botanical ingredients prepared and served like the traditional *Camellia sinensis* beverage are also considered to be types of tea. Often referred to as *tisanes*, these beverages can be created from blends of *Camellia sinensis* varieties, combinations of herbs and botanicals, or blends of *Camellia sinensis* with herbs and botanicals.

The diversity of source ingredients used to create tea result in a rich selection of flavor profiles, cultural associations, and functional benefits that appeal to a wide range of consumers. Beyond its traditional use as a hot beverage, tea is a versatile product that is often enjoyed in chilled, sweetened, pre-packaged, flavored, and even sparkling versions. In addition, tea leaves and tea liquor (the term for liquid tea) can also be used as an ingredient in specialty dishes such as tea-smoked duck and green tea ice cream.

HISTORY OF TEA

Legends relating to the discovery of tea date back some 4,500 years to the time of Shen Nong, the mythical Chinese emperor credited with introducing agriculture and the use of medicinal herbs to mankind. It is said that he was the first to drop tea leaves into boiling water and taste the resulting liquid.

More recently, the oldest physical proof of tea consumption has come from tea found in ancient Chinese tombs. *Camellia sinensis* leaves found with other food remains at a burial site verify that tea was consumed at least 2,100 years ago.

Tea cultivation and processing flourished across China over the centuries, leading to the development of dozens, and potentially hundreds, of distinct processing styles and *Camellia sinensis* plant cultivars. China remains the source for the widest range of tea processing styles and cultivars. The earliest white, green, oolong, yellow, black, and dark teas were all first developed in China.

With time, *Camellia sinensis* tea spread beyond China to reach other countries, many of which are now major tea producers. Buddhist monks from Japan learned of tea cultivation and processing during their visits to Chinese monasteries, and brought tea seeds and knowledge back to Japan starting in the 9th century.

Tea's first appearance in Europe wasn't until the early 17th century, when the Dutch East India Company brought tea leaves to Amsterdam. By the mid-17th century, tea was known in France and had been introduced to the English. European colonization was largely responsible for the spread of commercial tea plantations. For instance, tea was known in India for thousands of years as a medicinal plant, but it was not cultivated on a large scale until the British East India Company established commercial-scale tea production in the areas of Assam and Darjeeling, India in the middle of the 19th century.

Likewise, the first Sri Lankan tea plantation was established in 1867 by James Taylor, a British planter who had arrived in 1852. Not long thereafter (in the 1870s), coffee plantations in Sri Lanka were devastated by a fungal disease known as "coffee rust" or "coffee blight." This disease destroyed entire crops, and after experimenting with cinnamon and cinchona as an alternative crop, most farmers turned to tea. Commercial-scale tea production also began in Kenya while it was under British control in the 1920s.

When Europeans migrated to the Americas (including colonial North America) and elsewhere, they brought their appreciation of tea along with them.

Figure 2.1: Tea Plantation in Sri Lanka

TEA IN THE MARKETPLACE

While Americans have a tea-drinking history that dates back to early colonial times, the current culture of tea in the United States is built on habits popularized in the early 20th century. According to statistics from the Tea Association of the United States, roughly four out of five American adults report drinking some form of tea, with a total of approximately $11 billion consumer dollars spent on tea in 2014. In 2015, the United States imported 285 million pounds of tea, making it the third largest importer of tea after Russia and Pakistan.

Other trends that dominate American tea consumption include the following:
- Approximately 85% of tea consumed in the United States is iced tea.
- While loose-leaf specialty teas have increased in popularity, the vast majority of tea is prepared using either a traditional or pyramid-shaped tea bag.
- Restaurant menus are expanding to include more premium teas along with tea and food pairings.

- About 85% of tea consumed in the United States is black tea, but green teas and oolong (wulong) teas are growing in availability and popularity.

Worldwide, China is by far the largest consumer (and producer) of tea. However, on a per-capita basis, 2014 statistics from the Food and Agriculture Organization of the United Nations (FAOSTAT) cite the top five tea-consuming countries in this order (starting with the highest): Turkey (at 7.54 kg [266 oz] per person annually), Morocco, Ireland, the Republic of Mauritania, and the United Kingdom.

THE TEA PLANT

The tea plant, *Camellia sinensis*, is an evergreen plant that is indigenous to Asia. The plant is a shrub or small tree that can grow up to 30 feet (9 m) in height unless pruned. Commercially grown tea plants are pruned to 2 to 4 feet (0.6 to 1.2 m) in height for ease of picking. Tea is cultivated primarily in the tropics and sub-tropics because the plants require warmth and plentiful rainfall to thrive.

The tea plant produces a new growth of buds and leaves at the ends of its shoots multiple times per year. These new buds and leaves are called "flushes", and only the flushes are harvested. Depending on the location and climate where the tea is grown, tea flushes may be harvested one or more times per year.

In many tea-growing regions, the spring flush is the most important. After the longer, more dormant winter months, the first flush of the year can offer richer, more nuanced teas than those from later in the growing season. This is especially true in China and Japan where the first flush is important for green teas. India's Darjeeling teas are also known for their gentler, more fragrant 1st and 2nd flushes that are highly regarded. In comparison, the Monsoon (sometimes called Rains) and Autumnal flushes of Darjeeling are often considered duller teas.

Figure 2.2: Tea Plantation in Thailand

GROWING TEA

Commodity teas are grown on a commercial scale in a wide range of countries from as far south as Argentina to as far north as Japan. Specialty teas are grown in smaller quantities in places like New Zealand, Hawaii, and Scotland. A 2015 report from the Food and Agriculture Organization of the United Nations recorded these top tea-producing countries:

- China: 2.9 million tons
- India: 1.3 million tons
- Sri Lanka: 709 thousand tons
- Kenya: 480 thousand tons

The conditions most commonly associated with larger production areas include the following:

- Latitude: The major tea-producing areas are found within 35 degrees in both the northern and southern latitudes. This area includes the Equator, the Tropics of Cancer and Capricorn, and much of the growing areas of China, India, Kenya, and Japan.
- Elevation: Teas grown at higher elevations generally result in more complex, flavorful teas than low-grown teas. Taiwan and India have some of the highest tea plantations at elevations of over 6,500 feet (1,980 m) above sea level. Some places, like Sri Lanka, produce low-grown, mid-grown, and high-grown teas.

Other factors can significantly impact the quality of specialty teas. Examples of how environment and growing conditions affect specific teas include the following:

- Climate: Temperature changes occurring before or during harvest impact the quality of Taiwan milk oolong and Nilgiri frost tea.
- Geology: Wulong teas of China's Fujian Province are said to exhibit "yan yun," a set of distinctive flavor characteristics resulting from the absorption of minerals in the mountains where these teas grow.
- Cultivar: Certain varieties of tea have been cultivated to exhibit particular characteristics. Tea varieties used to create silver needle white tea were developed for their longer buds covered with silvery, hair-like filaments.
- Environmental: The presence of other organisms has been associated with certain tea characteristics. Taiwan's *dong fang mei ren* (Oriental beauty) oolong tea gets its signature flavors when the tea leaves react to being bitten by an insect known as the leafhopper.

HARVESTING TEA

In many places, tea is still harvested by hand (known as plucking), but labor and production costs require machine harvesting in other areas, such as Japan. On tea farms, the bushes are grown in compact rows and shaped to create a plucking table—a level top of uniform height that allows for easier harvesting. Bushes are trimmed between flushes to create a flat-topped surface across rows of plants. When the bushes begin to flush, the new sprouts noticeably shoot upward above the surface of the plucking table. This shaping of tea bushes allows for ease of both manual and automated harvests.

Depending on the type of tea produced and the time of the harvest, the pluck may include only the youngest sprout. Another common plucking standard is "two leaves and a bud," which refers to the two youngest leaves just below the bud that contains the underdeveloped next leaf. Two leaves and a bud is one of the most common plucking standards for Chinese green teas and finer Indian teas. In other places, like Taiwan, oolong harvests may extend down the branch from the bud to the first three to four leaves.

Figure 2.3: Tea harvest in Sri Lanka

TEA PROCESSING

The most common stages in the processing of tea include the steps of withering, fixing (or firing), oxidation, rolling and shaping, drying, and sorting. As there are many different methods for creating teas, there is not one consistent formula for the manufacturing process that applies to all. Some stages, like oxidation and shaping, may be done in different sequences or may be repeated several times for many hours.

The main categories of tea are classified, in part, according to the methods used during processing. The primary variables in tea processing are the level of withering and oxidation that are allowed to occur. If the degree of moisture is not controlled through withering, the product is not shelf-stable. If oxidation is not controlled, then the desirable flavor elements within the tea leaves may be lost or altered. These two factors come into play throughout the manufacture of tea.

Withering: Withering (which is sometimes referred to as wilting) is the beginning stage of the tea process. To begin, manufacturers allow a certain amount of moisture loss to occur. This makes the leaves limp, pliable, and easier to manipulate. In the manufacture of some white teas, withering may be the only process that takes place. In this case, the leaves are left to dry thoroughly enough that the enzymes that cause oxidation are deactivated and the tea is dry enough to be a stable product.

Fixing: The processing of green tea needs to involve the prevention of oxidation while allowing for the release of aromatic compounds within the leaf cells. To achieve this, green teas are "fixed." Fixing, which may also be called "firing" or "kill-green" involves applying heat to break down the enzymes that cause oxidation. Fixing can involve hot surfaces (pan firing), surrounding the leaves in hot air, or steaming the leaves. The Chinese green tea called dragonwell *(long jing)* is a classic example of a pan-fired tea. In this procedure, the leaves are pressed flat by hand as skilled processors press and circulate the leaves in the wok-shaped pan. These artisans have learned how to expose the leaves to just the right amount of heat to fix the leaves without burning them. In Japan, the most common method of fixing green teas is steaming. Varying durations of steam can create distinctions in the tea's character.

Oxidizing: Teas such as oolong and black tea undergo a form of fixing, but it occurs after a desired degree of oxidation takes place. As teas oxidize, the flavor and aroma compounds change. Throughout history, tea processors at various locations discovered they could highlight distinct tea flavor profiles by controlling the length of time the teas were oxidized. Chinese *tie guan yin* ("Iron Goddess of Mercy") wulong is a common example of a single kind of tea that can be oxidized to various degrees to create different characteristics. Some tie guan yin is barely oxidized at all, leaving bright green leaves that barely show any indication of the browning effects of oxidation. Other processors allow their tie guan yin to oxidize more fully, until the leaves become a more solid, rust-colored brown. Black tea processing allows for an even fuller amount of oxidation to occur.

Figure 2.4: Fresh tea leaves in the withering stage

Rolling and Shaping: Rolling and shaping may be done by hand or machine, and involves rolling the damp leaves lengthwise into strips and sometimes further into balls or spirals. Rolling releases the oils from the leaves that enhance the flavor of the final beverage. This step may be performed at different stages of the process, depending on the specific style of tea being produced. Green teas are often rolled or shaped during the fixing stage in order to release the aromatic compounds within the leaves. Wulong teas are often rolled after the fixing stage. In some instances, eighteen or more hours are allotted to alternating intervals of rolling and drying.

Drying: In this step, the leaves are dried to remove much of the remaining moisture content to prevent mold or rotting. The final leaf moisture content of most tea leaves is five or six percent.

Sorting: Before packing, many finished teas are graded and sorted according to size and quality—with whole leaves being the most valuable. These classifications include the following:
- Souchong: Large leaf
- Pekoe: Medium leaf (pronounced "peck-oh")
- Orange Pekoe: Small leaf; the term "orange pekoe" indicates the tea is produced from the two-leaves-and-a-bud plucking standard. The term is most often used with Indian and some other black teas.

Broken tea leaves are classified as brokens, fannings, or dust. Brokens are most often used in tea bags; however, there is a misconception that the teas used in teabags are, by default, lower quality. In actuality, any grade or quality of tea can be converted from larger leaves or leaf portions to become the fine pieces found in teabags. These small pieces of broken leaf infuse faster and more evenly than larger leaf pieces.

TRADITIONAL TEAS

The earliest teas imported to the West were *Camellia sinensis* teas brought from Asia to Europe in the early 17th Century. The beverage created from the steeped leaves of this plant was the first to be called tea. In modern times, this form of tea is categorized according to its degree of oxidation. Oxidation refers to the chemical reaction caused by exposure to oxygen. Just as a sliced apple or banana will turn increasingly brown as it is exposed to air, oxidation is the browning of tea leaves.

The major forms of traditional tea include the following:
- White tea: White tea is made from the buds of the tea plant. These buds have a silver-hued fuzz on them, which gives the tea its name. White tea is wilted but undergoes only the most minimal oxidation before the process is halted, making white tea typically the least oxidized and least processed form of tea. Chinese Silver Needle is an example of a white tea.
- Green tea: Green teas have little or no oxidation but are processed to shape (roll) the leaves and preserve the color and flavor of the green leaves before fixation. Following fixation, the green leaves are quickly shaped and dried. Green tea has medium flavor intensity, grassy or nutty flavors, and little or no bitterness. Japanese sencha is a green tea.
- Oolong (or wulong) tea: Oolong is a semi-oxidized tea popularized in South China. After wilting, the tea is oxidized for a short amount of time—longer than green tea but shorter than black tea. There are many different styles of oolong tea and a corresponding range of flavors. Taiwanese dong ding tea is an oolong (wulong) tea.
- Black tea: Black tea is a fully oxidized tea made using all of the production steps. Black tea tends to show robust flavors of earth and honey. Examples of black teas include Ceylon teas (from Sri Lanka), Indian teas such as Darjeeling, as well as Lapsang Souchong tea from China. In addition, most of the classically flavored and blended teas, such as Earl Grey and English Breakfast, are black tea blends.

Figure 2.5: Black tea leaves in production

Other, less common forms of traditional teas include:

- Yellow tea: Yellow tea was developed in China, and involves a process whereby the leaves are exposed to concentrated levels of warm, humid air for one or more set periods of time.
- Dark (pu'er) tea: Also known as post-fermented tea, this tea is not commonly found in the US market. Worldwide, the most common kind of dark tea is pu'er (sometimes spelled pu'erh), a specialty of the Yunnan province in China and named after Pu'er City. Dark tea leaves may be wilted and oxidized to some extent (similar to green or oolong teas) but also undergo a microbial-based fermentation based on the action of molds, bacteria, and yeasts. During this process, certain phenolics, carbohydrates, and amino acids present in the tea leaves are transformed, creating the tea's unique flavor profile. This type of tea may be aged for months or years before consumption, and it is often compressed into bricks or disks for sale. Post-fermented tea has earthy, mushroom-like flavors, a slight hint of bitterness, and a thick, rich texture.

TEA BLENDS

While single-origin or single-location teas are gaining popularity, most tea on the market is blended—the product of different pickings, processing, or plantations. Blending allows a tea producer to ensure consistency for a consumer who expects his or her tea to taste the same at every brewing. Examples of well-known combinations and tea blends include:

- English Breakfast: Although there is no single standardized formulation for English Breakfast tea, it is often a blend of black tea leaves from China, Sri Lanka, and Kenya.
- Earl Grey: Earl Grey tea may consist of a blend of black tea leaves or a single-origin tea combined with oil of bergamot—a type of citrus oil.
- Chai: There are many variations of chai. Most include an Indian black tea or rooibos (red tea) combined with a selection of spices that may include cinnamon, ginger, black peppercorns, cardamom, or others. The steeped tea and spices are then combined and served with warm milk.

Figure 2.6: Rooibos tea

HERBAL AND BOTANICAL TEAS/TISANES

Many herbs and botanicals have become popular as teas (sometimes called tisanes) in their own right, or in blends combined with *Camellia sinensis* tea leaves. These ingredients have their own distinct flavors and functional benefits that some tea drinkers prefer.

Some of the more common herbs or botanicals used in teas or as tea include the following:

- Rooibos: Rooibos ("red bush") tea is made from the leaves of the *Aspalathus linearis* plant, native to South Africa. Rooibos tea leaves undergo oxidation and produce richly-colored, red liquor when brewed. Its sweet and nutty flavors blend well with other ingredients, and its leaves are often used in place of *Camellia sinensis* leaves as a caffeine-free alternative.
- Chamomile: Chamomile has been used since ancient times as a remedy for various ailments. Tea made from chamomile flowers is a popular sleep aid.
- Mint: Spearmint and peppermint leaves can be steeped on their own or blended with other ingredients. Moroccan mint tea was created centuries ago from mint leaves and Chinese gunpowder green tea.
- Toasted rice: Genmaicha is a Japanese tea that combines toasted rice and Japanese green tea. It is frequently served at Japanese restaurants.

- Yerba mate: Yerba mate comes from the leaves of a plant in the holly family (genus *Ilex*). Indigenous peoples of South America have consumed Yerba mate tea for generations. Mate is currently the national drink of Argentina, and it plays an important role in cultural and social life in other South American countries as well.
- Guayusa: Guayusa is a highly caffeinated herbal tea produced from the leaves of a holly tree native to the Amazon Rainforest of Ecuador. Guayusa has a long history of use in Ecuador and throughout South America, and has recently become available in the United States.

In addition to those listed above, many other types of flowers, leaves, roots (such as ginger), bark (such as cinnamon), and fruits may be used in tea.

While some herbs and botanicals are used in place of caffeinated teas, not all herbal teas are free of caffeine. Yerba mate and guayusa are specific examples of herbal teas that have higher levels of caffeine than comparable servings of *Camellia sinensis* tea.

BREWING TEA

In general, the successful preparation of tea relies on four factors:
- The tea itself: As a general guideline, a teaspoon of dry tea leaf is used to prepare one cup of tea. When preparing a pot of tea, the general rule is a teaspoon per cup to be served, plus an additional teaspoon "for the pot." Variations in the kind of tea and the tea drinker's preferences (strength/ intensity of the tea) may require some degree of experimentation to achieve the ideal cup of tea.

- Water: As with coffee, water that is completely devoid of minerals (such as distilled water) will produce a flat-tasting brewed tea. Fresh, filtered water with a mild degree of hardness is best suited for making most teas.
- Temperature: The ideal water temperature will vary with each type and style of tea. Keep in mind that higher temperatures may not elicit the best results, and more delicate products such as Japanese green teas may be better suited to water closer to 160° F (71°C).
- Time: The optimal amount of brewing time is based on water temperature and water-to-leaf ratio. For example, some Chinese styles of tea preparation involve greater amounts of leaf steeped for shorter periods of time (sometimes as short as 5-10 seconds). This particular method allows for multiple successive steeps using the same leaves. In all cases, it is best to consult the tea's packaging for brewing guidelines.

Different types of tea should be brewed to accentuate their particular flavor characteristics using the manufacturer's suggested variables for water quantity, temperature, and brewing time in order to bring out the tea's unique subtleties. With very few exceptions, water used to brew tea should not be boiling, which tends to cook the tea leaves. Standard brewing guidelines for tea are: allow for 1 teaspoon of leaf per 8 ounces (30 ml) water just off the boil (195-205°F [91°C to 96°C]) for 2 to 3 minutes.

Table 2.1 provides more specific guidelines based on specific styles of tea.

Table 2.1: Suggested Tea Brewing Guidelines

TYPE OF TEA	WATER TEMPERATURE	BREW TIME
White Tea	175°F to 185°F (79°C to 85°C)	1 to 3 minutes
Green Tea (steamed)	158°F to 176°F (70°C to 80°C)	2 to 3 minutes
Green Tea (pan-fired)	176°F to 185°F (80°C to 85°C)	2 to 3 minutes
Oolong Tea	180°F to 190°F (82°C to 88°C)	3 to 5 minutes
Black Tea	206°F (97°C)	3 to 5 minutes
Dark (post-fermented) Tea	195°F to 206°F (91°C to 97°C)	30 seconds, flush, then 3 to5 minutes
Tisane	206°F to 212°F (97°C to 100C)	5 to 7 minutes

TEA SERVICE

Various cultures serve tea differently, and specialty tea service may require adhering to specific traditions. A few of the more common traditions include the following:

- English tea service: English tea service usually consists of an English Breakfast or Earl Grey tea, though many other black teas may be offered. The service often includes traditional British scones served with clotted cream, an array of pastries, or small sandwiches.
- Japanese tea service: Some Japanese tea ceremonies may be highly formalized, and can take months or years of study to perform properly. Simpler, more informal, Japanese tea service may include matcha, gyokuro, or sencha green teas with a small serving of traditional Japanese sweets.
- Chinese tea service: Although Chinese tea customs vary somewhat by region, more common Chinese tea services use an Yixing clay teapot, Chinese ceramic teapot, or *gaiwan* (lidded bowl). Small savory dishes, like dim sum, may accompany the service.

Figure 2.7: Oolong tea service

STORING TEA

Tea should be stored in airtight canisters away from heat, moisture, and light. These three general rules will help with the successful storage of tea to preserve freshness:

- Avoid humidity: Humidity is understood to dull tea and shorten its shelf-life.
- Stable temperature: Fluctuations in temperature alter air humidity levels and can affect the aromatic oils captured in tea leaves.
- Avoid contaminating aromas: Teas are known to absorb the aromas from their surroundings. Avoid placing teas with other aromatic products, and even be careful with different types of tea, as they can absorb scents from each other.

Some tea vendors in China and Japan will refrigerate (or freeze) their expensive teas—especially spring green teas that they wish to keep as fresh as possible. Critics argue that taking packages of green tea out of refrigeration, bringing them into warmer, more humid air, and then returning them to refrigeration allows vapor condensation to collect on the tea—thereby exposing the teas to unnecessary water. A compromise would be to refrigerate these teas in smaller parcels, thereby reducing the amount of tea exposed to temperature and humidity variations.

POTENTIAL HEALTH BENEFITS OF TEA

In addition to the wide range of flavor experiences offered by teas, many consumers are attracted to the health benefits of drinking tea. Numerous studies have pointed to the beneficial effects of *Camellia sinensis* tea. The Fifth International Scientific Symposium on Tea and Human Health found that tea could provide health benefits in relation to weight management, cognitive function, heart health, bone health, cancer prevention, and microbiome (beneficial bacteria and microbes found throughout the body).

Further research on various herbs and botanicals used in teas and tea blends suggest an even wider range of nutritional and functional benefits available to tea drinkers. Some tea blends are touted for their ability to help with relaxation, digestion, and detoxifying the body. These claims, however, must be viewed with scrutiny, as their basis on solid research may be questionable. Furthermore, guidelines by the FDA require that these teas not be labeled as a medicine, treatment, or cures for health conditions.

THE SENSORY EVALUATION OF TEA

While it is rare for a customer to find a flawed tea that has slipped through manufacture and grading, an awareness of the organoleptic (sensory) aspects of tea is helpful for evaluating the tea's quality and freshness, recommending teas to guests, and selecting teas to pair with foods.

The evaluation of tea includes an examination of the dry leaf, the wet leaf, and the liquor (the formal name for liquid tea). All of these are factors that determine the tea's freshness, quality, and complexity.

Dry leaf evaluation: Dry leaf evaluation involves noting the aroma, color and shape of the leaves. In particular, you may note the following:
- With specialty teas, whole leaves and leaf sets (two leaves and a bud) are generally preferred to broken leaves. In addition, whole leaves should not be intermingled with brokens, as whole leaves and broken leaf portions will not steep in the same manner.
- The aroma of the dry leaf will often give initial indications of the complexity, intensity, and duration of aromas to expect from the liquor.
- Fresher teas are generally brighter in color and offer richer aromas than older versions of the same tea.

Wet leaf evaluation: For wet leaf evaluation, it is generally preferable to steep the tea in the same manner that guests will receive the tea, and then smell the wet leaves after all the liquor has been removed. Wet leaf evaluation is useful in order to determine the optimal steeping parameters for a tea, and in doing so, it is helpful to note how variations in these parameters highlight particular aspects in

the tea's aroma. Note that teas that have been tightly rolled and shaped may not completely unfurl during the first steep.

Tea liquor evaluation: The steps of tea liquor evaluation are similar to the evaluation of wine and coffee in that they involve appearance, aroma, and in-mouth impressions. In the process of tea liquor evaluation, take note of the following:
- Before sipping the tea, it is helpful to note the color of the tea. White porcelain cups are useful in establishing a more consistent colored background for comparing the visuals of the tea liquor. Some teas may appear dull or cloudy. This character may not affect the overall taste of the tea, but may influence the tea drinker's overall impressions of the tea drinking experience.
- Smelling the aroma of the liquor may help in detecting variations compared to the aroma of the wet leaves.
- When it is time to sip the tea, many professionals will actually "slurp" the liquor. The powerful and rapid slurping of tea helps to convert the tea into a more vaporized form, and exposes more aromatic compounds to air so that they can be detected in the mouth. This method does not reflect the average guest's usual mode of tea drinking, so as an alternative, simply make sure as much surface area of the mouth and upper throat comes in contact with the liquor as possible. It is helpful to engage as many taste receptors in the mouth as you can, as well as allowing smells to travel from the back of the mouth to the nasal cavity (retronasal olfaction).
- Evaluating the liquor involves noting the number of flavors/aromas present, their intensity and their duration. It is often useful to look for certain categories of flavor/aroma in teas. General categories of tea aromas and flavors include mineral, floral, vegetal, fruit, and toasted/nutty/woody.
- With many teas, a certain level of astringency is a desirable factor, as the drying aspect of the tea creates a brisk, mouth-watering effect.
- Teas exhibit varying degrees of texture, ranging from thin and watery to thick and brothy. The components of the tea's aftertaste and the duration of the aftertaste should also be noted. Higher quality teas often exhibit richer, more complex, and longer-lasting aftertastes.

As a beginner in the practice of tea tasting, it can be helpful to record your notes and impressions. Given the wide range of teas available, and the variation in grades of quality for teas, consistent note-taking can help relate experiences of teas across years, seasons, or tea types.

Many of the standard practices described relate to the evaluation of single-origin, specialty teas, because those teas fetch higher prices and, therefore, are under higher scrutiny. However, these same practices can be applied to tea blends and herbal teas with similar usefulness. The ability to recognize and articulate the characteristics of any form of tea benefits the guest who needs help selecting tea and appreciating the tea experience. Tea evaluation also assists those responsible for purchasing teas and assuring their tea inventory has not become dull or stale.

WINE PRODUCTION

Wine is an alcoholic beverage produced by the fermentation of grapes or grape juice. Fermentation is a natural process whereby the sugar in grapes is converted into alcohol. Other agricultural products such as cherries, plums, apples, and rice may also be used to produce fermented beverages that are sometimes referred to as wine. However, in the United States, as well as in much of the rest of the world, the unmodified word refers specifically to a fermented beverage produced from grapes.

The combination of grape variety (or varieties), winemaking techniques, and the unique features of the vineyard landscape—often called terroir—produces thousands of distinctive wines sourced from many parts of the world. These range from crisp, sparkling wines to light, dry whites; robust, rich reds, and unctuous dessert wines—and everything in between.

This chapter begins with a look at the various categories and classifications of wine. This is followed by a discussion of the physical and chemical properties that are found in wine. The chapter then continues with a discussion of the production of wine—in still, sparkling, and fortified forms.

BASIC CATEGORIES OF WINE

The vast diversity found in the world of wine can be both exciting and intimidating. As such, a good place to begin is to look at the broad categories of wine grouped by style and color—such as red, white and rosé—as well as dry (not sweet) or sweet. As one delves deeper into the study of wine, other potential categories will become apparent, such as place of origin, naming scheme (regional, varietal, or other), grape variety (or varieties), flavor profile, food

affinity, and many other characteristics. Beginning with the basic categories of still wines, sparkling wines, fortified wines, and aromatized wines is another good foundation from which to expand.

Still Wines: Still wines are produced by fermenting the juice of freshly pressed grapes until some or all of the sugar has been converted to alcohol. Still wines are so named because they do not contain a discernible bubbling under the surface when opened. Still wines, like most wines, may be red (produced from red or black grape varieties), white (produced from white grape varieties [which often appear green or yellow in appearance] or by using just the juice from red or black grapes), or rosé (produced from red or black grapes with limited contact with the grape skins).

Sparkling Wines: Sparkling wines have a degree of dissolved carbon dioxide which will, upon opening the bottle and pouring the wine, create streams of cascading bubbles. Sparkling wines may contain as little as 1.5 to 3 atmospheres of dissolved carbon dioxide pressure (which might be described as a "fizzy" or *frizzante* wine) or as much as 6 atmospheres of pressure (in the case of fully-sparkling wines such as Champagne). Carbon dioxide may be introduced into the wine via several different production methods, which will be discussed later in this chapter.

Fortified Wines: Fortified wines are produced from a base wine (typically a still wine) that has had its alcohol content increased by the addition of brandy or another distilled spirit. Many of the world's most historic and famous wines—such as Port, Madeira, and Sherry—are fortified wines. The precise timing of the fortification—whether during fermentation or after fermentation—will determine a good deal about the finished character of the wine, particularly whether it is sweet or dry. Fortified wines generally contain between 15% and 20% alcohol by volume (abv).

Aromatized Wines: Aromatized wines are a specialized subcategory of flavored wines. Aromatized wines may be fortified or unfortified, dry or sweet, but will always contain a flavoring agent or agents. Vermouth, which is typically fortified, and retsina (which is typically unfortified) are two examples of aromatized wines. Fortified wines are typically flavored by botanicals, including a wide range of roots, flowers, leaves, spices, herbs, bittering agents, and even pine resin—among other compounds. Aromatized wines are further discussed in chapter 7.

A note about sweet versus dry: In retail platforms and wine lists, wines are often categorized by whether they are sweet or dry. Sweet wines of all types are typically grouped together under the heading of "sweet wines" or "dessert wines" (or something similar). This makes sense from a sales or menu planning point of view, as people tend to consider individual foods or certain meal courses in terms of these two basic styles: sweet or not sweet (savory). Wines may certainly be grouped by sweetness level, but in reality all of the broad categories of wine—still wines, sparkling wines, fortified wines, and aromatized wines—may be produced as a dry wine, a sweet wine, or as something in-between (often referred to as "off-dry").

Table 3-1 summarizes the basic categories of wine and provides additional examples.

THE COMPOSITION OF WINE

To the consumer, wine is a pleasurable drink found in a delectable range of colors and styles. However, a beverage professional should have a deeper understanding of the science behind what is in the bottle. This will enable you to comprehend what makes each glass so unique and communicate this to customers.

The differences between one wine and the next—be they visual, aromatic, gustatory (related to taste) or tactile (related to the sense of touch)—can all be attributed to its chemical makeup. Some of the chemical compounds found in wine originate within the grapes themselves, others are created during fermentation, and still others are created over time as the wine matures in a tank, barrel, or bottle.

The major components of wine include the following:

Water: Wine is typically 80% to 90% water. The water in wine is primarily from the grapes themselves, but under some circumstances small amounts may be added during winemaking.

Table 3.1: Basic Categories of Wine

Category	Definition	Examples
Still Wines	Produced by the fermentation of grapes; not sparkling	Oregon Pinot Noir (red) Barolo (red) Napa Valley Fumé Blanc (white) Soave (white) Tavel (rosé)
Sparkling Wines	Produced by the fermentation of grapes, contain an amount of dissolved carbon dioxide	Champagne Asti Prosecco
Fortified Wines	Wine that has had its alcohol content increased by the addition of a distilled spirit	Port (Porto) Sherry (Jerez) Marsala
Aromatized Wines	Wine that contains a flavoring agent	Vermouth Retsina

Alcohol: During fermentation, yeast metabolizes sugar and converts it into alcohol. Ethyl alcohol, also referred to as ethanol, is the main type of alcohol produced via fermentation. The typical range of alcohol in wine is generally stated at 10% to 15% alcohol by volume. However, there are many examples of wines that fall outside of this range. For instance, a semi-sweet, sparkling Moscato may be as low as 4.5% abv, and a fortified wine such as Port may be as high as 20% abv.

Alcohol is the intoxicating element in wine, but its importance to the overall flavor profile of a given product goes well beyond these properties. Alcohol is also highly volatile, meaning it evaporates easily. When it does so, it carries with it the wine's aromas to the nose. Alcohol is one of the compounds that contributes to a wine's body or mouthfeel. All other things being equal, wines that are higher in alcohol will be more full-bodied—and thus richer, rounder, or heavier in weight—than lighter-alcohol wines.

Acid: A variety of acids give wine much of its balance, structure, and flavor. The proper level of acidity in a wine is essential to give it its crisp, thirst-quenching refreshment, and yet keep it from tasting too sharp or sour. This balance often depends on harvesting the grapes at the precise time in the ripening process. Grapes should be picked at the optimal equilibrium between sugar and acid. When grapes are over-ripe, the winemaker sometimes has the option of adding additional acid prior to fermentation in order to "lift" the wine and give it structure. In sweet wines, the proper level of acidity is crucial in order to prevent a cloying sensation on the palate. The principal acids in wine include the following:

• Tartaric acid: The grape is one of the only fruits in nature that accumulates significant quantities of tartaric acid. Tartaric acid is a very sharp-tasting acid, and as such it plays a major role in the taste and structure of both grapes and wine.
• Malic acid: Malic acid has particularly high concentrations in under-ripe grapes or grapes grown in a cool vintage or climate. Malic acid is often associated with green apples and has a very particular, sharp taste.
• Lactic acid: Lactic acid is not a natural component of grapes, but may be produced in wine during fermentation or a separate winemaking process known as malolactic fermentation. Lactic acid

is the primary acid found in fermented dairy products such as yogurt and buttermilk and is softer than many of the other acids found in wine.
• Acetic acid: Acetic acid is a volatile acid found in most types of vinegar. Acetic acid is a natural by-product of fermentation and is thus found in small quantities in most wines. However, higher levels of acetic acid—which may be considered a defect in the wine—can result from certain chemical reactions or via the activity of *acetobacter* (spoilage bacteria).

Sugar: Sugars are organic chemical compounds produced by plants via the process of photosynthesis. In ripening grapes, two simple sugars—glucose and fructose—accumulate in the grapes until reaching between 15 to 28 percent sugar (also called brix) at harvest. Glucose and fructose are highly fermentable sugars and will be converted, through the action of yeast, into ethanol.

In the production of a dry wine (dry meaning a wine that has no discernible sweetness to the taster), fermentation is considered complete when the yeasts have converted as much sugar as possible into alcohol. Typically, this means that all or most of the sugar has been used up, and the yeasts have naturally expired. However, many wines contain varying amounts of sugar after fermentation arrests (whether naturally or due to certain winemaking procedures). The sugar that remains after fermentation is complete is referred to as residual sugar, and wines are often described in ascending order of sweetness as dry, off-dry, medium sweet, or sweet. A dry wine may actually have a small amount of residual sugar (typically less than 1% by volume) while sweet wines may have somewhere between 5% and 12% (or even higher).

Figure 3.1: Color compounds known as anthocyanins are typically found in the skins of red grapes

Phenolic Compounds: Also called phenolics, polyphenolics, or polyphenols, this is a large category of plant-related molecules that are responsible for a wine's color, structure, taste, certain aromas, and antioxidant properties. Some of the phenolic compounds typically found in wine include the following:

- Anthocyanins: Anthocyanins are compounds that give wine its blue, purple or red color. Anthocyanins are typically found in the skin of red grapes, although some grapes have red-tinted flesh as well.
- Tannins: Tannins are bitter compounds found in the stems, seeds, and skins of grapes as well as in oak barrels. They are responsible for a textural drying sensation on the palate and may contribute to the astringency found in some wines. Tannins also provide wines with longevity and structure, and are a natural preservative that helps to protect wines from oxidation.
- Resveratrol: Resveratrol, found in red grapes, red wine, and a variety of plants, is regarded as having potential health benefits due to its antioxidant properties.

Phenolics in grapes are primarily located within the skins and seeds. Red wines extract these compounds before, during, and sometimes after the fermentation process due to the fact that, unlike most white wines, the juice from red grapes is kept in contact with these grape solids. This accounts for the color, tannin, and higher resveratrol content of red wines.

MINOR COMPONENTS FOUND IN WINE

Esters: Esters are odiferous compounds that occur due to reactions between acids and alcohol. Esters represent the largest group of aromatic compounds found in wine. Most are desirable at low levels, but some are considered off-odors when found at high enough concentrations. One of the most common esters is ethyl acetate. In low concentrations, it imparts a fruity, floral aroma; however, at higher levels it is considered a fault and may impart an unacceptable aroma reminiscent of acetone or nail polish remover.

Dissolved Gases: Dissolved gases such as oxygen and carbon dioxide are present in most liquids, including wine. However, they are only sometimes present in concentrations high enough to be detected by the taster or to have a significant impact on the wine's overall chemistry. Carbon dioxide is a natural by-product of fermentation and, as such, is present in all wines in small amounts, but often goes undetected by the taster. Sparkling wines, of course, contain high enough levels of carbon dioxide (typically three to six atmospheres of pressure) to create cascading streams of bubbles once the wine is open and poured.

Oxygen readily dissolves in wine and promotes many chemical reactions through the process of oxidation. While small amounts of oxidation may promote desirable effects (particularly during the winemaking process), excessive oxidation may cause discoloration or a muting of a wine's aromas. Thus, managing a wine's exposure to oxygen is an important part of the winemaking process.

Sulfites: Sulfites are a group of chemicals based on the element sulfur. Sulfur compounds are formed in small quantities as a natural by-product of fermentation. However, winemakers often choose to use sulfur compounds at various stages during the winemaking process due to its powerful anti-microbial and anti-oxidant properties. Sulfur is an effective preservative when used properly in the production of wine, protecting the product against spoilage and oxidation. Wines that are sold in the United States containing sulfites at a concentration of more than 10 parts per million (ppm) are required by law to include the words "Contains Sulfites" on the label. Sulfites are classified as an allergen in the EU, and as such, most EU wine labels also contain this same notation.

Figure 3.2: Chardonnay grapes heading to the winery

WINE PRODUCTION

THE PROCESS OF FERMENTATION

Simply put, fermentation—often referred to as primary fermentation or alcoholic fermentation in the context of the wine industry—is the conversion of certain sugars into ethyl alcohol via the action of yeast. The primary yeast species used in the production of wine is *Saccharomyces cerevisiae*. These yeasts may be present on the grape skins themselves or introduced to the grape juice by the winemaker.

The actual mechanics of fermentation are quite complex, with many successive steps involving numerous progressive chemical reactions. However, the basic process can be described as follows: Yeast consumes sugar and converts it to alcohol, carbon dioxide, and heat.

Fermentation begins with the yeast cells attacking the sugar molecules and breaking them apart to release energy, some of which is given off as heat. The smaller molecules that remain after sugar is broken apart are ethyl alcohol (also known as ethanol) and carbon dioxide (most of which dissipates into the air). Specific steps in the fermentation process can also create small amounts of other chemicals, many of which are commonly found in wine. These include glycerol, succinic acid, acetic acid, ethyl acetate, and methanol (methyl alcohol).

Winemakers have many choices in terms of the fermentation process, beginning with the choice of yeast—native (also known as natural yeast) or a specific strain of commercial yeast. There are also various containers that may be used. Oak barrels (large or small) are appreciated for their ability to add oak flavors, a bit of oxidation, and complexity to the wine. Inert containers such as stainless steel, stone, or ceramic may also be used. Other factors that may be controlled during the fermentation process include the temperature of the fermenting juice and the length of time fermentation is allowed to continue.

Nearly all wines undergo a form of fermentation at some point during the production process. The sections that follow outline the fermentation process and other basic steps in the production of still wines (white, red, and rosé), sparkling wines, and fortified wines.

THE PRODUCTION OF WHITE WINES

White wines range in style from light, fresh, and fruity to full-bodied, well-oaked, and highly complex. As such, the specific process used in the production of any one wine will be somewhat unique. This section will thus focus on the typical steps used in the production of white wines, beginning with the hand off of the grapes to the winery.

While studying the methods of production for any type of wine, please keep in mind that winemaking is an art as well as a science. Many of these procedures are open to a wide range of possibilities, and in some cases, may even be considered optional.

Pre-fermentation: After the grapes arrive at the winery, they are sometimes treated with a form of sulfur that combines with oxygen to create sulfur dioxide. Sulfur may be added at many different points throughout the winemaking process in order to prevent oxidation, browning, or the uninhibited growth of yeast or bacteria. The grapes may also be sorted to remove leaves, under-ripe bunches, or other unwanted debris.

From the sorting table, the grapes are typically sent to be pressed. Most often, this is begun via a large piece of equipment known as a crusher or a crusher-destemmer. Crushing breaks the skins of the grapes and allows the juice to begin to flow. Typically in the production of white wine crushing is accompanied by—or quickly followed by—pressing, to extract the remaining liquid. Pressing is the process of removing the liquid (juice) from the skins, seeds, and other solids.

Once the juice is prepared for and ready to undergo fermentation, it is referred to as must. (Note: the term "must" refers to the juice or juice mixture that is prepared for fermentation, and in other types of wine production may include grapes skins, seeds, and/or stems.)

The cake of compressed skins and pulp left over after pressing the juice away from the solids is known as pomace. Pomace may be composted or otherwise used as a fertilizer, or it may be used to produce pomace brandies such as grappa or marc.

Fermentation: As discussed in the previous section, fermentation may be initiated through the use of naturally-present yeast, or with the use of a particular strain of yeast. Individual strains of yeast may be chosen for specific properties such as their ability to work quickly or their tolerance for certain circumstances (such as levels of acidity, sugar, or temperature).

Once the juice is inoculated, the yeast will start to multiply rapidly, causing the juice to bubble and foam with escaping carbon dioxide. The releasing energy will quickly cause the juice to grow warm, and the winemaker will most likely intervene to control the temperature. In order to retain the crisp acidity and fresh fruit flavors desired in most white wines, the temperature for white wine fermentation is typically held between 50°F and 60°F (10–16°C).

Fermentation for dry white wines usually continues for several days to several weeks and will naturally come to an end when all the sugar is depleted and there is nothing left for the yeast to consume. Fermentation will also start to end when the alcohol content of the liquid reaches 14% or higher by volume; at this point the yeast will not be able to survive. In other instances, such as in the production of an off-dry or semi-sweet white wine, the winemaker may intentionally stop the fermentation while there is still a degree of sugar left over. Such leftover sugar is known as residual sugar.

Malolactic Fermentation: Malolactic fermentation (MLF) is known as a "secondary fermentation," meaning that it does not produce alcohol. Malolactic fermentation, which is started by bacteria, may occur naturally or it may be induced or suppressed by the winemaker.

Malolactic fermentation converts a portion of the malic acid (a very tart acid) to lactic acid (which is milder). This results in a softer, smoother wine with less overall acidity. In the process, several chemicals are created, including *diacetyl*, which imparts a "buttery" aroma and flavor to the wine. For most white wines that rely on fragrant aromas, light body, and crisp acidity, malolactic fermentation is avoided; however, some white wines such as Chardonnay can often benefit from the added richness and complexity.

Figure 3.3: A sample of Chardonnay just after fermentation has completed

Post-Fermentation: After fermentation is complete, the sulfur level of the wine is typically checked again. Sulfur may be added if necessary to decrease the chance of microbial spoilage, browning, or additional fermentation.

At this time, the expired yeast cells, along with any other solid particles in the wine, sink to the bottom of the tank or barrel. The sediment formed by the yeast is known as the lees. During this stage, the winemaker may either separate the lees from the wine and continue on with the process of clarifying the newly-made wine, or may choose to leave the wine in contact with the lees for a period of time. Contact with the lees, known as *sur lie aging*, can lend a yeasty aroma, creamy texture, and increased complexity to a white wine.

Shortly after fermentation is complete (or after sur lie aging), most wines will be clarified in order to remove any cloudiness and solid particles. Several different methods, or a combination of methods, may be used. Racking, one of the gentlest methods, uses gravity to allow suspended matter to settle to the bottom of the tank before siphoning the wine off the sediment and into a fresh container. Fining uses an inert material, such as gelatin, to bind with the unwanted sediment. Filtration involves straining the wine through a filter to remove particles over a certain size. In large wineries, a centrifuge may be used to separate the wine from the heavier solids.

Aging and Bottling: Some white wines are bottled within a few months of fermentation. These wines may rest in stainless steel tanks during clarification, and soon thereafter be ready to bottle. Other white wines may benefit from months or even years of aging. Such aging may be done in a variety of containers, including oak barrels which can transform the wines with added touches of vanilla, oak, wood, coconut, or toasty aromas. Some examples of white wines that often benefit from oak aging include New World Chardonnay and Fumé Blanc (Sauvignon Blanc).

Shortly before bottling, many different vats of wine may be blended together to make the finished product. These vats may be different "batches" of the same wine, or may represent wine from different vineyards, grape varieties, or vintages. In the case of wines labeled by their grape variety—known as varietal wines—a minimum proportion of the wine must be produced using the named grape variety. The specific amount (typically 75% to 85%) varies by the country or region of production. This still leaves a bit of room for blending with other varieties in order to develop complexity or achieve balance. Other wines—often referred to as blends or blended wines—are typically produced from several different grape varieties. In such cases, various grapes may be fermented together (co-fermented), or the blending may occur just before bottling.

Once the wine is finished, the last task is bottling or otherwise packaging the wine for sale. Once the wine is bottled or packaged, it is stored until needed for shipment and sale.

THE PRODUCTION OF RED WINES

The process used in the production of red wine is quite similar to that used for white wines with one major difference—red wine is fermented in contact with the grape skins, seeds, and sometimes stems. The color, much of the taste components, flavors, and texture of red wine is extracted from the grape skins and introduced into the juice before, during, and after fermentation.

This section will focus on red wine production with an emphasis on those procedures that differ from the manner in which white wine is created. As with all styles of wine, keep in mind that many of the steps of red wine production are variable or optional.

Pre-fermentation: As red grapes arrive at the winery, they may be treated with a form of sulfur, and may be sent through the sorting table. The winemaker may also choose to destem or partially destem the grapes. These steps are considered optional. However, in nearly all cases, the red grapes are crushed in order to allow the juice to flow and to create a fermentable mixture of grape skins, seeds, and juice (and perhaps all or some of the stems) known as must.

The contact between the red grape skins and the grape juice allows for the extraction of phenolics, such as color, tannin, and flavor components, from the skins and into the juice. This process is known as maceration, and is generally allowed to run anywhere from a few days to a few weeks or even longer. Maceration begins at or before the start of fermentation and may be allowed to continue until well after fermentation ends.

If the winemaker chooses to begin maceration before fermentation, the must is chilled to below 55°F (13°C) in order to postpone fermentation. This technique is called a *cold soak*. The cold soak is one of the techniques that allows the winemaker to control the level of phenolics that are extracted from the grape skins during production.

Figure 3.4: Merlot grapes in the crusher

Fermentation: The fermentation process for red wines is similar to that of white wines. The main differences are caused by the presence of the grape skins in the must.

In order for the appropriate amount of phenolics to be extracted from the skins, contact between skins and the must needs to be maintained throughout the fermentation. Inconveniently, the carbon dioxide that is continuously produced during fermentation forms bubbles that push the grape solids to the top of the fermentation vessel, where they will eventually form into a fairly dense and compact mass known as the *cap*.

Once the cap forms, it becomes the winemaker's job to break up the cap and reintegrate the skins into the liquid, allowing for optimal extraction. This is known as *cap management* and may be accomplished via a range of practices, including pushing the cap down, breaking it up, or pumping juice from the bottom of the tank up and over the cap.

Red wine fermentations are typically conducted at higher temperatures than those of white wines, in part, because the light floral and fruit aromas emphasized by a cool fermentation are less important in most red wines. Warmer fermentation temperatures allow for increased extraction of phenolics, which creates a good foundation for robust, age-worthy reds. A winemaker might choose a moderate temperature of 60°F to 70°F (16°C to 21°C) for a light, fragrant Pinot Noir, or a warmer fermentation of 85°F to 95°F (30°C to 35°C) when producing a tannic blockbuster Cabernet Sauvignon.

Malolactic Fermentation: For a variety of reasons, malolactic fermentation is used quite often in the production of red wines. In most red wines, high acidity is unnecessary (possibly even undesirable) and the added complexity introduced by malolactic fermentation is a plus. MLF can also result in the production of a more microbially stable wine by reducing the amount of malic acid available for bacterial spoilage.

Post-Fermentation: After fermentation ends, the winemaker has the option of allowing the new wine to remain in contact with the grape skins for a period of time. This is known as extended maceration and may last for several days, weeks, or even longer if the fullest extraction of phenolics is desired.

Once the winemaker decides the maceration period is complete, the wine will be racked (drained off the solids). The remaining solids are then pressed to release any remaining wine. After pressing, the wine may be moved into a tank for one or more additional rackings. The wine might also go through further clarification via fining, filtration, or centrifuge.

Aging and Bottling: Aging in barrels can be very beneficial for red wines, particularly those high in tannin. The slow infusion of oxygen that seeps through the wood and into the wine helps the tannin molecules combine with each other in a process called *polymerization*. These long, polymerized tannins feel softer and richer in the mouth compared to the shorter, harder tannins found in grapes. The use of new or young barrels can also add vanilla, toasty, or woodsy aromas to the wine. When properly balanced with the fruit and other characteristics of the wine, oak aging can add substantial complexity to the finished product.

For these reasons, many mid- and upper-range red wines spend some time in barrels. The most exalted Cabernets and similar wines typically go into new oak barrels for several years or more. Less powerful or less expensive wines may be aged in stainless steel or less costly (or used) barrels. Once the winemaker determines that the aging stage is complete, the wine may be filtered, blended, or otherwise finished before being bottled (or otherwise packaged), and stored for shipment.

Figure 3.5: Cabernet Sauvignon aging underground

THE PRODUCTION OF ROSÉ WINES

Rosé is a pink wine made from red grapes. Although consumers in the United States often think of rosé as a sweet, simple wine, rosé may, in fact, be produced in any style from dry to sweet. In many parts of the world, dry rosé is considered a serious, sophisticated wine equal in many ways to the red and white wines of a particular region.

In the typical process of rosé production, the grapes are harvested, handled, and crushed in a manner very similar to that of red wine production. Fermentation is then allowed to begin; however, skin contact is limited. After a few hours (up to a few days) of skin contact and color extraction, the must is pressed and the still-fermenting, pink juice is separated from the grape skins.

The depth of the hue in rosé depends on the amount of time the fermenting juice is allowed to stay in contact with the grape skins. The longer the skin contact continues, the darker the wine will be.

After pressing the juice away from the skins, fermentation is allowed to continue in a manner very similar to the process used in white wine production. The sweetness (or dryness) level of the resulting wine will depend on how and when the winemaker decides to stop the fermentation process. Fermentation may be discontinued while there is still a good deal of sugar in the must, or after it has all been converted to alcohol (at which time fermentation will naturally end). While exceptions do exist, malolactic fermentation and barrel aging are rarely used in the production of rosé wines, as rosé is most often appreciated for its fruity, refreshing, crisp flavor profile.

THE PRODUCTION OF SPARKLING WINES

Sparkling wines contain a significant amount of dissolved carbon dioxide gas, sometimes up to six atmospheres of pressure. These festive, bubbly wines are beloved by many cultures and are often considered an integral part of holidays, weddings, or any celebratory occasion.

Sparkling wines may be produced in a variety of methods, each of which has a profound impact on the overall character of the finished wine. The main methods used in the production of sparkling wine are discussed in this section.

The Traditional Method: The Traditional Method of sparkling wine production is used to create the most famous and renowned sparkling wines in the world, including Champagne (where the process is referred to as the *Méthode Champenoise*), Italy's Franciacorta, Spain's Cava, and many of the finest sparkling wines of the New World. This is an elaborate process that involves creating the wine's many fine and stable bubbles via a second fermentation in the bottle.

The process begins with the production of a dry, low- to moderate-alcohol base wine. This wine is blended with a mixture of yeast and sugar, then immediately bottled and capped. The yeast and sugar will begin a process of natural fermentation—the second fermentation—inside the bottle, creating a small amount of additional alcohol. The carbon dioxide that is produced during this fermentation is captured inside the bottle and dissolves within the wine.

This second fermentation typically lasts about a month, after which the yeast cells die and settle inside the bottle. Next, the wine is allowed to age on the dead yeast cells (the lees) for anywhere from several months to several years or longer. It is during this stage that the unique aromas and flavors of Traditional Method sparkling wines, such as toast, brioche, and biscuit, are created. These aromas are sometimes referred to as the "Champagne Bouquet."

After the wine has finished aging on the lees, the dead yeast cells will be coaxed down into the neck of the bottle in a process known as *riddling* or *remuage*. The bottles are then quickly opened, and the yeast cells are expelled via the pressure built up in the bottle; this step is known as *disgorging* or *dégorgement*. In the final step, the liquid lost during disgorging is quickly replaced, the wines are adjusted for sweetness (if necessary), and the bottles are immediately re-corked. The Traditional Method of sparkling wine production generally produces wines with six atmospheres of pressure (atm) of dissolved carbon dioxide. At this level, cascading streams of small, stable bubbles are created once the bottle is opened and the wine is poured into a glass.

Figure 3.6: Champagne aging underground in Reims

The Tank Method: Also known as the bulk or *Charmat method*, the tank method of sparkling wine production is used primarily in the production of wines that emphasize a youthful, fruity character, such as those produced from Muscat or Riesling grapes. The process begins with a dry base wine, which is placed in a pressurized tank along with a measured amount of yeast and sugar. This mixture then ferments under pressure, keeping the newly-created carbon dioxide inside the tank and dissolved in the liquid. After the fermentation is complete, the wine may be allowed to age on the lees, although the typical style of wine produced via the Tank Method does not require this step. In either case, when the wine is ready to be racked it is pumped through a filter, adjusted for sweetness if necessary, and bottled for immediate release.

The Partial Fermentation Method: The partial fermentation method is used to produce low-alcohol, lightly-sparkling, sweet wines such as Italy's Moscato d'Asti and Brachetto d'Acqui (both from the Piedmont region). The partial fermentation method consists of a single fermentation that is allowed to proceed just long enough to produce a low level of alcohol (typically around 5% to 7%). The fermentation takes place in a pressurized tank, which seals in the carbon dioxide, and when the desired levels of alcohol and carbon dioxide are reached, the wine is sterile-filtered and bottled.

Carbonation: The least expensive method of making a sparkling wine is to inject carbon dioxide directly into a still wine, much like making a carbonated soft drink. This method creates bubbles

that are larger and shorter-lived than those produced via fermentation and, as such, is primarily used for wines in the lower price categories.

THE PRODUCTION OF FORTIFIED WINES

A fortified wine is a wine to which alcohol (typically grape spirits) has been added to raise the final alcohol level. Fortified wines will have higher levels of alcohol by volume than those produced via natural fermentation, with many as high as 20%.

Fortified wines are made in most wine-producing countries. Sherry (produced in Spain), Port and Madeira (produced in Portugal), and Marsala (produced in Italy) are among the world's best-known fortified wines.

The winemaking process for fortified wines begins by producing a base wine in the same way one would produce a basic table wine. In the production of sweet fortified wines, such as Vintage Port, the fermentation is interrupted via the addition of a distilled spirit. Enough of the distilled spirit is added so that the overall alcohol content by volume is high enough to quickly kill all the yeast, stopping the process of fermentation. The addition of the distilled spirit must be carefully timed so as to leave quite a bit of sugar remaining once the fermentation is halted, and many sweet fortified wines have residual sugar levels of 10% or higher.

In the production of dry fortified wines, such as Fino Sherry or other dry styles of sherry, the fermentation of the base wine is allowed to continue naturally until all the fermentable sugar is used up by the yeast cells. The distilled spirits are then added at the end of fermentation.

Aging, blending, and finishing regimens following fortification vary by region and also by the style of the fortified wine. Due to the preservative effect of the added alcohol, fortified wines are much sturdier than typical table wines, and many fortified wines are elaborately aged before being bottled.

SPECIAL WINEMAKING PRACTICES

The world of wine is wide and diverse, and there are a plethora of winemaking practices that may be used in special circumstances, or to create unique styles of wine. Some of these are discussed below.

Late Harvest: If growers wait beyond the typical, optimal ripeness point to harvest the grapes, the berries will continue to gain sugar as long as there are green leaves on the vine. The grapes will begin to lose some water as well, making them very sweet. However, they also lose acidity during this period, so this process should only be used with grapes that are naturally high in acid, and ideally in cool climates. Late harvest grapes are typically used to produce sweet wines, however, in some cases they may be fermented to dryness, resulting in richly-flavored and textured wines.

Botrytis: *Botrytis cinerea* is a fungus, sometimes referred to a "noble rot." Under the right conditions, botrytis forms on ripe or nearly-ripe grapes, causing the grapes to shrivel while drawing water out of them. This concentrates the sugar content in the grapes while simultaneously adding distinctive flavor elements such as the aromas of honeysuckle and beeswax. This most famously occurs in the Sauternes area of Bordeaux in France as well as the Loire Valley, where some of the most world-renowned dessert wines are produced. Sémillon and Chenin Blanc are two grape varieties that have a particular affinity for botrytis due to their thin skins.

Dried Grapes: After harvest, grapes can be allowed to dry out and become partially raisinated. This is an ancient tradition that is still practiced in many places around the Mediterranean. The grapes may be spread out on mats or hung from the rafters of a drying room for as long as several months, retaining sugar but losing water content. The dried grapes may be fermented into a dry, high-alcohol wine, as in Italy's Amarone, or more often, into a sweet wine.

Icewine: In some cold regions, primarily in Germany and Canada, growers may leave the grapes on the vine until the weather turns cold enough to freeze them. This may be as late as January or February in the Northern Hemisphere. By this time, the grapes have developed significant sugar content. Following harvest, the frozen grapes are pressed immediately, resulting in extremely sweet, rich juice that is used to produce some of the world's sweetest wines. Riesling, Gewürztraminer, Chenin Blanc, and some cold-hardy hybrids are the most common varieties used in these styles of wine, known as *icewine* (ice wine) or *Eiswein*.

Carbonic Maceration: Carbonic maceration is an alternative method of red winemaking involving an enzymatic fermentation that requires neither yeast nor bacteria. It will occur in whole, unbroken grapes in the absence of oxygen. To begin the process, grapes are carefully placed in an enclosed fermentation vessel and blanketed with carbon dioxide. In this environment, enzymes in the grapes themselves will begin to break down the grape sugars and create some alcohol within the berries, along with other compounds that may affect wine flavor. Carbonic maceration generally results in red wines that are low in tannin, brightly colored, and showing aromas and flavors of tropical fruit and red berries.

GRAPE VARIETIES

Due to their unique chemical structure, grapes are the ideal raw ingredient for the production of fine wine. Grapes contain a good percentage of water as well as an ideal level of the fermentable sugars glucose and fructose, and have the potential to retain high levels of acidity. Many of the substances found in grapes have the ability to transform, via alcoholic fermentation and other related chemical reactions, into hundreds of minute physical compounds. These compounds lend complexity of aromas and flavors—as well as, it is hoped, deliciousness—to a finished wine.

Wine grapes differ from table grapes in that commercial plantings are almost exclusively *Vitis vinifera*, a species that evolved from the wild vines of ancient times. Familiar names such as Cabernet Sauvignon and Chardonnay are just two examples of the many thousands of varieties within the vinifera species.

Grapes suitable for winemaking must be grown in areas where they can achieve optimal ripeness. Such areas are typically found within the temperate zone that falls between 30° and 50° latitude in both the Northern and the Southern Hemispheres. Wine regions in the North are typically warmer at corresponding latitudes in the South, mostly due to greater landmass.

Where the grapes are grown has an influence on the style of wine produced. In the Northern Hemisphere, higher latitudes usually indicate cooler regions and are more suited to early-ripening varieties that do not require large amounts of warmth or sunshine in order to ripen fully. Wines from cool regions tend to be lighter in color and body. Examples of cool-climate wines include Pinot Grigio from Northern Italy and German Riesling.

Wines from warmer latitudes closer to the equator often benefit from greater exposure to sunshine and are therefore deeper in color and body. Warmer climates favor late-maturing varieties that need lots of sunshine and warm temperatures to reach optimum ripeness. Examples of warm-climate wines include Grenache-based wines produced in the south of France such as Côtes du Rhône and Châteauneuf-du-Pape.

This chapter will focus on the typical flavor profiles and preferred growing regions of the most widely-planted and highly-renowned vinifera varieties.

WHITE GRAPE VARIETIES

CHARDONNAY

Chardonnay grapes can be made into many different styles of wine, depending on the terroir of the vineyard and the winemaking practices used.

In its finest expressions, Chardonnay produces some of the most prestigious and age-worthy white wines in the world, particularly in Burgundy. When winemakers began planting vineyards in the New World, they looked to the great wines of France as their model, and Chardonnay was the natural choice.

Chardonnay is adaptable to many climates and is capable of producing wines of good, basic quality just about anywhere grapevines can grow. It performs at its finest, however, in cool- to moderate-climate sites and on limestone soils. These conditions allow the grape to retain its lively acidity and flavors of citrus, tree fruit, and mineral. In warm to hot climates, the wines produced are lower in acidity, higher in alcohol, and fuller in body. These warm-climate Chardonnays are more noticeably fruit-forward and can have flavors of tropical fruit such as pineapple and mango.

Figure 4.1: Chardonnay vineyards in the commune of Meursault (Burgundy, France)

Chardonnay is a non-aromatic grape variety, meaning that its aromas are fairly neutral. This makes it particularly well suited to winemaking techniques intended to add flavor complexity, such as the use of oak, which can introduce aromas of vanilla and spice to the wine. Partial or full malolactic fermentation may also be undertaken depending on the acid level of the wine and the style the winemaker intends. Malolactic fermentation is often responsible for the buttery aromas that many people appreciate in a glass of Chardonnay. Lees aging can also add dimension, richness, and flavor to the Chardonnay-based wines.

Prominent Sites for Chardonnay:
• Burgundy (France)
• Chablis (District of Burgundy, France)
• Napa Valley (California)
• Sonoma County (California)
• Monterey County (California)
• Washington State
• Yarra Valley (Australia)

Food Affinities for Chardonnay:
• The dry, steely wines of Chablis are excellent with all manner of fresh seafood, particularly oysters
• Medium-bodied, lightly-oaked and fruity Chardonnay pairs well with roasted poultry and lean pork dishes
• Rich, full-bodied, oak-aged Chardonnays are a nice match with smoked fish, or rich dishes with strong flavors such as roasted garlic or coconut curries, roasted cauliflower with cream sauce, and Gruyère cheese

CHENIN BLANC

Chenin Blanc is native to the Loire Valley, where it has been grown for over a thousand years. It undoubtedly produces its most captivating wines here, from crisp and fruity Vouvray to the steely and nervy Savennières. Chenin Blanc is also widely planted in South Africa, where it is sometimes referred to as "Steen."

Chenin Blanc typically produces refreshing, dry, medium-bodied wines filled with crisp apple and herb flavors. Chenin Blanc retains its high acidity even when very ripe. This makes it an ideal grape variety for producing a broad range of styles. It is made into sparkling wines as well as off-dry and sweet wines, particularly in the Loire Valley. This vigorous grape variety is also planted extensively throughout California, including the warmer areas, which highlights its adaptability as to climate.

While generally consumed as a young, fresh wine, the finest examples of Chenin Blanc can age extremely well, due to their naturally high acidity and balance. Such wines can develop flavors of honey, toast, and lanolin with age. Sweet wines produced using late harvest or botrytis-affected Chenin Blanc grapes are highly regarded, and quite often age-worthy.

Prominent Sites for Chenin Blanc:
• Loire Valley (France)
• Stellenbosch (South Africa)
• California

Food Affinities for Chenin Blanc:
• Light-to-medium-bodied dishes with earthy flavors, such as mushrooms, avocado, zucchini, endive, and spinach
• Dry wines pair well with light fish and chicken dishes
• Off-dry versions are well-suited to cream-based dishes, as well as rich stews and casseroles
• Sweet wines are excellent with tangy, fruit-based desserts or cakes, foie gras, and blue cheeses

PINOT GRIS

Pinot Gris is technically referred to as a color mutation of Pinot Noir. What this means is that Pinot Gris is genetically identical or close-to-identical to

Pinot Noir and several other members of the family of grapes descended from the ancient Pinot Noir variety. However, the grape has a distinct appearance and produces wines that are unlike Pinot Noir.

Figure 4.2: Pinot Gris grapes on the vine in Oregon

Pinot Gris is a pink- or grey-skinned grape that produces several styles of white wine. In the French region of Alsace, it displays its characteristics most intensely. Here, the ample sunshine allows it to produce rich, weighty, almost oily wines with exotic, musky aromas of spice, smoke, honey, and stone fruit. This richer style of Pinot Gris is also produced in Oregon, where it is the leading white grape variety.

Pinot Gris is also widely grown in northeastern Italy, where it is referred to as Pinot Grigio. This well-known and well-loved style of wine is more "quaffable" in style, a result of northern Italy's cool climate, and the tendency to harvest it somewhat earlier to produce a crisper, cleaner, citrusy style of wine.

Prominent Sites for Pinot Gris:
- Alsace (France)
- Willamette Valley (Oregon)
- Friuli (Italy)
- Veneto (Italy)
- New Zealand
- Germany
- Austria

Food Affinities for Pinot Gris:
- Salads, antipasti, cured meats, olives, cheeses, vegetarian dishes
- Firm-fleshed fish, scallops
- Meals based on roasted chicken or turkey

RIESLING

Riesling is a late-ripening, cold-hardy variety and, as such, it performs well in the northern latitudes of Germany, Alsace, Austria, Washington State, and other cool climate areas. Many grape varieties lose acidity as they ripen, but Riesling grapes have an outstanding ability to maintain their acidity, even when allowed to over-ripen. Because of this natural acidic backbone, Riesling wines have a natural balance and a longevity that is unique among white wines.

Figure 4.3: Riesling vineyards in Germany's Mosel region

Riesling styles vary from bone dry to very sweet, but because of its high acidity, it remains beautifully balanced. Riesling is intensely aromatic and often shows aromas of stone fruit (peach and nectarine), apple, citrus, white flowers, and wet stones. As it ages, Riesling often takes on an aroma reminiscent of petrol (gasoline), which sounds strange to the uninitiated, but is well-loved by Riesling aficionados.

Prominent Sites for Riesling:
- Mosel, Rheingau (Germany)
- Austria
- Alsace (France)
- Clare Valley, Eden Valley (Australia)
- Finger Lakes, Long Island (NY State)
- Columbia Valley (Washington State)

Food Affinities for Riesling:
- Dry and off-dry versions of riper Rieslings go well with ham and pork dishes, shellfish, salads, and smoked fish
- Off-dry styles also work well with the fat content in duck and goose, as well as with spicy cuisine and Asian flavors

- Dessert-style wines are best with fruit-based desserts such as apple tart or lemon mousse

SAUVIGNON BLANC

Sauvignon Blanc is native to France, where it gained its well-deserved reputation as a versatile, food-loving wine. Several Loire Valley regions specialize in crisp, flavorful wines based on Sauvignon Blanc, as do the white wines of Bordeaux—where it shares its star billing alongside Sémillon, its frequent blending partner.

Sauvignon Blanc is quite versatile in the vineyard, and has become a solid producer in warmer areas such as California, Australia, and parts of South Africa. The grape also has a particular affinity for cooler climates, and is the leading grape in New Zealand and Chile's coastal Casablanca Valley. California producers created and popularized the oak-aged, complex style of Sauvignon Blanc often referred to as Fumé Blanc, and New Zealand can take credit for popularizing the pungent, citrus-infused and vibrantly herbal style it produces.

Figure 4.4: Sauvignon Blanc on the vine

A hallmark of Sauvignon Blanc is its vibrant acidity and, for this reason, it does very well in blends with lower-acid grapes (such as Sémillon). Sauvignon Blanc performs best in cooler sites where it can develop its characteristic herbaceous, green fruit, and citrus aromas. When grown in warmer climates, the flavors give way to riper melon, peach, and tropical flavors, and the distinctive grassy note disappears.

Prominent Sites for Sauvignon Blanc:
- Loire Valley (France)
- Bordeaux (France)
- Marlborough (New Zealand)
- Casablanca (Chile)
- Stellenbosch (South Africa)
- Napa Valley (California)
- Sonoma County (California)

Food Affinities for Sauvignon Blanc:
- Lemon-based sauces or other condiments with high-acidity
- Capers, olives, salty condiments
- Raw seafood
- Light dishes, such as those made with vegetables, fish, shellfish, or chicken
- Creamy cheeses, brine cheeses, goat cheeses, feta cheeses

OTHER WHITE VARIETIES

Gewürztraminer: Gewürztraminer is a highly aromatic, pink-skinned grape variety that displays heady aromas of perfume and lychee. It produces wines that are deeply colored (when compared to other white wines), full-bodied, high in alcohol, and low in acidity. Gewürztraminer may be dry or contain varying degrees of residual sugar. The best examples are from Alsace, France, Germany, and northern Italy.

Muscat: Muscat is one of the world's most ancient grape varieties and has spread to just about every wine-producing country in the world. Having mutated many times, Muscat forms a family of closely related varieties. Muscat Blanc à Petits Grains is considered to be the finest, with the most finesse and aroma. It is the grape responsible for Moscato d'Asti, the popular wine from Piedmont (In Italy), as well as a range of sweet, fortified wines from the south of France, Spain, and Australia. Muscat is primarily known for its sweet wines, but is actually made into every style of wine imaginable from dry to sweet and still to sparkling, as well as fortified. Muscat is one of the few white grapes that can thrive in warm-to-hot climates, but it is successful in cool climates as well. Muscat grapes are known for their musty, perfume-like floral aromas and the characteristic scent of white grapes.

Sémillon: Sémillon is a non-aromatic variety often blended with Sauvignon Blanc, as is done in the white wines of Bordeaux. Sémillon can also be made into a dry, varietal wine, excellent examples of which are produced in Australia's Hunter Valley. This thin-skinned grape is easily penetrated by *Botrytis cinerea*, creating super-sweet grapes with complex, concentrated flavors that are often fermented into long-lived, unctuous and complex dessert wines such as Sauternes.

Torrontés: Argentina's signature white grape variety, Torrontés is aromatically similar to Gewürztraminer yet less intense, with medium body and alcohol. The Torrontés of Argentina is believed to be a natural crossing created from vinifera grapes brought to Argentina from Italy or Spain. Torrontés is typically made into a dry (or off-dry), crisp white wine with unique floral aromas and flavors of fresh grapes, white peaches, lemon zest, and grapefruit.

Viognier: Viognier is an aromatic white variety with floral (honeysuckle), stone fruit (peach, apricot) and citrus (tangerine) notes. Its wines are medium- to full-bodied, with low to medium acidity and medium to high alcohol. Viognier is grown throughout the south of France, where its best expression is found in the prestigious regions of Condrieu and Château Grillet in the Rhône Valley. Viognier is one of the few white wine grapes that can thrive in warmer areas and, as such, has spread to many New World areas, such as California, Texas, and Australia. Viognier is also planted on the East Coast of North America, including the state of Virginia, where Viognier was recently declared the state's signature grape variety.

RED GRAPE VARIETIES

CABERNET SAUVIGNON

Cabernet Sauvignon is one of the most popular grape varieties in the world, for much the same reasons as Chardonnay—it will ripen reliably in many vineyard sites, and it is recognized and appreciated by consumers around the world.

Cabernet Sauvignon, like any other grape variety, gives remarkably distinct flavors depending upon its climate. In Bordeaux's cool climate vineyards, it is blended with Merlot and Cabernet Franc (as well as Malbec, Carmenère and Petit Verdot). This blend produces some of the world's most distinguished, long-lived (and expensive) red wines. Cabernet Sauvignon's thick skins are loaded with tannin, color, and aroma—the key elements for wines with longevity that are expected to evolve into complex, well-integrated wines with age.

In New World sites such as California and Chile, Cabernet Sauvignon is made into many different styles of wine, from inexpensive and easy-drinking, to deeply-colored and profoundly complex. Its level of herbaceous character varies with ripeness level.

The key to producing good quality Cabernet Sauvignon is to aim for *physiological maturity*. This means that the tannins as well as the grape sugars have achieved optimum ripeness and the resulting wines are apt to be velvety rather than astringent in tannic structure. Well-ripened Cabernet Sauvignon often shows aromas and flavors of blackcurrant, blackberry, and black cherry. Oak-aging and other types of maturation often yield a complexity of aromas and flavors, including vanilla, tobacco, eucalyptus, and cedar.

Prominent Sites for Cabernet Sauvignon:
- Bordeaux (France)
- Tuscany (Italy)
- Napa Valley, Sonoma County (California)
- Washington State
- Hawke's Bay (New Zealand)
- Coonawarra, Margaret River (Australia)
- Maipo Valley, Colchagua Valley (Chile)

Food Affinities for Cabernet Sauvignon:
- Roast beef, grilled lamb, dishes based on beef, lamb, or pork
- Rich vegetables such as eggplant, asparagus, or roasted tomatoes
- Rich dishes with herbal accents such as mint, rosemary, thyme, or oregano
- Hearty cheeses such as Cheddars or blue cheeses

Figure 4.5: Ripe Cabernet Sauvignon grapes in Stellenbosch, South Africa

MERLOT

Merlot has become one of the most commercially important grape varieties in the world. Its soft, accessible style and easy-to-pronounce name has made it popular with consumers. Like Cabernet Sauvignon, it hails from the region of Bordeaux, where it adds suppleness and rounds out the hard edges of the typically Cabernet-dominant wines of the region's Left Bank. In the vineyards of Bordeaux's Right Bank, it takes center stage, producing sumptuous, deep wines full of plum fruit flavors and a good ability to age.

Merlot ripens quickly to high sugar levels and performs best in cooler sites where its aromas may fully develop. Too much heat can cause its acidity to plummet, and it does not do well in areas with intense sunlight. It ripens earlier than Cabernet Sauvignon, and its tannin and acidity levels are lower. Merlot typically has flavors of black cherry, plum, and chocolate. Merlot's best quality may be its velvety smoothness, which makes it an approachable, easy-to-identify wine.

Prominent Sites for Merlot:
- Bordeaux (France)
- Napa Valley (California)
- Sonoma County (California)
- Washington State
- Northern Italy
- Chile

Food Affinities for Merlot:
- Beef, pork, and lamb
- Hearty dishes accented by mint, rosemary, onions, mushrooms, tomatoes, or fennel
- Grilled dishes
- Duck
- Tandoori and other spicy dishes
- Stewed and braised dishes

PINOT NOIR

Pinot Noir inspires both passion and frustration among grape growers, winemakers, and consumers alike. Great Pinot Noir can be one of the most revelatory of great wine experiences, while an inferior Pinot can be notably disappointing. In addition, it is often described as being a difficult grape to handle in both the vineyard and the winery. For these reasons, this grape has earned the nickname "the heartbreak grape."

Many people consider the best Pinot Noir in the world to be those from the Burgundy region of France. Pinot Noir is one of the few red grape varieties that is able to ripen fully and even thrive in cool climates, and for this reason, many New World winemakers eager to replicate the Burgundian style have had the best results when planting in similarly cool sites. California's Russian River Valley, Oregon's Willamette Valley, and Central Otago in New Zealand—all cool climate regions—are a few of the New World sites that now produce world-class Pinot Noir.

Pinot Noir leans towards red fruit aromas such as strawberry, red cherry, and cranberry. It is also known for herbal, floral, and earthy aromas (sometimes described as wet dirt, barnyard, or mushroom). Great Pinot Noir is known for its silky, supple texture in addition to low to moderate tannins and moderate to high acidity. With age, its earthy notes are enhanced, and are often described as leather, smoke, and dried flowers. Pinot Noir is known as a grape that can show quite differently based on the natural characteristics of the vineyard and the particular year in which is it grown.

Prominent Sites for Pinot Noir:
- Burgundy (France)
- Willamette Valley (Oregon)
- Central Otago (New Zealand)
- Casablanca Valley (Chile)
- Yarra Valley, Tasmania (Australia)
- Walker Bay (South Africa)
- Carneros, Russian River Valley, Sonoma Coast, Santa Lucia Highlands, Anderson Valley, Santa Barbara, Sonoma Coast, Mendocino (California)

Food Affinities for Pinot Noir:
- Pork-based dishes, beef-based dishes, beef tenderloin
- Duck, turkey, chicken, or other roasted poultry
- Mushrooms, eggplant, tomatoes, roasted red bell peppers, and other flavorful vegetables
- Salmon or other firm-fleshed fish

GRENACHE

Grenache is widely grown throughout Spain (where it is known as *Garnacha*), the south of France, and parts of Italy (where it may be known as *Cannonau*). Grenache is sometimes used as a stand-alone varietal in both red and rosé wines, but it is very often used as part of a blend. This blending tradition is strong in the Southern Rhône, where the mix of Grenache-Syrah-Mourvèdre has become known as "the Rhône Blend" or "G-S-M."

Figure 4.6: Old Grenache vines in Châteauneuf-du-Pape (Rhône Valley, France)

Grenache is a Mediterranean grape variety, performing best in warm to hot climates, and able to tolerate drought conditions quite well. It ripens to very high sugar levels, resulting in fruity, high-alcohol wines. It has moderate color density, moderate tannin levels, and fairly low acidity.

At the end of the 18th century, Grenache was brought to Australia, where it is used as a varietal wine as well as in G-S-M blends. In addition, it is increasingly grown in California, Washington State, Argentina, and Chile. Grenache-based red wines are typically full-bodied with plenty of juicy, red berry flavors and hints of savory spice and herbs. Grenache makes an excellent base for flavorful, dry rosé, as seen in many areas in southern France and Spain.

Prominent Sites for Grenache:
- Rhône Valley, Provence, Languedoc-Roussillon (France)
- Rioja, Priorat, Navarra (Spain)
- Sardinia (Italy)
- Australia
- California

Food Affinities for Grenache:
- Charcuterie
- Cheese dishes or dishes made with cream
- Roasted or grilled game or poultry
- Eggplant, mushrooms, roasted pepper

Food Affinities for Rosé styles:
- Cheeses, vegetable dishes, grilled vegetables
- Green olives, black olives, sun-dried tomatoes
- Hearty fish dishes, grilled poultry or fish, fish soups or stews such as bouillabaisse or cioppino

SYRAH

Syrah is a well-known grape of southern France, where it is employed as a blending grape with Grenache and other Rhône varieties. Syrah has not yet attained the international reputation enjoyed by Cabernet Sauvignon or Merlot; although under its alias, Shiraz, it has proven to be very popular and successful in Australia. Australia boasts the second-largest vineyard area for the grape after France. Plantings in New World regions such as California, Chile, Argentina, and South Africa are increasing.

Many interesting versions of Syrah can be found in very different climates throughout the world. In the Northern Rhône, it displays a dramatic expression of black pepper, violet, tar, wild berries, and game accompanied by a full-bodied, firm structure. In the Southern Rhône, it is used primarily in blends such as the G-S-M or "Rhone Blend," and may even be one grape out of a blend of ten or even more varieties in a single bottle. New World styles tend to be softer in tannin, lower in acidity, and medium to full-bodied with lots of juicy, often jammy, fruit and sweet spice.

Prominent Sites for Syrah:
- Rhône Valley (France)
- Australia
- Santa Barbara (California)
- Washington State
- Chile
- Argentina
- South Africa

Food Affinities for Syrah:
- Northern Rhône-style: wild game, beef, pork, lamb
- New World-style: barbecue, Indian dishes (not too spicy), duck, wild game
- Either style: roasted dishes, dishes with herbs, dishes flavored with green peppercorns, black pepper, or coarse-grained mustard

OTHER RED VARIETIES

Barbera: Barbera is one of the most widely grown red grapes in Italy, and like other Italian varieties, it has followed Italian immigration patterns to portions of the New World such as California, Argentina, and Australia. Wines produced from Barbera may be concentrated, oaky, and structured or un-oaked, fresh, and fruit-driven. The grape's high acidity, medium body, and sour-cherry flavors make Barbera-based wines well-suited to a wide range of foods, including pasta, poultry, or meat dishes with tomatoes, eggplant, or roasted peppers.

Cabernet Franc: Extensively grown throughout the Loire Valley in France, this red fruit, violet, and herb-scented variety is also used as a minor blending component in Bordeaux. Cabernet Franc is increasing in popularity in some of the cooler-climate regions of the New World, such as New York State and Canada. Cabernet Franc-based wines tend to be lower in tannin, body, and alcohol than wines made using Cabernet Sauvignon. The fresh quality of Cabernet Franc makes it a wonderfully versatile food wine, pairing quite well with grilled, braised, or broiled dishes made from just about any kind of meat or poultry.

Carmenère: While originally from Bordeaux, Carmenère has become the "signature" grape of Chile. It is believed that the grape was brought to Chile with European settlers in the 1800's, just as Phylloxera was beginning its rampage through the vineyards of France. Carmenère is still grown in small amounts in Bordeaux, and is increasingly planted in China, where it goes by the name Cabernet Gernischt. Medium to full-bodied with moderate alcohol, this variety often displays vegetal aromas reminiscent of green pepper with red and black berry nuances. Carmenère is excellent with meat or vegetables accompanied by herb sauces.

Malbec: Malbec was traditionally a major blending partner in the red wines of Bordeaux, and while Malbec is still grown in Bordeaux and other parts of France, it is planted quite sparsely. However, it does star in one French red wine, the "Black Wine" of Cahors, produced in the southwest of the country. These days, Malbec is mainly known for its leading role in the wine industry in Argentina, where it is—by far—the most widely planted grape. Malbec flourishes in the warm, dry climate of Argentina's Mendoza. Mendoza Malbec tends to make medium- to full-bodied wines with smoky, juicy, and wild-berry flavors. Malbec generally has firm tannins and moderate acidity. These wines can be great values, and the best examples may age well for ten to twenty years. Malbec pairs well with spicy foods and grilled meats.

Nebbiolo: Nebbiolo, one of Italy's most prized grape varieties, is widely grown in Italy, particularly in the northwestern region of Piedmont where it stars in the highly-regarded wines of Barolo and Barbaresco (among others). Wines made with Nebbiolo tend to be extremely tannic when young, and may need to be at least eight to ten years of age for the tannins to mellow, and to show their full range of aromas,

Figure 4.7: Nebbiolo grapes ready for harvest in Barolo

which include leather, tar, tea, rose, and truffle. However, some producers are now gravitating towards a more modern, approachable style of wine made from Nebbiolo, particularly in the southern parts of Italy. Nebbiolo is best suited to rich dishes such as grilled Tuscan steak or roast beef tenderloin.

Sangiovese: Sangiovese is the main red grape of Italy, and the primary variety found in Chianti and Brunello di Montalcino, as well as many of the other famous red wines of Italy. Sangiovese may be made into a stand-alone varietal wine, but it shines as a blending partner as well, and many of Italy's well-known Sangiovese-based wines (including some versions of Chianti) are blends. Sangiovese is also quite often blended with international varieties such as Cabernet Sauvignon, Merlot, and Syrah—both in the New World, and in the Old World where Sangiovese blends are often used in the production of the stylish, successful wines known as "Super Tuscans." Sangiovese is noted as being high in acidity, with characteristic sour cherry and orange peel flavors that make it the perfect companion for beef, pork, or poultry dishes served with tomato- or fruit-based sauces.

Tempranillo: Tempranillo is Spain's most important red grape, and the main grape variety in the famous wines of Rioja. Rioja has traditionally been made in an earthy style and is usually well aged in new American oak. However, some modern producers are moving towards a more fruit-forward, polished style and have replaced American oak with French. Tempranillo is known for having a fairly neutral aroma, faintly smelling of strawberries and leather, with a savory edge. It is grown in Portugal, where

it is sometimes used in the production of Port and other wines; in Portugal it goes by the name Tinta Roriz or Aragonêz. Tempranillo is also planted in increasing amounts in the New World, such as parts of California, Texas, Oregon, and Chile. It pairs very well with beef, lamb, veal, and pork dishes, and goes particularly well with grilled foods.

Zinfandel: Zinfandel is primarily known as a California variety, despite the fact that its rather long and complicated lineage can be traced back to Croatia. Zinfandel thrives in California, as it needs plenty of sunshine and is able to ripen to very high sugar levels. This can translate into rich, red wines with high alcohol levels, often upwards of 15%. Because of its tendency to ripen unevenly, some grapes in the bunch may become raisins before the entire bunch has fully matured; this gives many Zinfandels the "jammy" character they are known for. Zinfandel is often used in rosé wines, which range from semi-sweet wines often referred to as "White Zinfandel," to dry, extracted rosés.

WINES OF THE OLD WORLD

One of the most basic ways wines can be categorized is by dividing them into Old World and New World regions. Europe, which has been making wine for at least two thousand years, is referred to as Old World. Wine-producing countries that began as European colonies—such as those in the Americas, South Africa, Australia, and New Zealand—have only been making wine for a few centuries, and are referred to as New World.

The distinction between the Old World and New World of wine, however, is much more than just historical and geographical. There are also stylistic variations between wine types as a result of climatic, geological, and cultural (grape-growing and winemaking) influences.

While the distinction between the Old World style and the New World style is in flux, the following general characteristics can be applied:

Old World wines tend to have the following characteristics:
- Higher acidity
- Lower alcohol
- Less overt fruit character
- More "earthiness" or "minerality"
- In many cases, Old World wines are regulated by European Union laws that govern many aspects of production
- Often labeled by region of origin
- More history and tradition

In contrast, New World wines tend to share the following traits:
- Higher alcohol
- More fruit-forward
- More winemaking/winemaker influence
- Often labeled by grape variety
- Less bound by regulations and traditions
- More innovation and technology

In this chapter, we will first take a look at the wine laws of the European Union. Next, we'll study the major wine-producing regions of the Old World, particularly France, Italy, Spain, Portugal, Germany, Austria, and Greece, as well as several other smaller producers. For each region, take note of how the local climate, geography, and culture impact the historical and modern wines of the area.

WINE LAWS OF THE EUROPEAN UNION

The European Union (EU) is a group of countries that joined together in 1993 to act as a single entity among other countries, allowing them to compete in the global marketplace more effectively. Most of the major wine-producing countries are part of the EU, and their wine appellation laws are governed under the same framework.

Beginning in 2007, the EU introduced legislative reforms to bring various member countries' wine laws into accordance with other appellation laws that govern the production of cheeses, oils, and other agricultural goods. Prior to this, wines were categorized into table wines and quality wines. Within the table wine category, there was a further distinction between table wines with a geographical indication and those without. Quality Wines Produced from a Specific Region (known as QWPSR) were the highest tier, and adhered to strict appellation laws.

Under the new reform that is currently in effect, there are three quality tiers for EU wine. From highest to lowest, these are:
- Protected Designation of Origin (PDO): This is the highest level of regulation for production standards, and includes strict standards for

allowed grape varieties, place-of-origin, viticultural practices, winemaking procedures, packaging, and organoleptic (sensory) features of a wine.
- Protected Geographical Indication (PGI): Formerly referred to as table wine with a geographical indication. These wines are generally sourced from a broader region or appellation and have less stringent production requirements than PDO wines, often allowing for stylistic variance and the use of international varieties.
- Wine: Formerly referred to as table wine without a geographical indication. These can be sourced from anywhere within the country (or even within the EU), and is not required to state a geographical indication.

Each country may use its equivalent in their national language for these designations. Some countries have additional levels within the PDO category, such as Spain's DO (Denominacion de Origen) and the higher quality level DOCa (Denominacion de Origen Calificada).

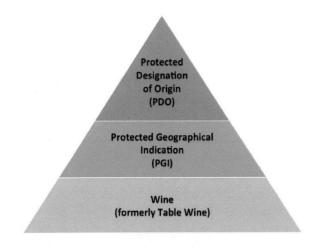

Figure 5.1: EU Wine Categories

The wine regulations of the European Union also include the following standards for wine labeling:
- If a PDO-categorized protected place name is stated on the label, 100% of the wine must be sourced from that region.
- If a vintage date is stated, at least 85% of the wine must be from that year.
- If a single grape variety is stated, at least 85% of the wine must be from that variety.

THE WINES OF FRANCE

France is one of the world's leading producers and consumers of wine. The wide range of climates and the diversity of its soils are so well suited to wine production that France, along with Italy and Spain, consistently ranks in the top three wine-producing and exporting countries (by volume) in the world. France is also one of the largest per-capita consumers of wine, underscoring not only the country's natural inclination towards wine production, but also the significance of its wine culture and winemaking tradition.

France is the native home of many widely-grown grape varieties that have been established around the world. The grapes have become known as *international varieties*, and include Chardonnay, Sauvignon Blanc, Pinot Noir, Cabernet Sauvignon, Merlot, and Syrah.

When these grapes began to be planted outside of their native homes, particularly in the New World, it was originally in hopes of re-creating the benchmark wine styles of France. Instead, these grapes have evolved over the years and adapted themselves to the diverse soils and climates of the world's vineyards. This adaptation to specific sites is the basis for the concept of *terroir*, a unique combination of a vineyard's soil, aspect, and climate that uniquely determines a wine of distinction.

The major white grape varieties of France include the following:
- Chardonnay: the major white grape of Champagne and Burgundy
- Sauvignon Blanc: one of the primary white grapes of Bordeaux and the eastern Loire Valley
- Sémillon: a variety used in Bordeaux and South-West France for blended, dry white wines; also planted in Sauternes and elsewhere as the major component of sweet, botrytis-affected white wines
- Muscat: a highly aromatic variety found in the South of France where it is used in the production of *vin doux naturel* (sweet, fortified wine) and other sweet wines
- Chenin Blanc: a versatile grape variety that is grown in the central Loire Valley.
- Ugni Blanc (aka Trebbiano): the most widely grown white grape variety in France, used primarily for the production of Cognac and Armagnac.

The major red grape varieties of France include the following:

- Merlot: widely grown throughout the country and the leading red grape of Bordeaux
- Grenache: a warm-climate grape that thrives in the Southern Rhône Valley as well as the Languedoc, Roussillon, and Provence
- Syrah: the leading red grape of the Northern Rhône Valley; also planted in the Southern Rhône Valley, and other areas of southern France
- Cabernet Sauvignon: closely associated with Bordeaux, where it thrives on the gravel soils of the Médoc; also grown throughout France's Southwest and the Languedoc-Roussillon.
- Cabernet Franc: favors the cooler climate of the Loire Valley, and is the third-most planted red variety in Bordeaux.
- Gamay: the leading grape variety of Beaujolais, also found in the Loire and other cool-climate areas
- Pinot Noir: the leading red grape of Burgundy and Champagne, grown in smaller amounts in Alsace and the Loire Valley

In the early twentieth century, France was the first country to devise a national system for legally protecting and restricting the use of place-names for wine regions, as well as for other traditional agricultural products such as cheeses and olive oils. This system became a model for the current regulatory system used throughout Europe.

The top tier of the French wine classification pyramid is the appellation d'origine contrôlée (AOC), "name of controlled origin," category. The name is sometimes shortened to appellation contrôlée or AC, and under the new EU system, the term appellation d'origine protégée (AOP) may be used. This category includes many of the great wines of France and carries with it restrictive regulations that ensure that a French place-name indicates a wine of quality to consumers. There are more than 300 AOCs, producing just under half of all French wine.

Major Wine Regions of France

Copyright: The Society of Wine Educators 2017

Figure 5.2: Major wine regions of France

THE WINES OF BORDEAUX (FRANCE)

The wine region of Bordeaux surrounds the city of Bordeaux in southwestern France. Near the city, two rivers, the Garonne and the Dordogne, meet to form the Gironde, a long estuary that flows into the Atlantic. These waterways divide the area into three sections: the Left Bank, to the west of the Garonne and Gironde; the Right Bank, east and north of the Dordogne and Gironde; and Entre-Deux-Mers, between the Garonne and Dordogne Rivers. Being so close to the Atlantic, Bordeaux naturally has a cool, maritime climate, but the climate is tempered thanks to the protective barrier formed by the Landes Forest along the western coast.

The Bordeaux region contains a total of sixty AOCs. Some are very small (as small as one estate) and are approved for only one type of wine, while others cover much larger areas and are permitted to produce more than one type of wine (such as dry red [rouge] and dry white [blanc]). Bordeaux also has several region-wide AOCs, such as the Bordeaux AOC which is approved for dry red, dry white, sweet white, and dry rosé wines produced from grapes grown anywhere in the region. Another regional appellation, the Crémant de Bordeaux AOC, is approved for Traditional Method sparkling wines with a minimum of 3.5 atmospheres of pressure; it may be either white or rosé.

A large proportion (as high as 89%) of the production in Bordeaux is red wine, and the region is home to some of the most prestigious dry red wines in the world. However, this very large region spanning over 250,000 acres (102,000 ha) of vines produces wines at all levels of quality and price, including value-priced wines, mid-range wines, and premium wines that are among the most expensive in the world.

Bordeaux wines are usually blends. The red Bordeaux blend consists of:
- Merlot
- Cabernet Sauvignon
- Cabernet Franc
- Malbec
- Petit Verdot
- Carmenère

Merlot is by far the most-planted red grape in Bordeaux with just over 170,000 acres (69,100 ha). Merlot is particularly heavily planted on the Right Bank and in Entre-Deux-Mers. It is followed by Cabernet Sauvignon, which is planted to just over 65,000 acres (26,300 ha) and especially concentrated on the Left Bank. At just over 28,000 acres, the third most widely planted red grape is Cabernet Franc. Malbec, Petit Verdot, and Carmenère are planted in much smaller amounts. While blending is not mandated, standard practice is to blend two or more of these varieties together to make red Bordeaux.

The primary white grapes of Bordeaux are
- Sémillon
- Sauvignon Blanc
- Muscadelle

Sémillon is the leading white grape of Bordeaux, at just over 17,000 acres (6,900 ha). It is followed by Sauvignon Blanc, which is planted to just over 12,000 acres (4,900 ha). A minor third grape is Muscadelle, which is sometimes added for its floral notes. A few other white grapes are permitted for limited use in some of the white wines of the region;

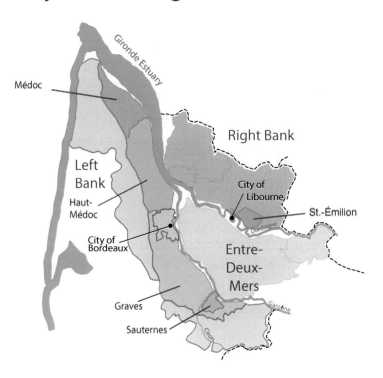

Major Wine Regions of Bordeaux

Copyright: The Society of Wine Educators 2017

Figure 5.3: Major wine regions of Bordeaux

these include Colombard, Ugni Blanc, and Merlot Blanc, among others. Almost all of the white grapes are found on the Left Bank, south of (upriver from) Bordeaux city, and in Entre-Deux-Mers.

The Médoc: The city of Bordeaux lies on the Left Bank. The area of the Left Bank north of Bordeaux city is called the Médoc; the area south and west of the city on the Left Bank is known as Graves. The Médoc is home to most of the area's most famous and prestigious wine estates (known here as châteaux) and specializes in Cabernet Sauvignon-dominant red wines. The renowned estates of Château Lafite Rothschild, Château Latour, and Château Margaux are all located in the Médoc.

Graves: The area around the city of Graves produces a range of wines and is especially famous for the sweet, botrytis-affected white wines produced in and around Sauternes. These sweet wines are normally Sémillon-based, with a small amount of Sauvignon Blanc added. They are harvested late in the season to achieve the highest possible sugar level and, in good years, to give botrytis a chance to develop. The resulting wines are rich, highly flavorful, and sweet. Château d'Yquem, located in Sauternes, is undoubtedly the most prestigious producer of this style of wine.

The Right Bank: The central areas of the Right Bank around St.-Émilion produce some top-quality, long-lived red Bordeaux. Right Bank red wines usually feature a substantial contribution from all three major red varieties, with Merlot often leading the blend. Château Cheval Blanc, Château Ausone, Pétrus, and Château Le Pin are among the most prestigious red wines of the Right Bank, which also produces a good deal of moderate and value-priced wine as well.

Entre-Deux-Mers: The soil of Entre-Deux-Mers, the triangular area between the Garonne and Dordogne Rivers, is more fertile than other parts of Bordeaux, so its wines tend to lack the concentration of those from either bank. The Entre-Deux-Mers AOC is approved for white wines only; however, a good deal of red grapes (primarily Merlot) are grown in this area as well. While there are a few small AOCs approved for red wines in the area, most of the red grapes grown here are made into "basic" Bordeaux AOC wine.

THE WINES OF THE LOIRE VALLEY (FRANCE)

The Loire Valley is really several different wine regions rolled into one, stretching roughly 250 miles (400 km) inland from the Atlantic coast. Its only common feature is the Loire River, the longest river in France. As a whole, the Loire Valley is known primarily for crisp white wines, light red wines, rosés, and some fine sweet and sparkling wines. However, each distinct subregion—(from east to west) the Pays Nantais, Anjou/Saumur, Touraine, and Eastern Loire—focuses on different grape varieties.

The Pays Nantais: The Pays Nantais is situated on low-lying terrain close to the ocean, and has a chilly maritime-influenced climate. The best-known grape variety of the Pays Nantais is Melon de Bourgogne, a white grape that tends to produce neutral, high-acid wines that are best consumed young. This grape represents three-quarters of Nantais vineyards and is the only grape variety allowed in four appellations: Muscadet AOC, Muscadet Coteaux de la Loire AOC, Muscadet Côtes de Grandlieu AOC, and Muscadet Sèvre et Maine AOC. In order to produce a more

complex and interesting wine, many producers of Muscadet put the wines through several months (or longer) of sur lie aging before the wine is finished and bottled.

Anjou/Saumur: The Anjou-Saumur is considered part of the Central Loire, along with Touraine, its neighbor to the east. Several well-known AOCs are located in the area, many of which produce their own unique styles of wine. These include:

- Savennières: a small region that produces dry, complex white wines based on the Chenin Blanc grape variety
- Rosé d'Anjou: a very popular, off-dry rosé wine produced from a variety of red grapes, including Grolleau, Cabernet Franc, Cabernet Sauvignon, and Malbec
- Quarts de Chaume: the highly regarded, sweet, white, botrytis-affected wine made using Chenin Blanc grapes has been granted the Loire Valley's only grand cru designation
- Saumur: the Saumur AOC is approved for many styles of wine, but is most well-known for its white and rosé sparkling wines

Touraine: Considered part of the Central Loire but located to the east of Anjou and Saumur, Touraine is home to Vouvray, one of the most well-known of the Loire appellations. The Vouvray AOC produces white wines based on the Chenin Blanc grape variety. Vouvray is typically a dry, still wine, but the style may range from dry to sweet, and some sparkling wines are produced as well. Across the river from Vouvray, its counterpart, Montlouis-sur-Loire, produces wines very similar in style.

Touraine is also home to Chinon, Bourgueil, and St.-Nicolas-de-Bourgueil. The highly regarded red wines of these appellations must be produced using a majority of Cabernet Franc, but often have a measure of Cabernet Sauvignon added for additional structure and complexity.

The Upper Loire: The Upper Loire (also known as the Eastern Loire) experiences less maritime influence and a warmer, drier climate. Vineyards in this area are focused on Sauvignon Blanc. Two of the AOCs of the Upper Loire, Sancerre and Pouilly-Fumé, are among the most famous of the Loire Valley and their white wines often rank among the

Main Wine Regions of the Loire Valley

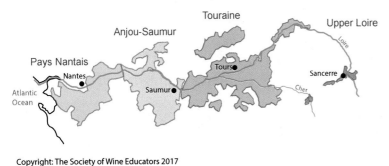

Copyright: The Society of Wine Educators 2017

Figure 5.4: Main wine regions of the Loire Valley

world's finest examples of dry, crisp, and elegant Sauvignon Blanc.

THE WINES OF CHAMPAGNE (FRANCE)

The Champagne region is the northernmost vineyard area of France, located about seventy-five miles northeast of Paris. This contributes to the overall cool climate of the area, making it ideally suited to the production of its famous sparkling wines.

The grapes grown in Champagne, which barely ripen by most regions' standards, are picked at high levels of acidity and low levels of sugar, which is essential in sparkling wine production. These grapes produce a crisp, rather neutral-tasting and moderate-alcohol wine that will be used as a base wine for Champagne. This base wine will undergo a second fermentation in the bottle that will capture up to six atmospheres of pressure of carbon dioxide. Carbon dioxide will become the bubbles that make this wine so famous. (Note: more detailed information on the Méthode Champenoise—the production process used in Champagne—may be found in chapter 3.)

Champagne is almost always made from one or more of the three main permitted grape varieties: Chardonnay, Pinot Noir, and Pinot Meunier. However, the region does allow the use of four additional grape varieties—Pinot Blanc, Pinot Gris, Petit Meslier, and Arbane. While somewhat obscure, these grapes are appreciated by some producers and are sometimes used in wines that emphasize the uniqueness of the grapes, such as Le Nombre d'Or (Golden Number) Champagne produced by the House of Aubry.

Styles of Champagne: Champagnes are almost always blends of different villages, vineyards, grape varieties, and vintages. Champagne is also made in many styles, which include the following:

- Nonvintage: the standard wine of a Champagne producer ("house"), made to a consistent "house style" by using a blend of wines from several vintages; this category accounts for three-quarters of Champagne production
- Vintage: Champagne from a single year's harvest; produced only in the best years
- Prestige cuvée, tête de cuvée, or cuvée spéciale: the top-of-the-line product produced by a Champagne house, using the finest grapes and most careful production techniques
- Blanc de blancs: wine produced from only white grapes, primarily Chardonnay
- Blanc de noirs: wine produced from only red grapes, primarily Pinot Noir, but sometimes with Pinot Meunier included
- Rosé: pink Champagne produced from base wines that have been allowed to macerate on the red grape skins for a short period of time, or by blending up to 20% red wine into the base wine

The sweetness level of Champagne is clearly marked on the label using terms such as the following:

- Extra Brut: quite dry, less than 0.6% residual sugar
- Brut: dry, less than 1.2% residual sugar
- Extra Dry: off-dry, between 1.2% and 1.7% residual sugar
- Sec: slightly sweet, between 1.7% and 3.2% residual sugar
- Demi-Sec: sweet, between 3.2% and 5.0% residual sugar
- Doux: quite sweet, more than 5.0% residual sugar

THE WINES OF BURGUNDY (FRANCE)

Located in east-central France, the renowned region of Burgundy has a northern continental climate with hot summers, cool autumns, and often-severe winters. The soils have varying amounts of limestone that produce grapes with good acidity. The majority of the wines produced in Burgundy are either dry white wines from Chardonnay or dry red wines from Pinot Noir. Small amounts of rosé and sparkling wine (produced under the Crémant de Bourgogne AOC) are produced as well.

Classic Burgundian Pinot Noir has red fruit flavors (cherry, strawberry, raspberry, sometimes rhubarb, cranberry, or pomegranate) that evolve with age to show earthy, smoky, and sometimes "gamey" notes. White Burgundy tends to be richer than many other versions of Chardonnay, with its fruit aromas (such as Meyer lemon, ripe pear, golden apple, and quince) enhanced by a subtle earthiness and, if the wine is oak-aged, a touch of nutty or toasty complexity. In general, the wines of Burgundy are medium bodied, with a good zing of acidity, and the reds show moderate tannins—all of which make them excellent food wines.

The wine-producing areas of Burgundy are divided into the four distinct vineyard areas of Chablis, the Côte d'Or, the Côte Chalonnaise, and the Mâconnais. The most renowned vineyards of Burgundy lie along the Côte d'Or, or golden slope. The Côte d'Or consists of two sections; the Côte de Nuits and, just to its south, the Côte de Beaune. The region of Chablis, which produces a very dry, mineral-scented white wine, lies to the north, and the warmer regions of the Côte Chalonnaise and the Mâconnais are located to the south.

Wine has been made in Burgundy for almost two thousand years, and its wine growers have a deep understanding of the land. This led to Burgundy being considered one of the most terroir-centric wine regions on earth, with its area being divided into more than one hundred separate AOCs. These appellations are often arranged with large, regional appellations encompassing smaller and smaller appellations. Typically, the smallest appellations are individually named vineyards.

The most highly regarded of Burgundy's wines are produced in its thirty-three grand cru vineyards. Each grand cru is a distinct AOC named after the vineyard.

Main Wine Regions of Burgundy

Figure 5.5: Main wine regions of Burgundy

These vineyards have been chosen due to the quality of the soil, micro-climate, and other aspects of terroir. Corton, Romanée-Conti, Montrachet, Chambertin, Richebourg, and La Tâche are among the best-known of the Burgundy grands crus.

THE WINES OF BEAUJOLAIS (FRANCE)

Beaujolais is situated along the Saône River directly south of the Burgundy's Mâconnais region. The red Gamay grape variety (technically known as Gamay Noir à Jus Blanc) comprises about 98% of Beaujolais's vineyards, with the remainder planted to Chardonnay, Aligoté, and Pinot Noir; small amounts of Melon de Bourgogne and Pinot Gris are found as well.

Nearly all the wines of the Beaujolais AOC are light- to medium-bodied, Gamay-based red wines with bright red fruit aromas and flavors. Some are produced using a specialized fermentation technique known as *carbonic maceration* that gives a unique tropical fruit aroma and produces exceptionally fruity, low-tannin wines with a vivid purple-ruby color. Such wines can be ready to drink almost as soon as the fermentation is complete. A considerable volume is bottled within weeks of the fermentation and sold worldwide, beginning the third Thursday in November, as *Beaujolais Nouveau*. The release of Beaujolais Nouveau is celebrated each year as one of the first French wines of the vintage.

The Beaujolais Cru: Despite the fact that Beaujolais is very well known for this light, fruity style of wine, grapes grown in the northernmost part of the district (where the granite soil is most prevalent) can have a more substantial character. Grapes from this part of the region are vinified using more typical production techniques rather than carbonic maceration, and produce wines that are often richer, more structured, and capable of improving for a few years after bottling. The best of these wines are grown in ten defined areas known as the Beaujolais Cru. Among the best-known are Moulin-à-Vent, Fleurie, and Morgon. As a group, the crus produce a third of the wine of Beaujolais.

THE WINES OF ALSACE (FRANCE)

Alsace is located at the northeast corner of France—stretched out in a north–south band seventy-five miles long—sandwiched between the Vosges Mountains to the west and the Rhine River to the east. Alsace has a cold continental climate due to its northerly location and distance from the ocean. It is also one of the driest areas of France as a result of the rain shadow created by the Vosges. The mountains block rain and humidity coming off the Atlantic and give the region an abundance of sunshine.

Alsace is overwhelmingly white grape territory, with Pinot Noir being the only red grape variety permitted in the AOC wines of the region. Placing emphasis on the grape variety, typical Alsace white wines are single variety, with aromatic, fresh-fruit-driven profiles and moderate acidity.

Figure 5.6: The town of Riquewihr and vineyards in Alsace

Varietal wines in the Alsace AOC may be produced from the following ten grape varieties: Riesling, Gewurztraminer, Pinot Gris, Pinot Noir, Pinot Blanc, Sylvaner, Muscat, Chasselas, Auxerrois, and Klevener de Heiligenstein (also known as Savagnin Rose). An eleventh grape, Chardonnay, may only be used in the sparkling wines of the region.

There are three types of appellations in Alsace: Alsace AOC, Alsace Grand Cru AOC, and Crémant d'Alsace AOC. Most wines fall under the general Alsace AOC, which covers the entire district. Under appellation rules, if a winery labels a wine with the name of a grape variety, it must be produced 100% from that grape.

There are currently fifty-one grand cru vineyards in Alsace, each of which is recognized as an individual appellation (AOC). With very few exceptions, the grand cru vineyards of Alsace are permitted to grow only the "noble varieties" of Gewurztraminer, Muscat, Pinot Gris, or Riesling.

Though Alsace, like Germany, specializes in aromatic grape varieties, Alsatian wines are quite different from German wines of the same variety due to differences in terroir. The wines of Alsace tend to be drier, more full-bodied, and higher in alcohol than their German counterparts. Alsatian Riesling is characterized by ripe stone fruit, steely minerality and high acidity. Gewurztraminer is quite aromatic and spicy, often golden in color with low acidity and high alcohol. Alsatian Pinot Gris tends to be rich and high in alcohol, with exotic musk and nutty aromas.

THE WINES OF THE RHÔNE VALLEY (FRANCE)

The Rhône Valley is best understood as two distinct wine regions that lie along the long Rhône River. These two regions are separated by a gap of about 30 miles (48 km).

The Northern Rhône Valley, while home to many prestigious wines, only represents about 5% of the total production of the entire Rhône Valley. The Northern Rhône is a region of very steep hills and

Figure 5.7: The crumbling castle in the town of Châteauneuf-du-Pape

a continental climate with hot summers and harsh winters. The red wines of the Northern Rhône Valley are based on the Syrah grape and tend to be deeply colored, powerful wines with high tannins and good acidity. The best-known red wines of the Northern Rhône Valley are produced in the AOCs of Côte-Rôtie, Hermitage, Cornas, St.-Joseph, and Crozes-Hermitage; some of these appellations produce a small amount of white wine as well.

While the Northern Rhône is indisputably red wine country, three appellations are approved for white wine only. Two of these, Condrieu AOC and the tiny Château-Grillet AOC, produce highly regarded wines from 100% Viognier. The Saint-Péray AOC produces still and sparkling white wines from a blend of Marsanne and Roussanne.

The Southern Rhône Valley covers much more ground than the northern vineyards and is the source for 95% of the Rhône's total production. The regional Côtes du Rhône appellation covers most of the area (including the Northern Rhône, although wine from the north rarely sacrifices a more famous appellation for the Côtes du Rhône label) and accounts for more than half of the Rhône Valley's output. Côtes du Rhône wines are produced in red, white, and rosé styles and may be produced using many combinations of over twenty permitted grape varieties.

The Southern Rhône Valley is home to several wines that have distinguished themselves sufficiently enough to warrant their own AOCs. Foremost among them is Châteauneuf-du-Pape, known for its hearty red blend of grapes as well as a small amount of white wine. (See table 5.1 for a list of grapes allowed in Châteauneuf-du-Pape.) The nearby AOCs of Gigondas, Lirac, Rasteau, Cairanne, and Vacqueyras are also known for hearty red blends, although some produce small amounts of white and rosé as well.

Table 5.1: The Allowed Grape Varieties of Châteauneuf-du-Pape AOC

Grenache–Noir, Gris, and Blanc
Mourvèdre
Syrah
Cinsault
Counoise
Bourboulenc
Roussanne
Brun Argenté (Vaccarèse)
Clairette, Clairette Rosé
Muscardin
Picardan
Piquepoul–Noir, Gris, and Blanc
Terret Noir

The Southern Rhône Valley is also home to several producers of sweet wine. Muscat de Beaumes-de-Venise is a vin doux naturel (sweet, fortified wine) made from the Muscat grape variety; it has an alcohol level of 15% or more and a minimum of 10% residual sugar. While usually produced as a white wine, rosé and red versions of Muscat de Beaumes-de-Venise are made as well, using red Muscat grapes in addition to white. Another vin doux naturel is produced in the Rasteau appellation. Rasteau vin doux naturel is generally a red wine based on Grenache; however, white, tawny, and rosé versions are also produced.

The Southern Rhône appellation of Tavel produces rosé exclusively. Tavel rosé, made primarily from Grenache and Cinsault, is considered one of the finest dry rosés of France.

THE WINES OF PROVENCE (FRANCE)

Blessed with nearly perfect Mediterranean climatic conditions, Provence produces a wide range of wine styles, but is particularly well known for rosé. Crisp, dry, and flavorful rosé accounts for nearly 88% of the wine produced in the region.

Provence rosé is generally made from a blend of grapes; the leading grapes include Grenache, Cinsault, Syrah, Mourvèdre, and Tibouren. Provence accounts for 40% of all AOC rosé production in France, making it at least partially responsible for France's position as the number one producer of rosé wine worldwide.

Provence produces only a small amount of red wine (9%), supplemented by an even smaller production of white wine (3.5%). Bandol, a communal AOC, produces Provence's best-known red wine as well as a deep, complex rosé wine. Bandol (both red and rosé) is made primarily from the Mourvèdre, Grenache, and Cinsault grape varieties.

THE WINES OF ITALY

Italy has an ancient winemaking history, with the earliest vineyards laid down by Greek settlers as far back as 800 BCE. The entire country of Italy is so well suited to wine production that it is consistently among the top wine-producing countries of the world (by volume).

Italy's most notable topographic feature is its long Mediterranean coastline. Shaped like a boot, Italy is suspended from the middle of the European continent into the Mediterranean Sea. The sea surrounds Italy everywhere except in the north, and few places in the country are more than 75 miles (121 km) from it. The Mediterranean acts as a moderating influence on the weather, reducing the summer heat by a few degrees and warding off the worst winter cold.

Copyright: The Society of Wine Educators 2016

Figure 5.8: Italy

Nevertheless, the country is 735 miles (1,180 km) long, and there is a considerable difference in climate between the cool, alpine north and the hot southern parts of the country.

Italy is home to a huge diversity of *Vitis vinifera*, and most of Italy's grape varieties are closely associated with one section of the country, even if they are also found elsewhere. For instance, although Sangiovese, the most widely planted red grape variety in Italy, can be found in many regions, it is known primarily as the grape of Tuscany. Other leading, red grape varieties include Nebbiolo, Barbera, Montepulciano, Negroamaro, and Nero d'Avola. Trebbiano (known as Ugni Blanc in France) is Italy's most widely grown white grape variety, along with Catarratto, Pinot Grigio, Malvasia, and Garganega. International varieties have, traditionally, not played a very large role in the Italian wine industry, but this is evolving with Chardonnay, Moscato (Muscat), Merlot, and Cabernet Sauvignon among the leading grapes of the country.

Politically, Italy is subdivided into twenty administrative regions: eighteen on the mainland, plus the two large islands of Sicily and Sardinia located in the Mediterranean to the west of the peninsula. The northern tier is the most prosperous part of the country, containing the majority of Italy's industrial infrastructure, including the cities of Milan, Turin, and Venice, the rich agricultural lands of the Po River Basin, and the highly respected wine regions of Piedmont and Veneto. Tuscany, located somewhat in the center of the Italian peninsula, is another internationally renowned Italian wine region, famous not only for its wines but also for its cultural sites and beautiful scenery.

Under modern wine law, PDO wines are divided into two categories in Italy. The primary designation is denominazione di origine controllata (DOC). The denominazione di origine controllata e garantita (DOCG) designates a higher-level classification among quality (PDO) wines. As of early 2017, Italy had 74 DOCGs and 334 DOCs, and this number is sure to remain in flux for the foreseeable future. Collectively, DOC and DOCG wine regions account for a little more than one-third of all Italian wine production. The indicazione geografica tipica (IGT) category, created in 1992, is a lower-tier—but

quite important—category of Italian wines which represents the wines with protected geographical indication (PGI) status. There are now more than one hundred IGT zones, producing almost 30% of all Italian wine.

THE WINES OF VENETO (ITALY)

Located in the northeast of the country, Veneto is the largest wine-producing region (by volume) in Italy. It is bordered by the regions of Trentino-Alto Adige to the northwest and Friuli-Venezia Giulia to the northeast. Its southern border sits along the Adriatic coast. The region's southern and eastern sections contain fertile soils well suited to high volume wine production, while the northern and western sections are more mountainous, with less fertile soils that are better suited to quality wine production.

The western section of Veneto is home to some of Italy's most popular exports, including Valpolicella DOC, a red blend made primarily from the Corvina and Rondinella grape varieties. Several variations of Valpolicella are produced, including Amarone della Valpolicella DOCG, a sturdy, often bitter-tasting version of Valpolicella made partially with dried grapes, and Recioto della Valpolicella DOCG, a sweet version (also made with partially dried grapes).

Bardolino DOC is often compared to Valpolicella, which makes sense as the wine is also based on the red Corvina grape variety. Bardolino DOC is also well known for its rosé version, known as *chiaretto*, and Bardolino Superiore DOCG, made from the same grape varieties but according to stricter standards in terms of yield and levels of alcohol.

Soave DOC, one of the best-known white wines of Veneto, is a widely-distributed, easy-drinking white wine. Its main ingredient is the Garganega grape, which must comprise at least 70% of the wine and may be blended with Trebbiano di Soave (Verdicchio), Chardonnay, or both. Soave is the third most-produced PDO wine in Italy (by volume), behind Chianti and Asti.

Veneto is particularly well known for Prosecco, a wildly popular sparkling white wine made from the Glera grape variety. A good deal of varietally-labeled IGT wines, particularly Merlot, Pinot Grigio, and Chardonnay, are also produced in Veneto.

THE WINES OF PIEDMONT (ITALY)

Piedmont—famous for its long-lived, complex red wines as well as its sweet, sparkling whites (and a few white wines as well)—takes its name from its position at the "foot of the mountains." Located in the northwest, it lies at the foothills of the Italian Alps alongside a portion of the Apennines. Piedmont is one of the few areas of Italy that experiences a continental climate, characterized by harsh winters, warm summers, and foggy autumns.

The majority of the wine produced in Piedmont is red, and the area's most famous grape is the tannic, high-acid Nebbiolo, which produces the region's blockbuster wines. However, the lighter, but still high-acid, lower-tannin Barbera is the most widely planted variety of the region. Other red varieties include Dolcetto, Freisa, Grignolino, and Brachetto. The leading white varieties are Moscato, Arneis, and Cortese.

The DOCGs of Barolo and Barbaresco are so famous that they are often referred to as "the king and queen of Italian wine." These two areas—as well as the other Nebbiolo-based DOCGs of Piedmont, including Gattinara and Ghemme—showcase Nebbiolo's potential for high quality, long-lived, full-bodied wines high in tannins and acidity. Nebbiolo is known for its unique aromas of rose, cherry, tar, and dried tea.

Figure 5.9: Vineyards in Piedmont surrounding the town of Barolo

The Barbera grape variety is used in a range of Piedmontese wines, including Nizza DOCG, Barbera d'Asti DOCG and Barbera d'Alba DOC. Barbera-based wines produced in Piedmont range from medium-bodied, refreshing, and fruit-focused with minimal to no oak treatment to sturdier wines best described as rich, bold and flavorful (and likely to have oak influence).

While mainly known for red wines, Piedmont produces outstanding white wines as well. Foremost among these are the Gavi DOCG, located in the southeast corner of Piedmont and producing crisp, floral white wines made from the Cortese grape, as well as the Roero Arneis DOCG, a highly regarded wine made from the fragrant Arneis grape variety.

Piedmont is also home to several well-known sparkling wines, including Asti, the very popular, intensely aromatic wine full of peach and apricot flavors made from 100% Moscato (Muscat) grapes. Asti DOCG is a spumante (fully sparkling) version; the calmer Moscato d'Asti DOCG is a frizzante (lightly sparkling) version. Brachetto d'Acqui DOCG is a unique, sweet red sparkling wine made from the Brachetto grape. Brachetto d'Acqui is known for its intense floral and berry aromas, and is an excellent choice with sweets (particularly milk chocolate or berry desserts).

THE WINES OF TUSCANY (ITALY)

Tuscany is a hilly region in central Italy with excellent sunlight exposure and a vast diversity of microclimates—from the warm interior to the cooler areas on the Mediterranean coast. Its primary cities are Florence, Pisa, and Siena. Tuscany is Italy's most famous wine region, due partly to its familiarity to tourists and partly to Chianti, one of Italy's largest-volume quality wines.

Only one other Italian region (Calabria) is more intently focused on red wines than Tuscany. Almost 90% of the region's output is red (including a small proportion of rosato). The traditional reds, all containing a majority of Sangiovese, are generally high in acid, moderate in tannin, and full of bright cherry and red berry aromas and flavors with a hint of flowers (roses, violets) and dried orange peel. Sangiovese generally produces medium- to full-bodied wines with high levels of acidity.

Chianti is a dry red wine produced primarily with Sangiovese, although in some cases a small proportion of other grapes—such as Canaiolo Nero and Colorino, or even international varieties such as Cabernet Sauvignon and Merlot—are blended in as well. The Chianti DOCG has seven sub-regions (Colli Aretini, Colli Fiorentini, Colli Senesi, Colline Pisane, Montalbano, Montespertoli, and Rufina). The original zone of Chianti wine, known today as the Chianti Classico DOCG, lies in the hills and valleys between Florence and Siena.

Another of Italy's best-known wines, Brunello di Montalcino DOCG, is produced in the idyllic hill town of Montalcino. Brunello, named for the local clone of Sangiovese, is typically a powerful wine that requires at least four years of aging before release (five for Riserva). Montalcino growers also have the Rosso di Montalcino DOC available to them for lighter, shorter-aged wines made from the same grape variety.

Vino Nobile di Montepulciano DOCG is another highly respected Sangiovese-based wine produced in Tuscany. Made in the village of Montepulciano, Vino Nobile is based on a minimum of 70% Prugnolo Gentile, another local synonym for Sangiovese.

Tuscany's best-known white wine, Vernaccia di San Gimignano DOCG, is produced from the Vernaccia grape in the area surrounding the town of San Gimignano. The indigenous Vernaccia grape is quite ancient, with historical evidence of its existence dating to the thirteenth century. Vernaccia di San Gimignano is a crisp, dry white wine with notes of citrus fruit, almond, and minerals.

THE WINES OF SPAIN

Spain is a moderately large country in southwestern Europe where, along with Portugal, it makes up the Iberian Peninsula. The country is very mountainous, with most of the interior raised on a large plateau known as the Meseta. Almost 60% of Spain lies above 2,000 feet (610 m) in elevation.

Spain has the largest area under vine of any country, yet due to the low density of its vineyard plantings,

it generally ranks third in wine production behind France and Italy. The country's mostly arid climate naturally restricts yields in many of its older vineyards.

Spain is characterized by several climate types: a cool, wet, maritime climate in the northwest; a Mediterranean climate running south to northeast; and a continental climate in the center. About half of Spain's vineyards are located on the central Meseta, a huge plateau about 2,000 feet (610 m) above sea level. Summers are hot, winters are cold, and there is a marked temperature variation between day and night.

In terms of quality wine production, Tempranillo is Spain's most important grape, at just over 20% of plantings. Tempranillo, a red variety, is widely grown around the country, and is known by many different names, depending on the region in which it is planted. Tempranillo is prized for its long-lived wines with moderate acidity and aromas of spice, chalk, strawberries, and tobacco, often accompanied by a hefty input from oak aging. Other well-respected varieties found in many parts of Spain include the red grapes Garnacha and Monastrell (known in France as Grenache and Mourvèdre) and the white Macabeo (also known as Viura).

The majority of the PDO wines of Spain are classified as denominación de origen (DO). These wines come from a demarcated zone and their production is managed with regard to grape varieties, crop yields, winemaking methods, and aging regimens. Each DO has a consejo regulador (regulating council) that controls local production areas and practices. As of 2107, there are 68 DOs in Spain, and this number is sure to change in the future.

The denominación de origen calificada (DOCa) status is reserved for standout regions among the DOs. Their standards are higher than those of the other DOs, and they must have demonstrated superior quality as a DO for at least ten years. So far, this classification has been awarded to only two wines—Rioja and Priorat. (Because Priorat is in Catalonia, the acronym may be seen in its Catalan equivalent, DOQ.)

Vino de pago (estate wine) is a category established in 2003 to recognize specific single vineyards of

Major Wine Regions of Spain

Copyright: The Society of Wine Educators 2016

Figure 5.10: Wine regions of Spain

Rioja makes a small amount of white wine based on the Viura grape and some excellent dry rosé, however, the majority of Rioja's production is red wine, based on the Tempranillo grape variety, often blended with Garnacha (Grenache). Other permitted red grapes include Mazuelo (also known as Cariñena or, outside of Spain, Carignan), and Graciano.

When young and with limited oak treatment, these wines possess aromas and flavors of strawberry and tobacco leaf. However, these wines are often aged in oak, with the aging period—such as Crianza, Reserva, or Gran Reserva—stated on the label. As the time in oak and the age of the wine increases, the wines become less focused on fruit and offer more earthy and savory characteristics.

distinction that consistently produce excellent wine. Some pagos lie within the established DOs; however, many of them do not. Pagos set their own appellation rules, but if they are located inside an existing DO, their standards must meet or exceed those of the surrounding DO. As of early 2017, there were fourteen pagos, but this number is expected to increase.

THE WINES OF RIOJA (SPAIN)

The Rioja DOCa is located in north-central Spain, closer to Bordeaux than to the Mediterranean Sea. It lies in the Ebro River Valley, mostly in the province of La Rioja, as well as in the neighboring Basque Country and Navarra. Rioja has a continental climate moderated by Mediterranean influences that come up the Ebro Valley, providing warm, sunny summers and mild winters. The Rioja DO has three subregions:

- Rioja Alta: the high-altitude, hilly area covering most of the western half of the region
- Rioja Alavesa: essentially, the part of Rioja Alta north of the Ebro
- Rioja Baja: the lower, flatter eastern part of Rioja

THE WINES OF PRIORAT (SPAIN)

The Priorat DOQ (known as "Priorato DOCa" in Spanish) is located in a mountainous region in the southwest of Catalonia. The area is only 18 miles (29 km) from the Mediterranean Sea, but mountains shield most of the region from the damp sea air and Ebro Valley winds.

Priorat is known for its *llicorella* soils of flat, easily breakable stones made of decomposed slate flecked with mica and other minerals. These famous soils impart a distinct herbal and mineral character to the powerful, deep red wines of the area. Garnacha is the primary grape of Priorat, but Cariñena is almost as prominent. Cabernet Sauvignon, Merlot, and Syrah are also listed among the allowed varieties. Some rosé (rosat in the Catalan language) is also produced in Priorat, as well as some white wine produced from Garnacha Blanca, Macabeo, Pedro Ximénez, and other approved white grapes of the region.

THE WINES OF GALICIA (SPAIN)

Galicia, also known as "Green Spain," is located in the northwest corner of Spain. This area is exposed to the moist air from the Atlantic Ocean and is therefore decidedly cooler and wetter than the rest of the country. Due to the climate, the wines produced here are notable for their high acidity compared to other Spanish wines.

The best known of Galicia's wines come from Rías Baixas DO. The area is known for a dry, fragrant white wine with high acidity made primarily from the Albariño grape variety.

Other well-known wine regions in Galicia include the Ribeiro DO, known mostly for white wines produced from a variety of grapes including Albariño, and the Valdeorras DO, known for white wines produced from the Godello grape and medium-bodied, fruity red wines made from the Mencia variety.

THE WINES OF JEREZ (SPAIN)

The Jerez DO (which often goes by the anglicized name Sherry) is one of the most renowned appellations for fortified wines in the world. The region of production is in Andalusia in southwest Spain. This is a hot, arid climate moderated by cool Atlantic breezes.

The primary grape is the indigenous Palomino, which is the sole or majority grape variety in most sherries. Sherry is produced in a wide range of styles from light and dry to rich and sweet, and is found in a wide range of colors from pale yellow, tan, and brown to nearly black.

Figure 5.11: Sherry aging in a solera

The majority of sherry is produced using a base wine that is fermented dry before it enters the aging and blending process known as the solera system. The solera is a complex series of barrels containing several "layers" known as criaderas. These layers are usually depicted as multiple rows of barrels with the solera (row) on the bottom and the progressively younger criaderas in the upper rows, but the actual positioning varies by winery. While in the solera, young wine is progressively blended together with a series of older, more complex wines.

This process is used to create the two basic styles of sherry–fino and oloroso–with a wide range of styles available within each of these two main categories.

- Fino sherries are typically pale, delicate, and dry wines that are influenced while in the solera by a unique organism known as flor yeast. Flor yeast floats on the surface of the wine in the barrel, and multiplies until it becomes a thick blanket on top of the maturing wine, thus protecting the wine from oxidation, and preventing it from darkening in color. This process is known as "biological aging."
- Oloroso sherries are aged without the influence of flor yeast, and are allowed to undergo considerable oxidation (oxidative aging) while in the solera. As it ages, oloroso sherry changes in color from its original shade of gold to light brown to deep brown and increases in body and aroma. Oloroso sherry may be dry or sweetened.

CAVA

Cava is a DO sparkling wine produced in several areas across Spain but centered in the Penedés region of Spain's Catalonia, near the city of Barcelona. Cava is produced in the traditional method, with the second fermentation occurring in the bottle followed by sur lie aging, as is the style in Champagne. Most Cava is white (technically a blanc de blancs), and is made from the three famous white grapes of the region: Macabeo, Parrellada, and Xarel-lo. Other allowed (but lesser-used) grape varieties include Chardonnay, Pinot Noir, Malvasia, Monastrell, and Garnacha Tinta. Cava may also be produced as a white wine or a rosé, in varying levels of sweetness, and in both vintage and non-vintage expressions. Cava is very popular as an inexpensive yet high-quality and delicious alternative to the more expensive sparkling wines on the market.

THE WINES OF PORTUGAL

Portugal has long had an excellent reputation for its fortified wines Port (Porto) and Madeira, as well as its delightfully crisp Vinho Verde. In addition, the country's recent increase in the production of dry, unfortified, red wine—such as those produced in the Bairrada, Dão, and Alentejo regions—has earned significant international acclaim.

Portugal occupies the southwestern section of the Iberian Peninsula, bordered by the Atlantic Ocean to the west and south, and by Spain to the north and east. It is a small nation, with nearly all the country covered by rugged ridges and valleys. If it weren't for the rough terrain, vineyards could thrive almost anywhere in Portugal.

Despite its small size, Portugal is made up of three distinct climates. The coastal part of northern Portugal, where Vinho Verde is produced, is lush and green with abundant rainfall. Continuing south along the coast, the climate becomes more Mediterranean, with warmer summers, mild winters, and very little precipitation during the growing season. Because of the patchwork of mountain ranges in Portugal's interior, the humidity quickly dissipates and the ocean no longer provides a temperature-moderating influence, so the climate turns decidedly continental and arid. The inland valleys, including those of the Douro Valley where the grapes for Port are grown, feature hot summers and very cold winters, with minimal precipitation.

The PDO wines of Portugal are labeled under the denominação de origem controlada (DOC) classification. There are thirty-one DOCs at present, including Porto, Madeira, and Vinho Verde.

PORT

Port (Porto in Portuguese), one of the world's most renowned fortified wines, is produced in Portugal's Douro region. The vineyards of the Douro begin approximately 40 miles (64 km) east of the city of Oporto and extend 60 miles (96 km) eastward to the Spanish border. For the most part, the Douro is rugged, wild, and remote. The area is divided into three sub-regions:

- Baixo Corgo: The westernmost section, relatively fertile and with ample rainfall
- Cima Corgo: The central core of the Port region, this subzone has hotter summers, colder winters, and less rain than the Baixo Corgo and contains the majority of the vineyards used in the production of Port
- Douro Superior: The upriver, eastern part of the valley, this subregion has extreme temperatures and very little rainfall

Port is typically produced as a sweet, red wine made from traditional grape varieties, particularly Touriga Nacional, Touriga Franca, and Tinta Roriz. A few wineries also produce

Wine Regions of Mainland Portugal

Transmontano VR
Trás-os-Montes DOC

Minho VR
Vinho Verde DOC

Duriense VR
Douro DOC
Porto DOC

Beira Atlântico VR
Bairrada DOC

Oporto

Terras de Cister VR
Távora-Varosa DOC

Lisboa VR
Bucelas DOC
Carcavelos DOC
Colares DOC
Lourinhã DOC
Óbidos DOC
Alenquer DOC
Arruda DOC
Torres Vedras DOC
Encostas d'Aire DOC

Terras do Dão VR
Dão DOC
Lafões DOC

Terras da Beira VR
Beira Interior DOC

Tejo VR
Do Tejo DOC

Lisbon

Alentejano VR
Alentejo DOC

Península de Setúbal VR
Setúbal DOC
Palmela DOC

Algarve VR
Lagos DOC
Portimão DOC
Lagoa DOC
Tavira DOC

Copyright: The Society of Wine Educators 2016

Figure 5.12: Mainland wine regions of Portugal

white Port, which is typically off-dry, using a range of white grapes including Gouveio and Malvasia Fina. Aside from these styles, Port is produced in a number of well-known variations, differentiated to a large degree by how long and in what type of container they are aged. The major styles of Port include the following:

- Ruby: This is the simplest of Ports, comprising a large share of all Port produced. Rubies have a vibrant red color and youthful aromas. Ruby Port is aged in large oak casks for about two years before being bottled and ready to drink.
- Tawny: Tawny Port has been aged in oak long enough for the color to oxidize from ruby red to a golden brown shade, developing richer, more oxidized flavors along the way. Those labeled "Reserve Tawny Port" are required to be aged in oak for at least seven years before bottling.
- Vintage: Vintage Port is the rarest and most expensive style of Port produced. Whereas most Ports are blends of wine from several harvests, vintage Port is made from the grapes of a single year's harvest and is only produced in the best years. Vintage Port is aged in oak casks, but must be bottled by July 30 of the third year after harvest. After bottling, the wine is usually cellared for many more years before release, and can be one of the world's most age-worthy wines.

Figure 5.13: Traditional boats on the Douro River

MADEIRA

Madeira, an island located in the Atlantic some 400 miles (644 km) off the coast of Morocco, is home to the second of Portugal's classic fortified wines. Back in the days of sailing ships, the fortuitous position of the island of Madeira made it an important resupply point for ships en route to the Far East or the Americas. Ships typically took aboard local wines, which had been fortified so that they would not spoil during the long voyage. It turned out that all the time spent in the stiflingly hot cargo hold of the ship as it sailed through the tropics did something to the wine that dramatically improved its character, resulting in an amber-colored wine with nutty, caramelized flavors. The term *maderization* was coined to describe this "cooking" process.

The grapes that are considered the "noble" grape varieties of Madeira are Sercial, Verdelho, Boal, and Malvasia (also referred to as Malmsey). The most widely planted variety on the island; however, is Tinta Negra Mole.

Madeira comes in both dry and sweet styles. The dry styles—made with Sercial, Verdelho, or Tinta Negra Mole grapes—are fortified after the wine has fermented to dryness. Sweet styles of Madeira, made from Boal, Malvasia, or Tinta Negra Mole, are fortified during fermentation, which halts the process while the wine is still sweet. All of these wines will then go through a maderization period to give them the true Madeira character, which includes aromas and flavors of dried fig, date, raisin, and nuts, as well as a high level of acidity.

VINHO VERDE

The Vinho Verde DOC is located in northwestern Portugal's Minho province, where the climate is cool and humid. The principal grape variety is Alvarinho (known as Albariño in Spain). Despite its name, which literally means "Green Wine," Vinho Verde can be red, white, or pink; the word green implies youth, meaning that the wine is meant to be consumed young. This is sometimes evidenced by a slight effervescence in these light, high-acid wines. There are fully-sparkling (*espumante*) versions as well.

THE WINES OF GREECE

Greece, located in southeastern Europe, has a long vinous history dating back at least 4,000 years. It consists primarily of a mountainous peninsula surrounded on three sides by the Mediterranean Sea, as well as the island of Crete and several archipelagoes with 3,000 smaller islands.

With the sea never far away, the climate throughout Greece is classic Mediterranean, with slight temperature variations from north to south and substantial differences due to elevation. High mountains run the length of the country, especially along the western side, blocking much of the rainfall and causing the rain-shadowed eastern side of the peninsula to be significantly drier than the west.

While few of Greece's appellations are particularly well known outside the country, the warm, sunny climate makes Greece a natural country for viticulture. Vines are planted throughout the mainland and on almost every habitable island. With over 300 cataloged indigenous grapes, Greece provides great diversity and originality in its wines. Leading red grapes include Xinomavro, Agiorgitiko, and Mavrodaphne, which is often used for sweet fortified wines similar in style to ruby Ports. The most respected white varieties include the pink-skinned Moschofilero, Muscat (known here as Moschato), and Assyrtiko, a high-acid white variety originally from the island of Santorini.

RETSINA
Retsina is a resinated wine (and, technically an aromatized wine) that has been produced in Greece for at least 2,000 years. The tradition of flavoring wine with pine resin originated with the practice of sealing ancient wine vessels with pine resin—particularly the resin from the Aleppo pine tree, native to the Mediterranean region. The pine resin helped to preserve the wine by keeping the air out, while at the same time, it infused the wine with resin aromas. When wine barrels (rather than clay amphorae) began to be used to store wine, the pine resin was no longer necessary; however, the resinated wine was popular enough that the use of pine resin to flavor wines continued. Today, Retsina is protected as a traditional appellation of Greece.

THE WINES OF GERMANY

Germany is home to some of the world's coldest climate vineyards. The northernmost winegrowing regions of Germany are well above the 50th parallel of latitude and are far from the moderating influence of a large body of water. Yet through determination, centuries of experience, and carefully chosen vineyard sites, Germans have found ways of producing world-class wines.

Germany's wine reputation is built upon its outstanding Rieslings. Riesling is the most widely planted grape in the country, taking up more than one-fifth of the vineyard acreage. It is especially dominant in the Rheingau and Mosel areas. Müller-Thurgau, a Riesling cross developed for hardiness but somewhat lacking in resemblance to Riesling with regard to taste and longevity, is the second most common grape. Several international varieties typically associated with cool climates are included among Germany's leading grapes, including Spätburgunder (Pinot Noir, the most planted red variety), Grauburgunder (Pinot Gris), and Weissburgunder (Pinot Blanc).

There are two levels of categorization for German PDO wines. Qualitätswein, the lower level of the two, is defined as "quality wine from a designated region." These wines represent the largest proportion of German wine output. Qualitätswein wine must come from one of thirteen Anbaugebiete (specified winegrowing regions of Germany), be made with the approved grape varieties, and reach sufficient ripeness for recognition as a quality wine.

Prädikatswein is the highest quality level designation. These wines may be defined as "quality wine with attributes." Prädikatswein must be produced from grapes grown within the same thirteen Anbaugebiete as the Qualitätswein. The Prädikatswein level has within it several subcategories known as the *Prädikate*, which are based on ripeness levels achieved in the vineyard.

The subcategories for Prädikatswein, in ascending order of grape ripeness, are as follows:
*   Kabinett: light- to medium-bodied wines made from grapes with the lowest ripeness level of the Prädikat

- Spätlese: wines made from grapes harvested after a designated picking date
- Auslese: wines made from grapes that have stayed on the vine long enough to have a required level of sugar
- Beerenauslese (BA): rich, sweet dessert wines made from individually harvested grapes which may be affected by botrytis (known in German as Edelfäule)
- Trockenbeerenauslese (TBA): wines from individually picked, very overripe berries that are often further shriveled by botrytis

Germany is also known for its sweet *Eiswein* (ice wine), wines made from frozen grapes harvested at a BA level of ripeness or higher. Having already become overripe from staying on the vine until as late as January, these grapes are harvested after they freeze in the vineyard. They are crushed immediately, and much of the water in the berries is discarded as ice, leaving grape must with a very high sugar level.

MAJOR WINE REGIONS OF GERMANY

Germany has thirteen recognized wine regions, known as Anbaugebiete, for PDO wines. Both Qualitätswein and Prädikatswein require a single Anbaugebiet as a place of origin. The best-known of these regions include the following:
- The Mosel: The Mosel is a valley along the Mosel River, located along the section of the river just before it joins the Rhine River in the north. The Mosel is one of the best-known wine regions of Germany, famous for its high-acid Rieslings. It is one of the larger areas in terms of production, responsible for almost one-sixth of the country's wine.
- The Rheingau: Located on the right bank of the Rhine River, this small region is protected by mountains. The south-facing vineyards enjoy optimal ripening conditions with dark slate soils that radiate heat back towards the vines, allowing for a long growing season. Riesling accounts for 80% of plantings and produces balanced, elegant and fruity wines with more body and richness than their Mosel counterparts.
- The Pfalz: The Pfalz enjoys plenty of sunshine and is sheltered from rainfall by a mountain range. It is located about 50 miles (80 km) south of the Rheingau and its climate is fairly dry.

This region is characterized by mild winters and warm summers. Because of its warmer weather, the Pfalz region produces exceptionally fine reds and more full-bodied whites than Germany's northern wine regions.
- The Rheinhessen: The Rheinhessen is located on the south and west bank of the Rhine across from the Rheingau and north of the Pfalz. It leads Germany's winegrowing regions both in area under vine and overall wine production.

THE WINES OF AUSTRIA

Austria is centrally located in Europe, southeast of Germany and northeast of Italy. The Alps cover much of the country, especially toward the west, so only the lower hills and plains in the eastern part of the country are really suitable for winegrowing. The cool continental climate of the vineyard areas favors the production of dry wines with crisp acidity and primary fruit aromas; about 70% of production in Austria is dry white wine.

The country's signature grape variety is the indigenous Grüner Veltliner, a spicy white grape that is internationally popular and known for citrus, white pepper, and mineral characteristics. Young examples provide fresh fruit and vibrant acidity, while wines produced from older vines and better vineyards are capable of aging for three to ten years. Approximately one-third of Austria's total acreage under vine is planted with Grüner Veltliner. Other leading white grapes include Riesling, Müller-Thurgau, Weissburgunder (Pinot Blanc), and Chardonnay.

The second most widely planted grape, and the most prominent red, is Zweigelt. This cross between Blaufränkisch and St. Laurent, when well made, displays a medium body and cherry flavors with a peppery finish. Other significant red grape varieties include Blaufränkisch (also known as Lemberger or Kekfrankos), and St. Laurent (a member of the Pinot family).

Wine Regions of Germany

Copyright: The Society of Wine Educators 2016

Figure 5.14: Wine regions of Germany

- Weinviertel DAC: The Weinviertel DAC stretches from the Danube Valley to the borders of the Czech Republic and Slovakia. Weinviertel DAC wines must be 100% Grüner Veltliner, and tend to be quite pungent, spicy, and peppery.
- Mittelburgenland DAC: This area produces red wines based on the Blaufränkisch grape variety. These wines are known for full body, deep color, and spicy aromas as well as red and black fruit flavors.
- Kremstal DAC and Kamptal DAC: These neighboring regions, located in western Niederösterreich (along the Krems and Kamp Rivers) produce some of the best-known white wines in Austria. The wines of either DAC may be either Grüner Veltliner or Riesling.
- Wiener Gemischter Satz DAC: The Wiener (Viennese) Gemischter Satz DAC was approved in 2013 for white wines produced using at least three grape varieties (from a list of fifteen). The grapes must be harvested, pressed, and fermented together, with no more than 50% from any single grape variety. The wines are meant to be fruit-forward and are not allowed to show significant influence of oak.

RUSTER AUSBRUCH

Ruster Ausbruch, a traditional sweet wine dating from the seventeenth century, is produced on the western shore of Lake Neusiedl in the town of Rust. The term Ausbruch may only be used in conjunction with the wines of Rust and refers to the use of a combination of extremely ripe, botrytis-affected grapes and less concentrated grapes harvested from the same vineyard. A range of grape varieties may be used, including Chardonnay, Pinot Blanc, Welschriesling, and Pinot Gris. The wine is aged before release, and is ranked among the finest dessert wines in the world.

Quality Austrian wines are classified according to grape ripeness at harvest in a Prädikat system similar (but not quite identical) to that of Germany. There are also several dozen broadly defined wine-producing regions that may be seen on wine labels. In addition, in 2003, Austria introduced a terroir-based appellation system that designates PDO-level, grape-growing regions as Districtus Austriae Controllatus (DAC). The DACs are considered to be the highest-quality wines of Austria.

The DAC designation can only be used for the specified grape varieties considered the most outstanding and most typical of the delineated region. Each DAC also specifies alcohol levels, aging regimens, and other specific details. There are currently nine designated DAC regions. The best-known of these include the following:

THE WINES OF HUNGARY

Hungary has a long history of wine production, and is home to one of the oldest vineyard classifications in the world (dating perhaps to 1700 but with final legal recognition in 1772) for its Tokaj region located in the northeastern section of the country.

Hungary's most famous wine, Tokaji Aszú, is a dessert wine made in the Tokaj region. The production of the luscious, sweet Tokaji Aszú has a centuries-old history and managed to survive Soviet control in the twentieth century. The primary grape varieties are the white grapes Furmint and Hárslevelü, which provide enough acidity and aromatic character to keep the wine from being cloying. The production of Tokaji Aszú starts with late-harvested, botrytis-affected grapes; in this condition, the grapes are called aszú. The aszú grapes are gently mashed into a thick paste and then mixed with a normally fermented base wine for a day or two, allowing the wine to absorb the sugar and flavors of the aszú. The wine is then racked and aged for a few years in small casks in underground tunnels where film-forming yeast, similar to the flor of the Sherry region, grows.

Over 70% of Hungary's wine production is white, including both dry wines and the well-known sweet wines of the country. However, one of the famous wines of Hungary is a full-bodied red wine known as Egri Bikavér (Bull's Blood of Eger). Egri Bikavér is traditionally made from Kadarka grapes blended with other red varieties such as Kekfrankos (Blaufränkisch), Kékoportó (Portugieser), Cabernet Sauvignon, Cabernet Franc, Merlot, Menoire, Pinot Noir, Syrah, Blauburger, and Zweigelt.

Wine Regions of Austria

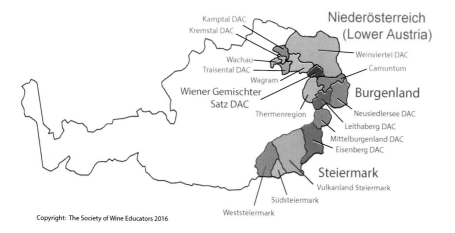

Copyright: The Society of Wine Educators 2016

Figure 5.15: Wine regions of Austria

WINES OF THE NEW WORLD

As European colonists established settlements in those areas that would become known as the New World, they brought vines, wines, and the culture of winemaking with them. As a result, unique wine cultures now exist in this New World, each with its own grape varieties, wine styles, export markets, and consumption patterns.

Unlike their Old World counterparts, New World wine laws are typically less stringent on what they regulate. For the most part, producers in New World wine regions may plant any grape variety they choose, determine their preferred maximum yield per acre, and decide at what sugar level to harvest the grapes. Some feel that this freedom permits New World winemakers to compete more easily in the world wine market, as they can quickly adapt to the ever-changing tastes of the consumer.

In the pages that follow, we will examine the wine cultures of the major producers of the New World of wine, including the United States (and other producers in North America), South America, Australia, New Zealand, and South Africa.

WINES OF THE UNITED STATES

Wine production in the United States now totals over 350 million cases, placing it just behind France, Italy, and Spain in terms of volume output. For the past several years, the US has been among the leading countries in terms of both exports and imports of wine. More recently, it has earned the title of the largest consumer of wine in the world; a statistic reflective of the fact that per-capita consumption continues to rise in the New World while falling in the Old. Furthermore, American wine drinkers overall tend to drink better quality and more expensive wines than their counterparts in most other countries. Thus, the United States, by many measures, now drives the global wine industry.

Within the United States, the center of the wine industry is firmly situated in California. Of the American total, California produces roughly 88%. Washington State, New York State, and Oregon are the next largest producers, typically followed by Virginia, Texas, Pennsylvania, Michigan, Missouri, Ohio, and Florida—although not necessarily in that order (which changes often). The other states contribute only a small fraction to the total, although many have thriving local wine scenes. There are more than 10,000 commercial wineries in the US, with at least one in all fifty states.

US WINE LAWS

The place-of-origin (appellation) system used in the United States is quite different from the appellation system of Europe. Unlike European appellations, there are no rules regarding approved grape varieties, minimum or maximum crop yields, planting densities, or vinification techniques that must be followed in order to be permitted to use the place-name.

At a general level, the place-of-origin of an American wine may be defined along political boundaries such as a country or state. However, these political units are not intended to define a unique winegrowing area. For that purpose, the Alcohol and Tobacco Trade and Tax Bureau (TTB), a department of the United States Treasury Department, maintains a list of American Viticultural Areas (AVAs) that may be used to describe the place of origin of a wine. As of early 2017, 239 distinct AVAs had been approved in over thirty different states; of these, 138 are in California (and these numbers are sure to increase in the future).

Beyond regulating the distribution of wine and approving AVAs, the TTB is also responsible for ensuring that wine labels meet federal labeling laws. Specifically, all wine labels in the United States, whether for wine made in America or imported from another country, require these elements:

1. A brand name
2. The class or type of wine
3. The alcohol content (in percentage by volume)
4. The name and address of the bottler or importer
5. The place of origin
6. The net contents (volume) of the bottle
7. A sulfite statement ("contains sulfites") if the wine contains ten parts per million or more of sulfur dioxide (which actually encompasses nearly all wines)
8. A health warning that includes the following two statements:
   - "Government Warning: According to the Surgeon General, women should not drink alcoholic beverages during pregnancy because of the risk of birth defects."
   - "Consumption of alcoholic beverages impairs your ability to drive a car or operate machinery, and may cause health problems."

The TTB also requires that a minimum percentage of the wine bottled come from the grape variety and vintage date stated on the label. These standards include the following:

- Varietal labeling: The basic rule for varietal labeling is that if a single grape variety appears on the label, the wine must contain a minimum of 75% of that variety, grown in the appellation of origin cited on the label. There are some exceptions, for instance, Oregon has adopted a more stringent definition than federal law, requiring some of its iconic varietals, such as Pinot Noir, Pinot Gris, and Chardonnay, to have a minimum 90% content of the named variety.
- Vintage dates: A vintage date is optional on a label, but if one is shown, the wine must meet the following criteria: if a wine's place-of-origin is a US state or county, a minimum of 85% of the wine must be from the stated vintage. If the wine has an AVA designation, a minimum of 95% of the wine must be from the stated vintage.

Additional items that may appear on a wine label include the following:
- Vintage date
- Grape variety (or varieties)
- Appellation of origin
- The term "estate bottled"
- Optional information about the wine, the winery, or related subject matter
- Label art

THE WINES OF CALIFORNIA

California is by far the largest wine producer of the fifty US states. It contains about 80% of the vineyard acreage in the country and makes nearly 88% of the wine. California is home to many diverse wine-growing regions, reaching from Mendocino in the north all the way down to San Diego, just north of the border with Mexico. While diverse and distinct, much of California's winegrowing areas are characterized by plenty of sunshine and moderate temperatures due to the cooling breezes and fogs generated by the Pacific Ocean. Some of the leading wine-producing regions of California are discussed below.

Napa County: Napa County, in particular the Napa Valley AVA and its sub-appellations, is undoubtedly the best-known wine region in the United States. Grapes have been grown in Napa since the 1830s, and the first winery in the valley was established in the 1860s. There are now more than 400 wineries in the county, growing a long list of grape varieties and producing wines of every type and style.

Napa's reputation has been built on the strength of Napa Valley's powerful Cabernet Sauvignons and Cabernet-led Bordeaux-style blends. These outstanding wines are produced by large, well-established wineries as well as numerous small boutique wineries that have achieved "cult" status, with demand far exceeding the supply—even at sky-high prices. Large wineries located in Napa include the Robert Mondavi Winery, Sterling Vineyards, and Beringer Vineyards; Harlan Estate and Screaming Eagle are excellent examples of the ultra-exclusive, smaller producers.

AVAs of Napa County

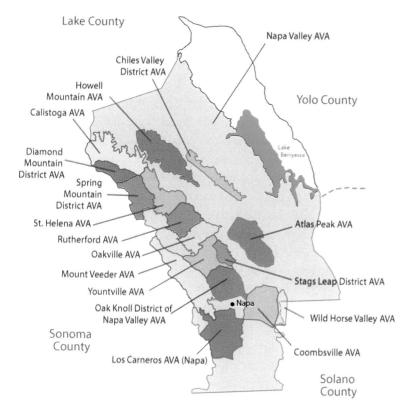

Lake County

Napa Valley AVA

Chiles Valley
District AVA

Howell
Mountain AVA

Calistoga AVA

Yolo County

Diamond
Mountain
District AVA

Spring
Mountain
District AVA

St. Helena AVA

Rutherford AVA

Oakville AVA

Mount Veeder AVA

Yountville AVA

Oak Knoll District of
Napa Valley AVA

Lake
Berryessa

Atlas Peak AVA

Stags Leap District AVA

• Napa

Wild Horse Valley AVA

Sonoma
County

Los Carneros AVA (Napa)

Coombsville AVA

Solano
County

Copyright: The Society of Wine Educators 2016

Figure 6.1: AVAs of Napa County, California

Napa County is located just east (inland) from Sonoma County. The Napa Valley AVA takes up most of the area within Napa County itself, save for the portion of the county surrounding and north/ northwest of Lake Berryessa. The heart of the Napa Valley, stretching north from the city of Napa, includes the valley floor appellations of Yountville, Stags Leap District, Oakville, Rutherford, St. Helena, and Calistoga. This is prime Cabernet Sauvignon territory and home to the majority of the county's most famous wineries.

The AVAs of Oak Knoll District of Napa County, Coombsville, and Carneros (which is shared with Sonoma) are located in the cooler, southern section of the county, closer to San Pablo Bay. These areas are well known for Pinot Noir and Chardonnay, some of which is used in the area's sparkling wines.

One of California's most famous wines, Fumé Blanc, was created at The Robert Mondavi Winery in Napa in

the 1960s. As the story goes, the newly-established Mondavi Winery had produced some excellent wine using purchased Sauvignon Blanc grapes—however, it wasn't selling. Mr. Mondavi believed the problem was either the searing acidity of the wine, or the hard-to-pronounce name of the grape, which at the time was unfamiliar to Americans. Remembering the wonderful Sauvignon Blanc-based wines he had tasted in the Loire Valley's Pouilly-Fumé region, Mondavi decided to soften the wine a bit by oak aging, and to re-name the wine using the easier to pronounce moniker of "Fumé Blanc." The wine was a success, and sold very well. The name was purposely not trademarked, and wine producers throughout California (and beyond) began to use the term for their oak-aged Sauvignon Blanc, thus ensuring the popularity of the grape for years to come. (Note: while technically [according to TTB standards], Fumé Blanc is a synonym for Sauvignon Blanc, most consumers assume that the term implies oak aging.)

Sonoma County: Sonoma County is less widely known internationally than Napa, but it is generally considered Napa's equal in terms of quality wine production. Sonoma's commercial wine industry began in the 1850s, with quality vinifera grape varieties introduced to the area in the 1860s.

Sonoma is located along the coast and, as such, is more strongly influenced by the ocean than the more-inland areas like Napa, and the immediate coastal zone is a marginal winegrowing region. However, the coastal ridges that parallel the shoreline either block or channel the fog and keep a barrier between the cold ocean water and the majority of the vineyard areas of Sonoma.

About two-thirds of Sonoma's wines are red, with Cabernet Sauvignon and Pinot Noir as the leading red varieties. Merlot and Zinfandel are also important red grapes. The single most widely planted variety, however, is Chardonnay, which accounts for the majority of white wines produced.

The Sonoma Valley AVA, a cool-climate AVA, is located in the southern and inland part of the county, and contains the sub-appellations of Bennett Valley, Sonoma Mountain, Moon Mountain District Sonoma County, and the Sonoma half of the Carneros AVA.

In the county's center, inland of the Russian River's cut through the coastal range, is another cool region, the Russian River Valley AVA, an ideal spot for Pinot Noir and Chardonnay, produced in both still and sparkling versions. Within the Russian River Valley AVA, the Chalk Hill AVA takes its name from the chalky appearance of the area's volcanic white soils. The Chalk Hill AVA, which is slightly warmer than the surrounding areas, is well known for robust Chardonnays and Sauvignon Blancs.

In the north and east of the county, the average temperatures steadily rise, with the inland areas possessing much hotter climates than those closer to the sea. Here, the warm Dry Creek Valley AVA has a good balance between maritime and inland influences, resulting in concentrated Zinfandels. The Alexander Valley and Knights Valley AVAs are

known for Cabernet Sauvignon and Merlot as well as ripe Chardonnay.

Mendocino County: Mendocino County, located north of Sonoma, is mostly mountainous and forested; however, the area contains several AVAs and 17,000 acres (6,900 ha) of vineyards.

Within the broad Mendocino AVA is the Anderson Valley AVA, one of the coolest winegrowing areas of California. This long, narrow valley in the south-central part of the county has a marginal climate that has proven excellent for Pinot Noir and sparkling wine production. Located in the hills along the coast, the Mendocino Ridge AVA is unique in that it is noncontiguous, as only the areas at elevations of 1,200 feet (366 m) above sea level or higher are included. As such, this appellation is often referred to as "Islands in the Sky." Because of its location above the fog line, the vines receive plenty of cool-climate sunshine.

Most of the other vineyards of Mendocino lie along the eastern side of the county, connecting with the adjacent Lake County. This relatively flat land in the watershed of the Russian River is well protected from maritime influence by the coastal mountains and therefore can get quite hot in midsummer, but the warm days are tempered by the area's cool nighttime temperatures. This wide diurnal variation permits grapes to reach full maturity while retaining vibrant acidity. Cabernet Sauvignon, Zinfandel, Petite Sirah, and Rhône varieties can be found here.

The Central Coast AVA: The Central Coast AVA covers a huge amount of ground, taking in almost the entire area along California's Pacific coast between San Francisco and Santa Barbara. As the AVA was delineated primarily using county boundaries, the region includes some inland areas on the eastern side of the mountains, as well. This means that within the large Central Coast AVA there exists a wide range of climates and terrains, from the cool, low-lying regions along the actual coast, to several small mountain ranges, and some warmer inland areas on

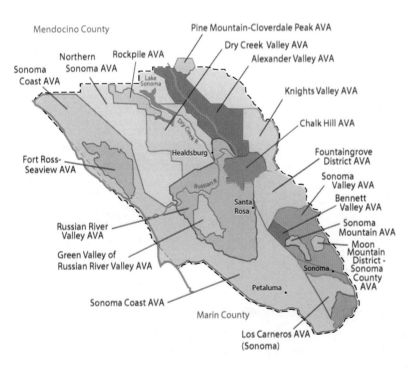

AVAs of Sonoma County

Copyright: The Society of Wine Educators 2016

Figure 6.2: AVAs of Sonoma County, California

the eastern side of the mountains as well. The main wine-producing counties of California's Central Coast AVA include the following:

- Monterey County: Monterey County is one of the top five wine-producing California counties, and grows a great deal of the state's Chardonnay. The cool-climate AVAs of Monterey County, including Arroyo Seco and Chalone, are also well known for Pinot Noir, Riesling, Pinot Gris, and Chardonnay. In the warmer, southern portion of the county, the San Lucas and Hames Valley AVAs are known for Cabernet Sauvignon and Rhône varieties.
- San Luis Obispo County: San Luis Obispo County is home to the Paso Robles AVA. Paso Robles is a large region once thought of as a hot, inland area known for growing Bordeaux varieties, Rhône varieties, and Zinfandel. While this remains somewhat true, in November of 2014, eleven sub-appellations were approved, demonstrating the great diversity of soils, climates, and elevations that existed in Paso Robles all along. Farther south in San Luis Obispo, the Edna Valley AVA and the Arroyo Grande AVA are known for cooler-climate viticulture featuring Chardonnay and Pinot Noir.
- Santa Barbara County: Santa Barbara County, a ninety-minute drive north of Los Angeles, is geologically unique in that it is one of the few places on the California coast where both the coastline and the mountain ranges run east–west as opposed to north–south. Six AVAs are currently located within Santa Barbara County: Santa Maria Valley, Santa Ynez Valley, Ballard Canyon, Los Olivos District, Sta. Rita Hills, and Happy Canyon of Santa Barbara.

Lodi: The Lodi AVA is located in California's Central Valley, where most of the area is considered to be too hot for the production of quality wine. However, Lodi is directly east of San Francisco and the Golden Gate entrance to San Francisco Bay—the largest gap in California's Coast Range. This gap provides access for the cool winds off the Pacific Ocean to penetrate inland, following the natural inlet of the San Joaquin/Sacramento River Delta to the foothills of the Sierra Nevada Mountains.

California's Central Coast

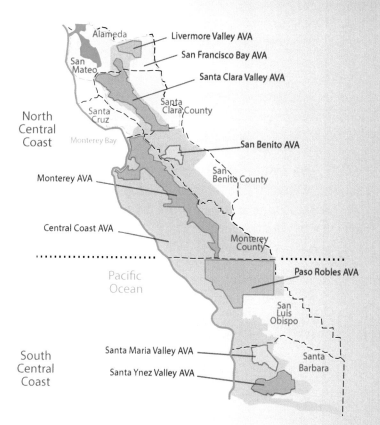

Figure 6.3: Main AVAs of California's Central Coast

The Lodi AVA has over 100,000 acres (40,500 ha) of vines and a surprisingly Mediterranean climate. During the growing season, the Lodi area is typically sunny, with warm daytime temperatures, cooling "delta breezes" in the afternoon, and a significant drop in temperatures at night. Diurnal temperature shifts can be as much as forty-five degrees Fahrenheit and allow for development of rich fruit flavors and bright, crisp acids in the grapes and the wines made from them. The Lodi AVA grows over seventy different varieties of grapes and has gained a reputation for old-vine Zinfandel, Petite Sirah, Cabernet Sauvignon, and Viognier, as well as other Rhône, Italian, and Spanish varieties.

THE WINES OF WASHINGTON STATE
The state of Washington is the second largest producer of vinifera wine in the United States after California. Washington is divided by the high-altitude Cascade Mountain range into a cool and very rainy western part and a larger zone to the east that has desert-like conditions with hot summers, very cold winters, and very little precipitation.

Almost all of the state's vineyards are located in this area east of the Cascades, which form a rain shadow that creates the near-desert conditions. Despite the lack of rain, runoff from the mountains' snowpack finds its way into the Columbia River and well water. This provides ample water for irrigation, without which viticulture would be impossible. The state's northerly latitude provides long days in midsummer and, in fact, offers more sunshine hours than California.

Washington's vineyards are almost equally divided between white and red varieties. Cabernet Sauvignon and Merlot are the red leaders. While grown in less quantity, Syrah often draws some of the highest critical acclaim. Washington State is considered one of the premier New World regions for Riesling, and it produces a good deal of Chardonnay as well.

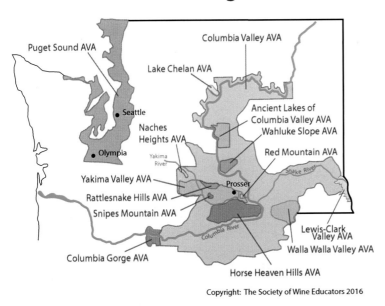

Copyright: The Society of Wine Educators 2016

Figure 6.4: AVAs of Washington State

As of early 2017, Washington has fourteen AVAs; some of these are discussed below.

The Columbia Valley AVA: Located in the southeast section of Washington State, the Columbia Valley AVA is one of the largest appellations in the country and the largest in Washington State. It encompasses most of the state's vineyard land as well as a small section crossing into Oregon. This essentially

guarantees that every Washington wine qualifies for AVA status. The Columbia Valley AVA is located in the rain shadow of the Cascade Mountains and surrounds the Columbia River and its tributaries, the Walla Walla and Yakima Rivers. Most of Washington State's smaller AVAs are included within the borders of the Columbia Valley AVA.

The Yakima Valley AVA: The Yakima Valley AVA, located completely within the larger Columbia Valley AVA, was the state's first appellation and today accounts for over one-third of the vineyards. Its primary grape is Chardonnay, followed by Merlot and Cabernet Sauvignon. However, Riesling and Syrah take up considerable acreage and are on the rise. The Red Mountain, Rattlesnake Hills, and Snipes Mountain AVAs are all located entirely within the larger Yakima Valley AVA.

The Horse Heaven Hills AVA: Located between the Yakima and Columbia Rivers, the Horse Heaven Hills AVA benefits from tempering winds and steep slopes. Some of the state's highest-rated wines hail from this appellation.

The Columbia Gorge AVA: The Columbia Gorge AVA straddles the Columbia River and the border between Washington State and Oregon. Located where the Columbia River cuts a very narrow passage through the Cascade Mountains, this area encompasses a wide range of climates, soils, and geology.

The Walla Walla Valley AVA: The Walla Walla Valley AVA spills over into Oregon and has been home to grape growing since the 1850s, when grapes were first planted by Italian immigrants. Although Cabernet Sauvignon is the leading grape, a wide range of varieties are currently planted.

The Puget Sound AVA: The Puget Sound AVA is where the Washington wine industry began, but today it is responsible for less than 1% of the state's wine production. This is the only Washington State AVA located on the western side of the Cascade Mountains, and it has so little sunshine that ripening grapes can be quite difficult. This cooler, wetter part of the state is much better known as the home of the state's population centers of Seattle, Tacoma, and Olympia. However, because this AVA is close to residents and the tourist trade, many Washington State wineries maintain production facilities and tasting rooms here.

THE WINES OF NEW YORK STATE

Winegrowers in the eastern states face more difficult viticultural conditions than those in the west because of potentially harsh winters and high summer humidity, which fosters mold and disease. Nevertheless, several states maintain flourishing wine industries, and New York played a significant role in the wine and grape industry of the United States before Prohibition. In recent years the wine culture of the state has grown, evolved, and modernized considerably.

The Finger Lakes AVA and its two sub-AVAs, Seneca Lake and Cayuga Lake, comprise the largest wine-producing region and account for 85% of New York's production. The climate here is akin to Germany's, and the area is becoming quite well-known for excellent Riesling. Cabernet Franc and cold-hardy hybrids such as Vidal, Seyval Blanc, and Cayuga are widely planted here as well.

Other AVAs of interest within New York State include the Long Island AVA, located just two hours east of New York City. With the first vines planted in 1973, the region is relatively young. This area is divided into the island's two "forks," including the North Fork of Long Island AVA and the Hamptons AVA in the South Fork.

The Hudson River Region AVA, located north of New York City, is home to the oldest continuously operating winery in the United States, the Brotherhood Winery, established in 1839. Despite its history, the Hudson River Region AVA has seen much of its growth in the past decade, with many of its wineries only a few years old.

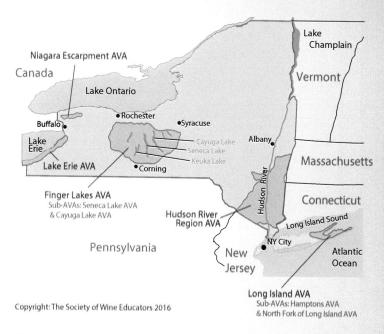

AVAs of New York State

Copyright: The Society of Wine Educators 2016

Figure 6.5: AVAs of New York State

THE WINES OF OREGON

The Oregon wine industry, dominated by small, often family-run vineyards, consistently ranks as one of the top four largest producers of wine in the United States. The wines of Oregon, particularly Pinot Noir, Pinot Gris, and sparkling wines, are highly acclaimed both in the United States and abroad.

Most of Oregon's wineries are west of the Cascades, primarily located in the valley of the north-flowing Willamette River between the Coast Range and the Cascades and as such, the majority of Oregon's wine regions are cooler than many New World vineyards, best suited to cool-climate grape varieties. There are additional vineyard areas in the southwest of the state, in the valleys of the Umpqua and Rogue Rivers.

Oregon's premier grape variety is unquestionably Pinot Noir, which makes up more than 62% of the vineyard acreage. The top white variety is Pinot Gris, followed by Chardonnay and Riesling. The region's Pinot Noir and Chardonnay are often made into Traditional Method sparkling wines. To a lesser extent, some producers are working with Syrah, Viognier, and other Rhône varieties, most of which are sourced from the warmer Rogue Valley in southern Oregon.

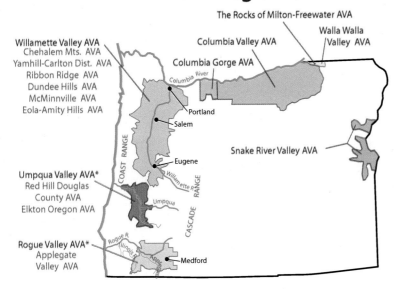

AVAs of Oregon

The Rocks of Milton-Freewater AVA

Willamette Valley AVA
Chehalem Mts. AVA
Yamhill-Carlton Dist. AVA
Ribbon Ridge AVA
Dundee Hills AVA
McMinnville AVA
Eola-Amity Hills AVA

Columbia Valley AVA

Walla Walla
Valley AVA

Columbia Gorge AVA

Columbia River

Portland

Salem

Snake River Valley AVA

COAST RANGE

Eugene

Willamette R.

Umpqua Valley AVA*
Red Hill Douglas
County AVA
Elkton Oregon AVA

Umpqua

CASCADE RANGE

Rogue Valley AVA*
Applegate
Valley AVA

Rogue R.
Illinois

Medford

*Note: The Umpqua Valley AVA and the Rogue Valley AVA (and their sub-appellations) collectively form the Southern Oregon AVA.

Copyright: The Society of Wine Educators 2016

Figure 6.6: AVAs of Oregon

Oregon wine law is unique in that it requires key varietal wines to contain a minimum of 90% of the grape variety stated on the label. Thus, many of Oregon's best-known wines—including Pinot Noir and Pinot Gris—will contain a minimum of 90% of the named grape variety. In 2007, this regulation was loosened a bit to allow exceptions for Bordeaux varieties (such as Cabernet Sauvignon, Merlot, and Sauvignon Blanc) and Rhône varieties (such as Grenache and Syrah), as well as Sangiovese, Tempranillo, and Zinfandel.

Nearly three-quarters of Oregon's vineyards fall within the Willamette Valley AVA, situated only one hour south of Portland. The Willamette Valley AVA is divided into six sub-appellations: Dundee Hills, Ribbon Ridge, Eola-Amity Hills, McMinnville, Yamhill-Carlton District, and Chehalem Mountains.

THE WINES OF CANADA

Canada has a small modern wine industry that dates back to 1974, when the first winery license was granted following Canada's own version of Prohibition. The country's wine production is concentrated in Ontario and British Columbia, although small amounts of wine are made in Nova Scotia and Quebec as well.

In the province of Ontario, the majority of grapes are grown on the shores of the Great Lakes, with approximately 85% of the vines located in the Niagara Peninsula appellation, which radiates around Lake Ontario. This close proximity to water mitigates the seasonally cold weather and allows Canadian producers to grow a substantial quantity of vinifera grapes, including Chardonnay, Riesling, and Cabernet Franc. Of course, the winter cold plays an essential role in the making of icewine, one of Canada's specialties.

British Columbia is the other major source of Canadian wine. As in Washington State, the ideal conditions for winegrowing are found east of the Coast Range in the dry interior valleys. The premier growing area is the Okanagan Valley, which is planted almost exclusively with vinifera varieties led by Merlot, Pinot Gris, Chardonnay, and Pinot Noir.

THE WINES OF MEXICO

Wine is produced in at least seven Mexican states, with 90% of modern production centered in Baja California. Principal white grape varieties include Chenin Blanc, Chardonnay, Sauvignon Blanc, and Viognier; principal red grapes include Cabernet Sauvignon, Merlot, Malbec, Grenache, Barbera, Syrah, and Tempranillo.

The main wine region here is the Valle de Guadalupe near the city of Ensenada, where vines are planted at elevations ranging from 1,000 feet (305 m) to 1,250 feet (380 m), and where the area enjoys a Mediterranean climate.

The Mexican state of Coahuila, located in northeastern Mexico adjacent to the US border, is the home of Casa Madero, the oldest winery in the New World. Casa Madero was founded by Don Lorenzo de Garcia in 1597 as Hacienda de San Lorenzo. The estate was purchased by Don Evaristo Madero in 1893, and the name was changed to Casa Madero. Casa Madero continues to be one of the most important wine and brandy producers in Mexico.

THE WINES OF ARGENTINA

Argentina occupies the largest portion of suitable viticultural land in South America and is the leading wine producer on the continent. The huge cosmopolitan city of Buenos Aires is the primary market for Argentine wine, but the country's wine industry has become increasingly export oriented.

Argentina is a wedge-shaped country lying between the long chain of the Andes Mountains to the west and the Atlantic Ocean to the east. The soaring Andean ridgeline, which also forms the border with Chile, creates a formidable barrier to the prevailing westerly winds and results in a significant rain shadow that keeps the vineyard areas of western Argentina quite dry. The combination of dry air, plentiful irrigation water from Andean snowmelt, high elevations, and almost unlimited sunshine produces exceptional winegrowing conditions in Argentina's western foothills.

Argentina's modern wine industry focuses on two key grapes: Malbec and Torrontés. Malbec, a French grape from Bordeaux and the surrounding areas, was imported to Argentina long ago and has become the country's signature red grape variety. Argentine Malbec tends to be deeply colored, often inky black, with corresponding fruit flavors of blackberry and plum. Torrontés, a white grape, produces a unique, light-bodied wine with pronounced floral aromas. Other leading red grapes of Argentina include Cabernet Sauvignon, Bonarda, and Syrah; other leading white grapes include Chardonnay and Sauvignon Blanc.

The province of Mendoza, located in the "Cuyo" or Central Region of Argentina, accounts for more than 70% of the country's vineyard acreage and is home to many of its internationally renowned wineries. Most of Mendoza's vineyards are planted between 2,000 and 4,000 feet (610 to 1,220 m) above sea level. The leading grape variety is Malbec, followed by Cabernet Sauvignon, a few Italian varieties, Tempranillo, Torrontés, and Chardonnay.

The province of Salta, located in the northern portion of the country, is home to some of Argentina's highest-altitude vineyards, where the abundant sunshine allows grapes to ripen nicely, and a combination of warm days and cool nights ensures good acidity levels at harvest. Salta is particularly known for its ultra-high altitude Torrontés, particularly from its sub-region of Cafayate—where vineyards can be found as high as 7,000 feet (2,100 m) above sea level. Molinos, another sub-region of Salta, is home to a vineyard named *Altura Maxima*, which, at an altitude of 10,206 feet (3,111 m), is reported to be the highest vineyard in the world.

Argentina is one of the few New World wine producers to attempt a European-style system of regulations, and while the system is still in its infancy, they have established two denominación de *origen controlada* (DOC) regions, controlled and enforced by a local *consejo*, or council. The DOC regulations spell out geographic boundaries, permissible grape varieties,

Wine Areas of Argentina

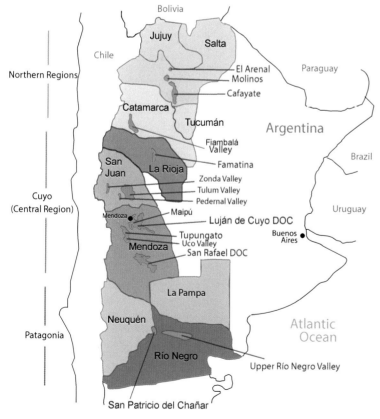

Copyright: The Society of Wine Educators 2016

Figure 6.7: Wine Regions of Argentina

planting densities, and other requirements. The two established DOC regions, both located within the province of Mendoza, are the Luján de Cuyo DOC (approved for Malbec) and the San Rafael DOC (approved for Malbec, Cabernet Sauvignon, and Chardonnay).

THE WINES OF CHILE

Chile is the second largest wine producer in South America and the continent's largest exporter of wine. Chile stretches almost 3,000 miles (4,828 km) in length, occupying a good portion of South America's Pacific coast. The country is very narrow, rarely more than a hundred miles wide over most of its length, and squeezed between the ocean and the Andes. In the north is the Atacama Desert, one of the driest places on earth, and the frozen archipelago of Tierra del Fuego is in the south. Thanks to these natural barriers and Chile's strict quarantine laws, the country holds the distinction of being considered phylloxera-free.

Stretched along the Pacific Ocean, Chile has a cold ocean current flowing along its shores from the polar seas, called the Humboldt Current. The prevailing westerly winds bring cool, moist air inland. Vineyard areas directly influenced by these breezes have low average temperatures and less sunshine. In many areas, the coastal hills block the fog and chilly air, so the inland vineyards are warm, dry, and sunny throughout the growing season. The climate is Mediterranean, and most of the rain falls during the winter. Summer temperatures rarely exceed 90°F (32°C), and humidity is low.

Many of Chile's vines were brought to the area from Bordeaux during the mid-1800s. These varieties include Cabernet Sauvignon, Sauvignon Blanc, and Merlot. Cabernet Sauvignon is by far the most widely planted grape variety, and many people believe that Chile is

ideally suited for the production of world-class, high-quality Cabernet Sauvignon. Other grapes from France, such as Syrah, Sauvignon Blanc, and Chardonnay, are also well represented.

Carmenère, another variety that arrived from Bordeaux, has an interesting history in Chile. During the time before phylloxera, Carmenère was widely planted in Bordeaux and a regular ingredient in the red blends of the region. However, after phylloxera ravaged France, Carmenère was not widely replanted in Bordeaux, but it continued to thrive in Chile, where it was often mistaken for a particular style of spicy Merlot.

This misidentification was discovered in 1994 when Professor Jean-Michel Boursiquot of the Montpellier School of Oenology noticed the distinctive character of Merlot from Chile and determined that much of what was considered to be

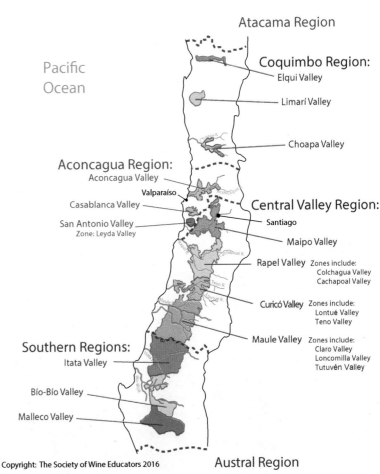

Wine Areas of Chile

Figure 6.8: Wine Regions of Chile

Chilean Merlot was, in actuality, Carmenère. Today, Chile is one of the few areas in the world that grows Carmenère on a significant, commercial basis, and it is considered a "signature" grape of Chile.

The major wine-producing regions of Chile include the following:

The Maipo Valley: The Maipo Valley, surrounding the capital city of Santiago, is the historical heart of the country and the center of Chile's winemaking culture. Not surprisingly, this area has some very old vines. The urban sprawl of the capital city has pushed much of the winegrowing out of this area, but it is still an important source for well-balanced reds. Maipo's specialty is Cabernet Sauvignon, with lesser plantings of Merlot, Chardonnay, Carmenère, Sauvignon Blanc, and Syrah.

The Rapel Valley: The Rapel Valley, located to the south of the Maipo Valley, is overwhelmingly focused on red wine production. The area has two well-known sub-zones, the Cachapoal and Colchagua Valleys. The Cachapoal Valley has a warm, but not hot, climate and is largely a producer of Cabernet Sauvignon, Merlot, Syrah, and Carmenère. To the south, Colchagua Valley produces full-bodied, premium reds from Cabernet Sauvignon, Syrah, and Carmenère.

The Casablanca Valley: The Casablanca Valley is the most coastal wine area within Chile. Its proximity to the ocean provides it with the benefits of a maritime climate, including frequent morning fogs. Not surprisingly, Casablanca specializes in white varieties, which make up 75% of all plantings, particularly Chardonnay and Sauvignon Blanc. The area is also gaining a reputation for its Pinot Noir.

Since 1995, Chile has had a set of geographic place-of-origin laws, the *denominación de origen* (DO) system, which is essentially identical to the United States' system of American Viticultural Areas. Under Chilean wine law, the minimum requirements for place of origin, vintage, and variety on a wine label are all set at 75%.

THE WINES OF AUSTRALIA

Australia has been making wine with traditional European grapes since the 1800s, and today, Australia is among the world's heavyweights in the wine industry, consistently ranking among the top ten countries for wine production. Australia also has a well-deserved reputation for innovation, as evidenced by the positioning of Shiraz as a uniquely Australian style of Syrah, the use of nontraditional blends, and the widespread use of alternative labels and packaging.

Australia is a large country, roughly the size of the continental United States, situated in the South Pacific Ocean southeast of the Asian landmass. It extends well into the tropics, but the southern third of the country is within the temperate latitudes that begin at 30° south. This is where almost all of the vineyards are found, mainly in the states of South Australia, New South Wales, and Victoria, but also in Western Australia and the offshore state of Tasmania.

The grape variety for which Australia is best known is Shiraz (known in France as Syrah). Australian Shiraz has proven very popular around the world, and it is the country's most widely planted grape, accounting for more than a quarter of vineyard acreage. Other prominent red grapes include Cabernet Sauvignon and Merlot, followed by Mourvèdre and Grenache. Australia is well known for blended wines, which might be a uniquely Australian Cabernet Sauvignon-Shiraz blend or a more typical blend such as G-S-M (Grenache-Shiraz-Mourvèdre). The cooler areas of the country, particularly Tasmania, also grow Pinot Noir—some of which makes its way into sparkling wines.

Chardonnay is by far the most prevalent white grape in Australia, followed by Sauvignon Blanc, Semillon, Riesling, and Chenin Blanc. Muscat is grown in the hotter areas and is often used in sweet wines as well as fortified wines.

Australia's place-of-origin system is similar to that of the United States in that the appellations, officially known as *geographical indications* (GIs), are simply areas on a map. They place no restrictions on the viticultural or winemaking procedures of grape

Major Wine Areas of Australia

Figure 6.9: Wine Regions of Australia

Rutherglen: Located within the state of Victoria, the Rutherglen Region has a markedly continental climate that brings very hot summer days, while frosts are common in the spring and fall. It is known for fortified Muscat wines and big reds, especially from Shiraz.

Mornington Peninsula: Located in the eastern outskirts of Melbourne in the state of Victoria, this is a cool growing area with high humidity but little summer rain. The Mornington Peninsula Region is noted for Pinot Noir and Chardonnay.

Margaret River: Located in the state of Western Australia, the Margaret River Region experiences constant sea breezes from the Indian and Southern Oceans that keep the area very cool in what would otherwise be an extremely warm Mediterranean climate. While both red and white grape varieties are planted here, Margaret River is especially prized for its white wines, including elegant Chardonnays and intense Sauvignon Blanc–Semillon blends.

Coonawarra: The Coonawarra Region, located along South Australia's Limestone Coast, is well known for its bright red soil called terra rossa, which rests over a free-draining limestone base. This region, thanks to its soil composition, is famous for its Cabernet Sauvignons.

Barossa Valley and McLaren Vale: These two regions, located within the state of South Australia, enjoy a Mediterranean climate that is generally warm and dry, becoming relatively cool in higher-elevation vineyards. Some of the finest Shiraz-based wines of Australia are grown in these regions.

Clare Valley and Eden Valley: These two regions, both well known for Riesling, surround the city of Adelaide and are somewhat cooler than most of the surrounding areas. The Clare Valley's cold nights and Eden Valley's high altitudes help to retain the much-needed acidity in the grapes of both areas.

growers or winemakers within their boundaries. The place of origin for a wine can be the country as a whole or one or more states, such as Victoria or South Eastern Australia. These states in turn may contain many more GIs: the larger areas are called *zones*, most of which contain at least one smaller *region*—which may in turn contain *subregions*. Some of the best-known wine areas of Australia are discussed below.

Hunter Valley: Located within the state of New South Wales just north of the city of Sydney, the Hunter Valley Zone is particularly well known for its varietally-labeled Semillon.

Tasmania: Tasmania is a state located 150 miles (241 km) off the coast of Victoria. Tasmania has a very cool climate with a short growing season. The wine industry here is still small, but it is growing based on its reputation for high-quality wines. It is especially known for Chardonnay, Pinot Noir, and sparkling wine.

Copyright: The Society of Wine Educators 2016

THE WINES OF NEW ZEALAND

New Zealand has been making wine since the 1850s; however, a good deal of the industry was wiped out due to phylloxera in the 1920s, and it took until the 1970s for the country to once again establish a viable wine industry. With New Zealand's relatively recent entrance into the global wine industry and its limited landmass, its wine production is fairly small, but the country has quickly made a name for itself as a producer of high-quality wine.

New Zealand is situated in the Pacific Ocean approximately 1,200 miles (1,930 km) east of Australia and a long way from any other large landmass. It is comprised of two main islands, the North Island and the South Island, and lies completely within the temperate winegrowing latitudes, spanning 36° to 45° south.

The primary topographic feature of the country is the Southern Alps, a high mountain chain that runs the length of the South Island along the western coast. Given that the winds normally blow from the west, these mountains keep the eastern part of the island drier and sunnier than it would otherwise be. The North Island does not have the same mountain chain, but it does have a few high volcanic mountains that perform a similar function in places. Thus, most vineyards are found in the rain shadow of the Southern Alps or the North Island volcanoes, along the east coast of both islands, or in the warmer northern part of the North Island.

With New Zealand's cool climate, it makes sense that the majority of the country's vineyards are planted to white grapes, led by Sauvignon Blanc. New Zealand Sauvignon Blanc tends to feature a combination of tropical fruit flavors, stone fruit flavors (peach, nectarine, apricot), and grassiness that is both unique and very popular among consumers. Chardonnay, Pinot Gris, and Riesling are the other leading white grapes here. Pinot Noir is the leading red grape, and the one red international variety that ripens adequately throughout New Zealand. Other red varieties such as Cabernet Sauvignon, Merlot, and Syrah are planted (in small amounts) in the warmer areas of the country.

The leading wine regions of New Zealand include the following:

Major Wine Regions of New Zealand

Copyright: The Society of Wine Educators 2016

Figure 6.10: Wine Regions of New Zealand

Marlborough: The Marlborough region, located on the northern edge of New Zealand's South Island, is home to over 75% of all of New Zealand's vines and grape production. In particular, the explosive growth in Sauvignon Blanc has taken place primarily in this area. Cloudy Bay, which gave its name to a now-famous Sauvignon Blanc producer, and Clifford Bay are both situated along the coast of this region.

Hawke's Bay: Hawke's Bay is the second largest of New Zealand's wine regions, both in terms of acreage and production. Located on the North Island, this is one of the country's warmest regions as well as the leading producer of red wines other than Pinot Noir. A key feature of the region is the Gimblett Gravels area, a relatively warm region with unique soil made up of a mix of greywacke (a sedimentary sandstone) and a variety of mineral and rocky fragments (the gravels).

Central Otago: Located on New Zealand's South Island, Central Otago is the most southerly wine region in the world. This relatively new winegrowing area is heavily focused on Pinot Noir and has established a positive reputation for its wines. Pinot Noir grown here is associated with the flavors of red fruits, raspberries, and herbs.

THE WINES OF SOUTH AFRICA

South Africa has a long history of wine production that dates back to the seventeenth century, when travel, trade and transportation of goods between Europe, the colonies, and the East meant sailing around the entire continent of Africa. The harbor at Cape Town, at the southern extremity of Africa, was a mandatory stop for ships to replenish their supplies, and wine was one of the items that the cape could provide to passing ships. Vines from Europe were first planted in 1655, with the first wine made in 1659.

The South African winelands, located in the southwest of the country around Cape Town, have a surprisingly Mediterranean climate. Most of the vineyards are located within fifty miles of the coast, and the prime winegrowing areas are those with direct influence from the ocean winds, generated near the point where the chilly waters of the South Atlantic meet the warmer waters of the Southern Ocean. Other influences include the Benguela Current, a cold current that flows up the western coast from Antarctica, bringing moist fogs and cooling breezes, as well as a southern wind known as the *Cape Doctor* that helps dry out the vines.

Chenin Blanc, sometimes referred to by the local name "Steen," has long been the most widely planted variety in South Africa and presently accounts for 18% of all grape production. South African Chenin Blanc is made into many styles of wine, including both oaked and unoaked table wines, as well as a range of sparkling wines. Dessert wines, including late-harvest wines and botrytis-affected wines (often referred to as Noble Late Harvest) are also crafted using Chenin Blanc. Other leading white grapes include Chardonnay and Sauvignon Blanc.

The leading red varieties are Cabernet Sauvignon and Shiraz (Syrah). Another popular red variety is Pinotage, an indigenous crossing of Pinot Noir and Cinsault that was developed almost a century ago at Stellenbosch University. In addition to showing up as a varietally labeled wine, Pinotage is used in Cape Blends in which a minimum of 30% (to a maximum of 70%) is blended with traditional Bordeaux red varieties. Pinot Noir itself is grown only in the coolest regions, such as those found around Walker Bay.

Quality wines in South Africa are highly regulated by the South African Wine and Spirit Board. South Africa's labeling requirements, known as the Wine of Origin (WO) Scheme, were introduced in 1973 and are quite typical of the New World, comprising differing sizes of geographical areas that define place of origin without any major restrictions on the types of wine made therein.

South Africa's main wine-producing area, the Western Cape, surrounds Cape Town and is home to most of the country's regions, districts, wards, and vineyards. Some of the more outstanding areas within the Western Cape are discussed below:

Stellenbosch: The Stellenbosch District, located just east of Cape Town, is one of the oldest and most respected winegrowing areas of South Africa. Cabernet Sauvignon is the leading red wine of the area, which is also known for Chardonnay, Chenin Blanc, and Sauvignon Blanc.

Paarl: The Paarl District lies north of Stellenbosch and is a bit warmer, although it is still reasonably close to the ocean. This larger area is home to some of the more familiar South African brands including the Fairview Wine Farm, known for such brands as Goats do Roam and La Capra.

Constantia: The Constantia Ward is located on the peninsula just south of Cape Town, with a cool maritime climate and decomposed granite soils. The first vines in South Africa were planted here in the 1600s. Vin de Constance—the luscious, sweet wine of the area—became quite famous in Europe during the 18th century and was for a while a leading export. However, the wine faded out of existence after phylloxera devastated the vineyards, and for

Wine Areas of South Africa

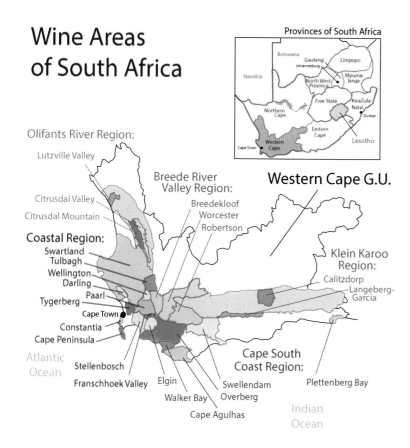

Provinces of South Africa

Olifants River Region:
Lutzville Valley
Citrusdal Valley
Citrusdal Mountain

Breede River Valley Region:
Breedekloof
Worcester
Robertson

Western Cape G.U.

Coastal Region:
Swartland
Tulbagh
Wellington
Darling
Paarl
Tygerberg
Cape Town
Constantia
Cape Peninsula

Klein Karoo Region:
Calitzdorp
Langeberg-Garcia

Atlantic Ocean

Stellenbosch
Franschhoek Valley
Elgin
Walker Bay
Cape Agulhas

Cape South Coast Region:
Swellendam
Overberg
Plettenberg Bay

Indian Ocean

Figure 6.11: Wine Regions of South Africa

a while seemed to be forgotten. Today, however, the once-famous dessert wine is being produced once again, by both the Groot Constantia and Klein Constantia wineries. The region is also being revived as a winegrowing site for dry white and red table wines.

Walker Bay: The Walker Bay District is located in the southernmost part of the country, close to the shore and subject to winds off the Southern Ocean. Proximity to the sea near Hermanus and Cape Agulhas makes this one of the most maritime-influenced of all South African areas, and therefore one of the coolest winegrowing regions of the country. This zone is ideal for Pinot Noir and Chardonnay.

AROMATIZED WINES

Aromatized wines, referred to as *vini aromatizzati* in Italian, are wine-based beverages flavored with aromatic botanicals. They may have additional spirit alcohol added for the purpose of stabilization and as such may technically be classified as fortified wines. Sugar, natural flavorings, and caramel colorings are allowed. Well-known styles of aromatized wines include vermouth, quinquina, and americano.

VERMOUTH

Undoubtedly the most famous of the aromatized wines, vermouth is produced using a wine base that has been flavored with some version of the Artemisia herb (commonly known as *wormwood* in English), along with any other approved natural herbs, fruits, spices, or flavorings. The type of wine base varies, as do the botanical formulas used by each producer. Most vermouth is fortified with spirits to stabilize the product. Some styles are produced with enhanced complexity via oxidative barrel aging and exposure to the elements.

Vermouth was originally consumed either straight or diluted with other liquids to create a tonic beverage designed to stimulate the appetite and enhance digestion. Over the centuries, however, vermouths have been used as flavoring ingredients in mixed drinks and cocktails, and vermouth now constitutes a major segment of the cocktail industry. Many classic cocktails, such as variations of the Martini, the Manhattan, and drinks in the Americano/Negroni family, include vermouth.

There are several dominant vermouth-producing regions as well as several types of vermouth recognized, primarily in Europe but increasingly in other parts of the world. Among the most highly prized and widely distributed are the following examples:

Chambéry: Located in the French Alps, the city of Chambéry at one time had numerous producers of fortified and aromatized wines and was considered one of the centers of vermouth production. Today, however, only the Dolin House remains. Dolin pioneered the light, dry style of vermouth in France in 1832 and later earned appellation d'origine contrôlée (AOC) status for Vermouth de Chambéry. Chambéry is known for its clean, fresh, floral style of vermouth. Chambéry remains the only vermouth with designated AOC status in France.

Noilly Prat: The Noilly Prat brand is today's main producer of Marseilles-style vermouth. As a port city, Marseilles was once another large center of vermouth production. The Marseilles style of vermouth is noted for its oxidative, lightly wooded, almost marsala-like properties. Founded in 1813, Noilly Prat is produced in Marseillan, France.

Figure 7.1: Wormwood (Artemesia)

Torino-Style Vermouth: The city of Torino (Turin) in the Piedmont region of northwestern Italy is the uncontested center of Italian vermouth production. Torino-style vermouth is, in turn, quite likely the dominant style of red/rouge vermouth worldwide. This style of vermouth tends to favor slightly more sweetness through the addition of sugar. Also, it emphasizes floral notes and spices over the herbal components. One notable producer of Torino-style vermouth is Carpano, founded in Turin in 1786 by Antonio Benedetto Carpano. Antonio Carpano is often credited with being the "original inventor of vermouth."

While many styles of vermouth are produced in the area, a specific product referred to as *Vermouth di Torino PGI* has protected geographical indication status in the European Union. Under these standards, which were updated in early 2017, Vermouth di Torino PGI must be produced within the province of Piedmont using a base of Italian wine, and must be fortified with the addition of spirits. The main flavoring must be Artemisia (with additional herbs and spices allowed) and the alcohol by volume must be between 16% and 22%. The standards also allow for a *Vermouth di Torino Superiore PGI*, with a minimum of 17% alcohol by volume. At least 50% of the base wine and the flavorings used for Vermouth di Torino Superiore PGI (aside from the Artemisia) must be grown in Piedmont.

Spanish Vermouth: Spanish vermouths are abundant but are generally not familiar to Americans, for the simple reason that, until very recently, Spanish vermouths were not exported to the United States. Of the many commercial producers throughout Spain, the three that are most well known outside the country include Perucchi, Yzaguirre, and Primitivo Quiles. These are discussed below.

- Perucchi: Dating back to the mid-1800s, Perucchi vermouths from Catalunya are available in rojo, blanco, and extra-dry. Perucchi vermouths are cited for characteristics of chamomile, ginger, lemon verbena, cinnamon, mint, and orange blossom.
- Yzaguirre: Yzaguirre is located in the province of Tarragona in Catalunya, Spain. In 1884, it began producing a range of vermouths, including red, white, rosado, and reserva versions, plus special releases. Yzaguirre is a classic "mistela"

vermouth, using grape must fortified with spirits to arrest fermentation. It is cited for a distinctive balsamic character.
- Primitivo Quiles: Primitivo Quiles vermouth, better known by its label as P. Quiles, is produced in the Alicante area of Spain. Primitivo Quiles has been producing traditional "alpine style" vermouths in a bodega dating back to 1780. While the majority of vermouths are made with white wine and gain their color from the botanical ingredients, P. Quiles vermouth uses red wine made from Mourvèdre grapes and, because of this, has a natural deep coloration. P. Quiles cites cinnamon, clove, ginger, and nutmeg as part of its proprietary formula of botanicals.

Figure 7.2: The Negroni, a vermouth-based cocktail

New World Vermouth: Many craft wineries and distilleries throughout the New World, particularly in the United States, are beginning to explore the creative possibilities of aromatized wines. Some strive to produce classical but proprietary versions of Old World vermouths, while others are creating entirely new styles and flavor profiles. This highly creative sector of the US beverage industry changes frequently; however, the following new brands have established themselves as vermouth producers to watch:
- Vya Vermouth from California
- Sutton Cellars Vermouth from California
- Imbue Bittersweet Vermouth from Oregon

- Ransom American Vermouth from Oregon
- Atsby Vermouth from New York City
- Uncouth Vermouth from Brooklyn

Other American wine and spirits companies have been producing vermouth for quite some time. Among the best known, Gallo Wine Company has long produced a modestly priced, widely distributed line of red and white vermouths. Another line of vermouth, the low-priced Tribuno brand, has been produced for many years by the Wine Group.

QUINQUINA

Quinquina wines, like vermouths, are flavored and fortified, but cinchona bark (the original quinine base used to treat malaria), rather than wormwood, is the primary botanical. The bark, which is generally from either Peru or India, is either chipped or powdered and then macerated in the wine. Sugar and other botanicals, as well as fortifying spirits, may be added. Europe has a long history of using cinchona bark, which is also known as *quina*, *kina*, or *china* (pronounced *kina* in Italian), for medicinal and beverage purposes.

Two of the best-known versions of quinquina are Lillet and Dubonnet, as discussed below:
- Lillet: Lillet, a mild quinquina, was created in Podensac, Bordeaux, in 1887 from locally sourced wine, fruits, and herbs. The original product, based on white Bordeaux wine, was dubbed Kina Lillet. This original Lillet was reformulated in 1986 to make it a bit less bitter and a bit less sweet. It is now known as Lillet Blanc. The change did not sit well with some people, so there are many consumers who still mourn the loss of the "original" Kina Lillet.
- Dubonnet: Dubonnet was originally created as Quinquina Dubonnet in 1846 in Paris, France; the name was later simplified to Dubonnet. It is generally considered to be one of the lightest products in the quinquina category. Since World War II, American Dubonnet has been produced, via licensing agreement, by Heaven Hill Distilleries in Kentucky. That said, there is some question as to how closely the American version follows the European version. In any case, the

original Dubonnet was rouge. The blanc version of Dubonnet was a later addition, made only for the American market.

Figure 7.3: Cinchona Bark

AMERICANO

Americano is a category of aromatized, fortified wines that may be flavored with wormwood or gentian (a type of flowering plant). The americano group is considered to be a subcategory of the quinquina group. In reality, as many of these products defy neat categorization, the families somewhat overlap.

These aromatized wines, despite the name americano, are not to be confused with the popular Americano cocktail, which is a concoction of Campari, sweet red vermouth, soda, and citrus peel. In this instance, the word does not reference America, but amer, the French word for bitter.

Some of the better-known examples of americano are described below:
- Cocchi Americano: Produced in Piedmont, Italy, by the same firm that also produces a range of vermouth and other products, the classic white version of Cocchi Americano is based on Moscato d'Asti wine and is flavored with cinchona bark, citrus peel, spices, and other botanicals. A red version, based on a wine produced from a blend of Brachetto and Malvasia grapes, contains the same flavorings as the white version with the extra addition of rose petals and ginger. The white

version of Cocchi Americano is considered to be the one contemporary product that comes closest to the flavor of the "original" Kina Lillet. It is often mentioned as a substitute in classic drink recipes that list Kina Lillet as an ingredient, such as the Vesper Martini—ordered by James Bond in Casino Royale—and the Corpse Reviver #2.

- Contratto Americano: The Contratto Winery of Piedmont, Italy, was founded in 1867 and has been producing aromatized wine since the 1890s. A former producer of Vermouth di Torino, Contratto currently produces red and white vermouth, fernet, and americano rosso, along with a portfolio of still and sparkling wines. Contratto Americano Rosso is based on white wine made from the Cortese grape (a specialty of the Piedmont region), botanicals steeped in brandy, caramelized sugar, and over thirty other ingredients including mint, ginger, hibiscus flower, nettle, wormwood, lemon peel, licorice, angelica, and bitter orange peel.

WINE SERVICE

In the service of wine, whether at a formal restaurant, a catered event, or even a casual diner, the role of the wine professional is to enhance the customer's experience by assisting with the selection and service of wine while providing the establishment with an appropriate margin of profit.

In the following sections, we will study the roles and responsibilities of the hospitality professional in regards to the service of wine, including the storage of wine, recommending wines, food and wine pairing, and the standard procedures for wine service. The responsible service of alcohol is another important facet of restaurant wine service and is addressed in chapter 14.

WINE STORAGE

The vast majority of wines are meant to be consumed in their youth. The fresh acidity and fruit character of these wines will be enjoyed best during the first few years after their release. With time, wines lose some of these favorable attributes as chemical and phenolic reactions occur within the bottle. Thus, only a small percentage of wines should be held to age for any considerable period of time.

However, proper wine storage conditions should be available even to wines that will only be in storage for a few weeks to a few months. Proper wine storage, whether it entails a large, formal wine cellar or just a small closet, should ideally provide the following:
- Cool temperatures (50°F–60°F/10°C–15°C)
- A moderately humid environment (65%–75%)
- Constant temperature or minimal temperature fluctuations
- An environment with no vibrations
- No light, especially sunlight

- Store wine bottles on their sides or at an angle, so that the cork remains moist and does not dry out.

Wine may be stored with the labels face-up to prevent scuffing, although some people recommend storing the labels face-down to prevent them from getting dusty.

RESTAURANT WINE SERVICE

To prepare for service, it is necessary to gather the required tools and equipment in advance. The glassware should be free of soap and spots. This is particularly important for flutes or other glassware intended for sparkling wines, as any soap residue on glassware will deaden the bubbles in a sparkling wine.

After being washed, glassware should be rinsed or steamed with clean, hot water and polished free of streaks, residue, and fingerprints with a clean, dry, lint-free cloth. Handling the glassware by the stem will eliminate finger smudges.

Depending on the restaurant's policies and facilities, there are two different options for serving chilled wine—using a wine chiller that maintains the service temperature, or using an ice bucket to further chill a wine. When white or rosé wines are stored under refrigeration, it is best to ask the guests whether they prefer the wine served in an ice bucket or chiller.

Chillers must be stored under refrigeration prior to service, and there needs to be sufficient storage space available. If ice buckets are used, they should be prepared in advance on busy nights by filling them two-thirds full with ice. When needed, water should be added to the bucket. The ice and water combination chills wine more quickly than ice alone.

Serviettes (napkins, towels, or small linens) should be neatly folded and ready to be placed on top of each bucket to wipe the bottles after they have been submerged.

Sufficient quantities of each wine offered on the list should be available and accessible to supply the day's needs. Reds should be served at cool room temperature; whites and rosés should be chilled. Note, however, that some people prefer high-acid reds such as Beaujolais, Barbera, and Chianti to be slightly chilled as well. The suggested serving temperature ranges are noted below in Table 8-1:

Table 8-1: Suggested Wine Service Temperatures

Wine Style	Suggested Service Temperature
Sweet white wines	43°F–47°F (6°C–8°C)
Dry Sherry	43°F–47°F (6°C–8°C)
Sparkling wines	43°F–50°F (6°C–10°C)
Light white wines and rosés	45°F–50°F (7°C–10°C)
Medium- to full-bodied, dry white wines	50°F–55°F (10°C–13°C)
Light-bodied red wines	50°F–55°F (10°C–13°C)
Tawny Port and sweet Sherry	54°F–61°F (12°C–16°C)
Medium-bodied red wines	55°F (13°C)
Full-bodied and aged red wines	59°F–64°F (15°C–18°C)
Vintage Port	64°F–68°F (18°C–20°C)

TAKING THE ORDER

To begin the process of wine service, it is first necessary to determine who will be responsible for ordering the wine for the table. In the context of wine service, this person is referred to as the host. If it is not immediately apparent who at the table is to assume this function, you should politely ask. When doing so, be careful not to assume that a male guest will serve as the host, as this may alienate the female guests. While taking the order and sampling the wine, stand to the right of the host whenever possible.

While some guests may be very comfortable with wine and know precisely what they wish to order without the need for assistance, many will appreciate some guidance. Accordingly, you should be familiar with the restaurant's wine list, including details concerning each wine on the list and how those wines pair with the items on the food menu. It is also helpful to ask the guest about which wines he or she has enjoyed in the past (and which ones he or she hasn't) to get a better understanding of what wine the patron may like. It is a best practice to develop a dialogue with the guest in order to build trust and confidence.

Once a wine selection has been made, repeat the selection back to the customer, along with the vintage, to confirm the order. It is also important to ensure that the correct information is relayed to the bartender or other on-premise colleagues who may be responsible for obtaining the specific bottle of wine.

SERVICE OF STILL (NON-SPARKLING) WINE

Once the wine is ordered, select the appropriate glasses and carry them to the table on a beverage tray. The glasses should be set to the right of the water glass, above the knife on the right side of each place setting. Presuming that the table is freestanding, the glasses should be placed on the table from the right-hand side of the customer, with the server walking around the table in a clockwise direction.

After the glasses have been set, the wine should be brought to the table. The bottle is presented to the host from the right side by holding it at an angle, label facing up, so that the selection can be confirmed. The brand name of the wine, its appellation, and the vintage should be repeated back to the guest, and the bottle should not be opened until the guest has accepted the wine.

During the process of removing the cork, the bottle may be held in one hand or placed on a table. To begin the process, use the knife of the corkscrew to cut around the capsule below the raised lip or bulge of the bottle's neck. If using a wine opener that has a foil cutter, a clean cut can be made above the raised lip.

The top of the capsule should be removed and placed in an apron or pocket (as opposed to in the ice bucket or on the table). If the foil tears while cutting it, the entire capsule should be removed. If the wine is sealed with a screw cap, simply unscrew the cap and

Figure 8.1: Presenting the Bottle

the host, without placing the bottle on the table, if it hasn't already been. In formal service, a side plate or tray is used to present the cork. This tradition dates back to the days when the winery's seal, emblazoned on the cork, was a guarantee of authenticity.

Taking a clean napkin, wipe the rim of the bottle and, holding the bottle approximately 2 inches (5 cm) above the glass, pour the host a sample (1 to 2 ounces [30 to 59 ml]) so that he or she can evaluate and accept the beverage.

If a customer is dissatisfied with the wine, you should, without confrontation, determine the cause, such as cork taint or a sulfur-based fault. Whatever the cause, if the wine in question is indeed faulty, the guest's glass should immediately be replaced with a new one, and a fresh bottle of the same wine should be presented, with service beginning again. Restaurants and retailers are often able to obtain a credit from their distributor when returning faulty bottles.

However, if the guest simply doesn't like the wine, you will need to follow the restaurant's policies and possibly suggest that the customer try a different wine. If possible, find out what the guest doesn't like about the wine so that an appropriate substitute can be recommended. A hostile attitude should never be taken. Bottles that have been returned and are in good condition may be used in by-the-glass programs.

Presuming that the wine is sound and has been accepted by the guest, move around the table to give each guest a serving of the wine. While some restaurants are moving away from long-established norms of service, the traditional wine service pattern is as follows:
- Moving clockwise, female guests are served
- Moving clockwise, male guests are served
- Finish with the host (regardless of gender)
- If there is a guest of honor present, this person may be served first regardless of seat location or gender

Wine is poured from the customer's right unless at a booth or otherwise unreachable. The glasses should not be lifted from the table, and they should be filled only one-third to one-half full, depending on the size of the wine glass. As there are five 5-ounce (148-ml) glasses of wine in a wine bottle, a table of up to

place it in your pocket (or otherwise out of sight of the guest) and proceed with service.

The label of the bottle should, whenever possible, face the guest while the wine is being opened and served. To remove the cork, insert the tip of the corkscrew's spiral into the center of the cork from a 45° angle and twist it into an upright position. While holding the bottle with one hand, turn the corkscrew until the entire spiral—save for one turn—has entered the cork. Next, place the corkscrew lever on the lip of the bottle and hold it in place with a finger of one hand, and used the other hand to slowly and gently pull the handle of the corkscrew upward in order to extract the cork. Corks should be removed from the bottle as quietly as possible. At all times, avoid having your fingers touch the mouth of the bottle.

Once removed from the bottle, the cork should be taken off the corkscrew and placed to the right of five people will be adequately served in this fashion. With large tables of six or more, the pour should be adjusted appropriately to ensure that all guests get an equal amount of wine.

To avoid dripping wine at the completion of each pour, the bottle is given a slight twist when lifting it from the glass and the rim of the bottle is wiped with a serviette to catch any drips. If there is wine left in the bottle when you are finished pouring, place the wine bottle on the table to the right of the host or, in the case of white wines, in an ice bucket (also to the right of the host). In formal service, the wine may be placed on a coaster instead of directly on the table, or at a side table or station.

If a second bottle of the same wine is ordered, the host should be brought a fresh glass for tasting the new bottle. Upon approval, the table is served. If the second bottle of wine ordered is different from the first, fresh glasses are needed for everyone. If a second set of glasses is required, the second glass is placed directly behind the first. Any dirty glasses remaining on the table should be removed.

Serving older red wines requires careful handling, as these wines can have quite a bit of sediment in the bottle. The usual practice is to stand these wines upright for a while, and then remove the cork and decant the wine off the sediment.

If the cork breaks off in the neck of the bottle, the corkscrew should be gently reinserted to try to salvage the remaining section. If it can be extracted cleanly from the bottle, the wine continues to be served as described above. If it is unsalvageable, ask the guest if it is acceptable to decant through a piece of cheesecloth or a specifically designed decorative wine funnel that has a filtering screen to catch any bits of cork that have fallen into the wine.

SERVICE OF SPARKLING WINE

Bottles of sparkling wine take a little extra care when opening, and proper service has as much to do with safety as ceremony. First, it is important to be sure that the bottle has not been shaken or roughly handled en route to the table. Next, ensure that the bottle is properly chilled, as cold reduces the pressure inside the bottle and allows for more

control of the cork. Finally, make sure that the bottle and your hands are dry; wet bottles are slippery and difficult to control.

Care must be taken when opening such bottles, as a Champagne cork is capable of flying across a room at 65 mph (this is not just a myth). Many injuries have resulted from lack of attention when opening a bottle of sparkling wine. In addition, the bottle can slip from one's hands if it isn't held tightly. During the process of opening a sparkling wine, the bottle may be held in one hand or may be placed in the ice bucket.

To begin the process of opening a bottle of sparkling wine, pull the small tab in the foil to allow a clean tear along the perforation of the capsule. Alternatively, using the knife from a corkscrew, make a cut in the foil beneath the wire cage. Remove the foil from the top of the cork and place it in your pocket. Next, place a cloth napkin over the bottle; and, with one hand, grip the neck of the bottle and place a thumb on top of the cork. With the other hand, unfasten the wire cage by untwisting it in a counterclockwise fashion, usually for six twists. Removing the cage can allow the cork to be suddenly expelled, so it is best not to remove the cage—or one's thumb—from the cork.

Holding the bottle at a 45° angle, rotate the bottle while tightly holding onto the cork. The cork should not be twisted or turned, as the top section of the cork may break off. It is important to ensure that the cork is not pointing at anyone or at anything

Figure 8.2: Sparkling Wine Service

breakable. After a few turns of the bottle, the cork should slide gently into the napkin with a soft hiss. If the wine is not quite as cold as it should be, try to hold the cork in place so that the escaping CO2 can be released from the side of the cork as it is being expelled. A loud pop, although festive, allows too much carbon dioxide to escape and may deflate some of the bubbles.

If the sparkling wine begins to foam out of the bottle after the cork is popped, it is possible that it was not properly chilled. To prevent the loss of good wine, return the bottle to a 45° angle for a few seconds. It should stop foaming immediately. Present the entire cork, including the cage, to the host (or place at his or her right side), and proceed with service.

DECANTING AND AERATION

Most fine red wines improve if allowed to breathe for a while, although just how long the process should be allowed to last is a hotly debated issue. The preferred method to allow a wine to breathe is to aerate the wine by carefully pouring it into a decanter or carafe.

The purpose of decanting is to allow the wine's aromas and flavors to develop by exposing the wine to oxygen. For those wines that are not overly delicate, vigorously splashing the wine as it is poured into the decanter further aerates the wine. The few moments it takes to decant a wine is roughly equivalent to hours of time spent simply letting the wine stand opened.

Decanting may be appropriate in the following cases:

- Young, robust red wines: Many wines are released into the market so quickly after bottling that they are still heavily tannic. This can mask the fruit and coat the mouth with astringency. Decanting softens and mellows these tannins through exposure to air; this same exposure allows the fruit flavors to emerge more fully.
- Complex wines with moderate aging: Some wines, such as Nebbiolo-based reds and various Cabernet Sauvignons, are dense, compact, and complex, able to age for decades. Wines of this type with limited age may be improved by being decanted for an hour or so, which allows the aromas to open and expand.

- Wines with sediment: Certain wines may have sediment in the bottle. Ideally, these wines should be stored in a decanting cradle or placed upright for an hour or so to allow the sediment to sink to the bottom of the bottle before service. The wine can then be carefully decanted over a lit candle to allow the server to see when sediment reaches the shoulders of the bottle.

THE SENSORY EVALUATION OF WINE

This section describes how to perform a systematic sensory evaluation of a wine. When tasting several wines, evaluate the color and appearance of all the wines first, and then quickly smell them all to get a fresh impression. Next, smell each wine in detail, making notes. Finally, begin the process of actually tasting the wines by taking a sip of the first wine and noting its tastes, flavors, and textures before moving on to the next. Be sure to rest as needed during the process in order to avoid sensory adaptation and palate fatigue. A serving of water for hydration and unsalted crackers or bread for palate cleansing are also suggested.

APPEARANCE

This first stage of wine evaluation involves a visual inspection of the wine for clarity, color, legs (or tears), and, in some cases, the bubble display.

Clarity: To inspect for clarity, hold the wine up to a bright source of light such as a clear light bulb or candle. Modern-day technology allows for most wines to be made clear and bright, if that is the style the winemaker intends. Some unfiltered, unfined, or similarly styled wines may be somewhat cloudy or turbid by design. While not necessarily a fault, any sign of cloudiness or haziness should be investigated. Terms used to describe clarity include (in order of increasing clarity) dull, clear, and brilliant.

Color: To evaluate a wine's color, begin by holding the wine glass over a white surface. Tip the glass at an angle to view the edge of the wine, observing both color and hue. Is the wine color-saturated at its rim, or does the color appear to fade at the edge? Intense color that extends to the rim may indicate a young wine, a wine high in extract and flavor, or both. A degree of fading along the edge, known as the meniscus, may indicate a certain grape variety or production method. It is also quite a reliable indicator of age. To compare the colors of several wines, place the glasses on a white surface, fill them to equal depths, and inspect the wines from above.

- Terms used to describe the color of red wines include purple, ruby, and garnet. Purple indicates a touch of blue, ruby indicates mostly red, and garnet implies a hint of orange or brown. Older red wines with a noticeable brown hue may be described as tawny, amber, or brown.
- Terms used to describe rosé include pink (the most common term), to salmon (if the wine shows a hint of orange) to orange (which is quite rare).
- The most common term used to describe the color of young white wines is yellow. However, white wines made from under-ripe grapes or from a cool climate (or year) may have a hint of green resulting in a yellow/green color. An aged white wine, or one produced from grapes grown in a warmer climate (or year), may have a hint of orange or brown in the hue and might be described as gold, amber, or (in the extreme) brown.

Figure 8.3: Red Wines Arranged by Color

Legs or tears: The rivulets known as legs or tears may be indicators of a wine's high alcohol content. Because water and alcohol evaporate at different rates, legs will form on the inside of the glass after the wine is swirled due to the change in surface tension. Dessert wines and other wines with high residual sugar will also have higher viscosity and thick, slow legs. The presence of such legs is an indicator of the body or weight of a wine.

Bubbles: Evaluating the bubble display of sparkling wines requires keen attention to the stream of bubbles and the size of the bubbles. Although there are other benchmarks of quality in sparkling wine, all other things being equal, the smaller the bead (bubble) and the more continuous and persistent the bubble streams, the higher the quality.

AROMA

For many, the aromatic evaluation of wine proves to be the most difficult step in the process. Therefore, a high level of concentration may be needed for this part of the sensory analysis. You may find it helpful to look at a wine aroma checklist, such as is provided in table 8-2, for a list of descriptive terms often used in the process of wine evaluation. Follow these steps to perform a thorough aromatic analysis of a wine:

- Before swirling the wine, put your nose into the glass above the wine and sniff quickly and deeply.
- Next, reflect on the aromas, and note your impressions on paper. Refer to the wine aroma checklist found in table 8-2 for help with the terminology that may be used to identify specific aromas in your wine.
- Hold the glass by the stem (unless the wine in it has been served too cold and you want to warm it). Swirl the wine in the glass for several quick revolutions. Put your nose back into the glass and take one or two quick, deep sniffs. Record your impressions, and note any associations you make with the wine's aromas. These will help you file and recall the aromas of this wine and others like it. Each time you taste, you are adding a mental "reference library" of standards with which to compare other wines of this type when you taste them.
- Rest 15 to 45 seconds as you reflect and record your impressions.
- Swirl the glass briefly and sniff again. Once again, note your impressions.

Table 8-2: Wine Aroma Checklist

This wine aroma checklist presents many of the most common wine aromas and classifies them for ease of detection and recognition. The categories on the checklist are not mutually exclusive and are not intended to represent an absolute or a standard; checklists such as this are merely meant to be a tool to help the student identify some of the many aromas that may be recognized in wine.

Aroma Category	Specific Aromas
Tree Fruit	Apricot, nectarine, peach, yellow pear, red apple, white peach, red plum, quince
Citrus Fruit	Grapefruit, lemon, lemon curd, lemonade, lime, orange, mandarin orange, orange peel, orange zest, tangerine
Green Fruit	Gooseberry, green grape, green apple, green pear, green plum
Tropical Fruit	Papaya, mango, pineapple, guava, banana, kiwi, lychee, melon, passion fruit
Red Fruit	Red cherry, sour cherry, raspberry, strawberry, pomegranate, red plum, red currant, rhubarb, grape, grape juice
Black Fruit	Blackberry, black cherry, black currant (cassis), black plum, blueberry, boysenberry, mulberry
Dried Fruit	Dried cherry, fig, raisin, golden raisin, prune, jam, fruit cake, baked apple, apricot jam
Floral	Acacia, chamomile, dried flowers, jasmine, honeysuckle, lavender, orange blossom, perfume, rose, rose petal, violet, wildflower, elderflower, geranium
Vegetal	Green bell pepper, eucalyptus, fennel, menthol, fresh tobacco leaf, tomato leaf, green olive, black olive, asparagus
Fresh herbs	Dill, lemon grass, mint, rosemary, bay leaf, thyme, sage
Dry Herbs	Hay, straw, dried herbs, herbs de Provence, dried tobacco
Grassy	Green grass, freshly cut grass
Minerality	Flint, graphite (pencil lead), salt air, gunpowder, steel, slate, wet concrete, wet stone, chalk, wet chalk, fresh rain, gravel, granite
Butter	Butter, buttered popcorn, butterscotch
Yeast	Yeast, bread dough, brioche
Toast	Toast, burnt toast
Nuts	Almond, hazelnut, marzipan, walnut
Oak	Oak, fresh-cut lumber, cedar, cigar box, pine, sandalwood, smoke
Vanilla	Vanilla, vanilla cookies
Coconut	Coconut
Honey	Honey
Botrytis	Musty, moldy, honey, honeysuckle, beeswax, apricot
Earthy	Barnyard, bramble, smoke, dirt, wet dirt, wet leaves, dusty, forest floor
Mushroom	Mushroom, truffles
Tea	Black tea
Coffee	Coffee, espresso, burnt coffee, mocha
Leather	Leather, leathery, wet saddle
Spice	Anise, baking spices, black pepper, cinnamon, clove, ginger, nutmeg, white pepper, incense

ON THE PALATE

Once you have taken a sip of the wine, you can begin to evaluate the tastes, flavors, and tactile sensations of the wine. These characteristics are often referred to as "in-mouth impressions."

To begin this stage of wine evaluation, use the following steps:

1. Place a small amount of wine (about a tablespoon) in your mouth. Move the wine all over your tongue and the inside of your mouth with a chewing motion so that all your taste buds come into contact with the wine and the tactile receptors in your mouth can sense it.
2. Next, allow the wine to warm in your mouth so that more of the volatile compounds can escape. If you hold the wine in your mouth a little longer, you will be able to appreciate more of its flavors.
3. Draw some air into your mouth and through the wine to extract the volatile components and force them up to your olfactory epithelium through the opening in the back of your mouth. This will cause some "slurping noises" so this step may not be appropriate for all occasions, but it should be acceptable in a serious wine tasting.
4. Using a paper cup or a designated spittoon, spit out the wine. Consuming alcohol will alter your abilities of perception, and you want to keep them sharp.
5. Repeat steps 1–4, and, if the situation is appropriate, swallow a small amount of wine. Water, crackers, or bread may be offered as a palate-cleansing option between wines. However, cheese, fruit, salty items, or other foods should be avoided, as their aromas, tastes, and composition will greatly impact the way the wines are perceived.

While using the steps outlined above, you can draw your attention to the taste components (sweetness, acidity, and bitterness) of a wine as well as its level of tannin, level of alcohol, body, and flavors. The following guidelines offer some terms that may be used when describing these aspects of wine or when writing tasting notes.

Sweetness: Sweetness in wine relates to the remaining sugar left over after fermentation; such sugar is typically referred to a "residual sugar" (RS).

Sweetness in a wine may be described using the following terms: dry, off-dry, or sweet.
- Dry: Use this term if the wine has no discernible residual sugar.
- Off-dry: Use this term if a wine has a barely or slightly discernible level of sweetness.
- Sweet: Use this term for any wine that is obviously sweet, including all true dessert wines.

Acidity: In evaluating acidity, pay attention to the sensations that are both tasted and felt on the palate—acidity is often accompanied by a "zing" or "tingling" effect felt on the tongue as well as the mouthwatering effect of the acidity. Acidity in a wine may be described using the following terms: low, medium, or high.
- Low: Use this term if the wine has a "just barely detectable" level of acidity.
- Medium: Use this term if the level of acidity reminds you of the acidity of a fresh red apple.
- High: Use this term if the wine is very acidic; almost seeming (but not quite) sour; such as you might experience when eating fresh green table grapes.

Bitterness: For many people, bitterness is perceived on the back of the palate and will be one of last sensations to be perceived. The levels of bitterness in a wine may be described using the following terms: none, low, medium, or high; and may be defined as follows:
- None: Use this term if the wine contains no discernible bitterness.
- Low: Use this term if you detect just a slight "tingle" of bitterness on the back of the tongue or throat, particularly on the finish.
- Medium: Use this term if the wine has a noticeable bitter sensation, yet it is pleasant and in balance with the other taste components of the wine.
- High: Use this term if the wine has a noticeable level of bitterness that is the leading taste component of the wine.

Tannin: Tannins are mostly found in red wine, although it is possible for white wines made with oak influence or skin contact to show some tannin as well. Tannins are a major contributor to the weight of red wines and are also responsible for the textural drying sensation of many red wines. When evaluating a wine for tannin, it may help to use the formalized tasting technique of drawing some air into the mouth or before swallowing or spitting. The level of tannin in a wine may be described using the following terms: none, low, medium, or high.

- None: Most white and rosé wines will show no evidence of tannin.
- Low: Use this term if, after tasting the wine and drawing some air into the mouth, you detect just a slight drying sensation on the palate, and/or if the drying sensation is confined to the back of your mouth.
- Medium: Use this term if the drying sensation from the tannin is easily detectable not just on the back of the mouth or the tongue, but also closer to the middle of your tongue or on the gums.
- High: Use this term if the tannins are easily detectable with both texture and dryness all over the tongue and on the sides of the mouth. In some cases, you may even be able to detect dryness on the roof of your mouth.

Level of Alcohol: Alcohol affects the flavor of a wine as well as body, aroma and texture. The other components of flavor must be in balance with the alcohol, or the wine will have a "hot" (burning) taste or feel. High-alcohol wines, all other things being equal, will seem viscous and full-bodied, while low-alcohol wines may seem a bit lean or even watery (unless there is a bit of residual sugar to enhance the mouthfeel). The level of alcohol in a wine may be described using the following terms: low, medium, or high.

- Low: Use this term for wines that have up to 11% alcohol by volume.
- Medium: Use this term for wines that have between 11.5% and 13.5% alcohol by volume.
- High: Use this term for wines that have 14% alcohol by volume or higher.

Body: Body, sometimes referred to as "mouthfeel" or "weight" is the textural or tactile sensation of a wine. Alcohol, residual sugar, and tannin are the main components of mouthfeel for most wines. Conversely, high levels of acidity can make a wine seem lighter in body. The body of a wine may be described using the following terms: light, medium, or full.

- Light: A light-bodied wine will seem just slightly more viscous than water, and is most likely low

alcohol, medium-to-high in acidity, and delicately flavored. Many young, fruity, and/or unoaked white wines will fall into this category.
- Medium: The medium-bodied indicator is often appropriate for wines moderate in alcohol, tannin, and/or acidity. Flavorful white wines such as Viognier or oaked Chardonnay, as well as the lighter styles of red wines such as some Pinot Noir and Beaujolais are likely to be medium-bodied.
- Full: A wine that is medium-to-high in alcohol and/or tannin, and bold in flavor may be described as full-bodied. Red wines are more likely than white wines to be full-bodied (although there certainly are some full-bodied white wines). Very sweet dessert wines (of any color) are also likely to be full-bodied.

Flavors: Flavors in wine may be described using the same terminology used in the description of aromas. However, you may find that the flavors experienced on the palate are quite different than the aromas you previously recognized, and you may find that the flavors present themselves at different levels of intensity than the aromas did.

Figure 8.4: Sensory Evaluation of Wine

OVERALL IMPRESSIONS

After you have analyzed the wine for its separate components, you will want to take a step back and consider the wine as a whole. This stage of wine evaluation may include an assessment of the wine's balance, finish, complexity, and intensity; and by considering these four characteristics, you can reach a conclusion about the overall quality of the wine.

Balance: One of the most desired traits in a wine is good balance, where the concentration of fruit and sugar is in harmony with the levels of acidity and tannin. In a balanced wine, all of these components seem to be in proportion and appropriate to the style of the wine.

Finish: A wine's finish includes its aftertaste (the tastes, aromas, and flavors that linger on the palate after the wine has been spit out or swallowed) and its length (how long those sensations last). A wine's finish may be lean, cleansing, mouth-filling, or warm (among other possible descriptors), but, above all else, it should be pleasant. The finish of a wine is typically described by its length using the following terms: short, medium, or long.

- Short: Use this term if the finish lasts for five seconds or less.
- Medium: Use this term if the finish lasts for between six and thirty seconds.
- Long: Use this term if the finish lasts for longer than thirty seconds; a finish lasting for a minute or longer may also be described as "lengthy" or "persistent."

Complexity: Complexity is one of the most subjective descriptions used in wine evaluation. Complex wines have a lot going on and tend to hold one's interest. Complex wines have "layers" of scents and flavors, many of which are revealed only as the wine evolves in the glass. A high-quality wine is almost always a complex wine; think of it as the complete opposite of a simple "porch sipper."

Intensity: A wine's aromas and flavors may be described in terms of their intensity (sometimes referred to as "concentration"). If a wine's aromas or flavors seem to leap out of the glass and take no effort to notice or recognize, the wine could be described as having a high level of intensity. If the aromas need to be coaxed out the glass or the flavors are somewhat hard to describe, the wine may have a light or medium level of intensity. Wines of marked quality are typically expected to have a high level of intensity of aroma and/or flavor.

Quality: The concept of "quality" in wine is subjective at best, and even the most revered wine critics will often disagree on the quality level of any given wine. Adding to the confusion is the fact that price should—but does not always—reflect quality, and that even within a specific batch of wine the quality of an individual bottle (or serving) may vary based on the care taken and conditions found in the transportation, storage, and service of the wine. However, there is a standard vocabulary used to describe the favorable attributes of wine. It is expected that a high-quality wine will be well balanced, have an appropriate level of intensity of flavors (concentration), have a long and pleasant finish, and be high in interest and complexity.

Quality in wine can be described, in a simplified manner, by using the following terms: poor, acceptable, good, very good, or excellent. In order to be described as "excellent," a wine should demonstrate good balance, a long and pleasant finish, a high level of complexity, and an intensity of aroma, taste, and/or flavor.

- Poor: Use this term if a wine does not show any of the features of quality (balance, finish, complexity or intensity).
- Acceptable: Use this term if a wine shows one out of the four possible features of quality.
- Good: Use this term if a wine shows two out of the four possible features of quality.
- Very good: Use this term if a wine shows three out of the four possible features of quality.
- Excellent: Use this term for a wine that demonstrates all four possible features of quality, and is described as having (as noted above) good balance, a long and pleasant finish, a high level of complexity, and an intensity of aroma, taste, and/or flavor.

On a final note, we should not leave the topic of wine quality without mentioning sheer physical pleasure. In other words, did the customer (or consumer) enjoy it? Many would argue that this is the most important aspect of a wine's character. In light of this seemingly obvious appraisal, we must always keep in mind that just because a wine is of the highest quality, does not mean that everyone will appreciate it!

WRITING A TASTING NOTE

A wine tasting note can be simple or complex, analytical or pure poetry, or all of the above. You may have even come across tasting notes that make you laugh. While there is no set standard and many "correct" ways to describe wine, a tasting note should clearly communicate the basic characteristics of a given wine, and—when used to describe wines to customers—should include the information that the customer wants to hear without intimidating or confusing them.

Consider, for example, the following tasting note: "Captain's Winery Monterey County Chardonnay 2015 is a yellow-hued white wine with brilliant clarity. The aromas include green apple, lemon, peach, vanilla, and smoke. It is medium-bodied and dry, with a high level of acidity, medium alcohol, and flavors of peach, green apple, and spice. This is a well-balanced, excellent quality wine with a long finish."

You will note that all of the information presented in the tasting note was discussed in detail in the previous section and—if you have already read the previous section—should be easy to understand.

Writing a tasting note does not need to be difficult, nor should you feel that you need to include every possible bit of available information in a tasting note. Table 8-3 includes a template that can be used to write a basic wine tasting note.

Table 8-3: Suggested Template for a Wine Tasting Note

Characteristic:	Suggested terminology:	Example:
Name of the wine	Include (as applicable) the name of the producer, the type of the wine, the region of origin, and the vintage date	*Captain's Winery Monterey County Chardonnay 2015*
Type	White, Rosé, Red, Fortified, Sparkling	
Color	White: Yellow/Green, Yellow, Gold, Amber, Brown Rosé: Pink, Salmon, Orange Red: Purple, Ruby, Garnet, Tawny, Amber, Brown	*This is a yellow-hued white wine with brilliant clarity*
Clarity	Dull – Clear - Brilliant	
Aromas	See Table 8-2 (Wine Aroma Checklist)	*The aromas include green apple, lemon, peach, vanilla, and smoke.*
Sweetness	Dry – Off-dry – Sweet	*This wine is medium-bodied and dry, with a high level of acidity and medium alcohol. The wine has no tannin and no discernible bitterness.*
Acidity	Low – Medium - High	
Bitterness	None – Low – Medium – High	
Tannin	None – Low – Medium – High	
Alcohol	Low – Medium – High	
Body	Light – Medium – Full	
Flavors	See Table 8-2 (Wine Aroma Checklist)	*The flavors include peach, green apple, and cinnamon.*
Finish	Short – Medium - Long	*The wine has a long finish.*
Other characteristics	Balance, complexity, intensity, or others	*This is a well-balanced, highly complex, and intensely aromatic wine.*
Quality	Poor – Acceptable – Good – Very Good – Excellent	*This wine is of excellent quality.*

RECOMMENDING WINES

Recommending wines is an integral part of the wine server's role. To be skillful at this, one needs to have thorough knowledge of the restaurant wine list and the styles of wines on offer. One should be able to clearly and concisely describe the characteristics of the wine being suggested, and be able to offer alternatives with ease.

When describing wines, be sure and use terminology that wine consumers can relate to, and aim to describe the overall style of the wine. For example:
- Is it dry, off-dry, or sweet? Some guests may even be confused by a term such as 'dry,' so be prepared to describe what you mean.
- Is the wine light- or full-bodied?
- What are its dominant flavor characteristics? Red fruit? Citrus fruit?

As an example, suppose a guest suggests a grape variety, such as Chardonnay. The server must be familiar with the wide range of styles of Chardonnay-based wines available and respond accordingly, guiding the customer to the style—such as tropical fruit versus citrus fruit, full and oaky versus lean and crisp—that best fits their taste, food selection, and budget.

You also need to understand the restaurant's menu, including ingredients and cooking preparations. The ability to describe the dishes on the menu and make suggestions for wine pairings can help drive sales by leading customers to specific wines that they might not otherwise have considered.

Strive to be enthusiastic and project confidence in your ability to recommend wines. Telling a story or sharing an anecdote about the winemaker or vineyard is a sure way to spark the customer's interest in a certain wine. The key to keeping your customer's trust is to communicate effectively and knowledgeably while avoiding arrogance or intimidation.

Figure 8.5: White wine and seafood is a classic pairing

PAIRING WINE AND FOOD

The objective of food and wine pairing is to enhance both the wine and the dish; however, this is not an exact science—there is no "perfect" wine for each dish, as even slight variances in seasoning can change the perception of a wine on the palate. Furthermore, in a restaurant setting, one may need to choose one wine for the entire table, which may entail finding a wine that can pair with a variety of dishes; in such a case, a good by-the-glass program can help.

While there is no such thing as a set of "rules" that will always guide one to a successful matchup, there are some guidelines that will predict how the wine and food will interact. These guidelines take into consideration the components—such as sweetness, acidity, bitterness, intensity, and flavor—of the food and the wine as well as the cooking methods used to prepare the food. Some of these guidelines are discussed below.

SWEETNESS

While it may seem counter-intuitive, sweetness in food will diminish the perception of sweetness in a wine. This can be an advantage when serving ice wines and late-harvest wines that seem overly sweet when tasted on their own; served with sweet foods, the wine is perceived to be less sweet and, to some people, more balanced. Another important time to remember this concept is when serving a dish that has a bit of sweetness in it, such as pork loin with cherry sauce or chicken with apricot glaze. An off-dry wine is a good choice for such dishes, as the sweetness in the food will actually make the wine taste drier. For the same reason, serving a sweet food with a dry wine will most likely bring out the wine's acidity and may result in a negative impact on the wine's flavors.

ACIDITY

In a similar reaction to that which occurs with sweetness, pairing wines with acidic foods will actually decrease the perception of acidity in the wine. Therefore, it is best to pair high-acid foods—such as those dressed with lemon, other citrus juices, tomatoes, or vinegars—with high-acid wines such as Sauvignon Blanc, Riesling, or Barbera. This is a situation where very high-acid wines, such as New Zealand Sauvignon Blanc or white Bordeaux, can really shine; the food will take the "edge" off the acidity and the wine will likely still taste well-balanced. At the same time, keep in mind that high-acid foods will make anything but a correspondingly high-acid wine seem flat.

BITTERNESS

In contrast to the taste dynamics of sweetness and acidity, where the components tend to cancel each other out, bitterness in food enhances the bitter tastes in wine. Unless this is desirable, one should try to pair bitter tastes in food with wines that are low in bitterness. Wines that are medium-to-high in acidity and those with some residual sugar typically pair well with bitter tastes in food. Keep in mind that oak-aged wines have a bitter component to them. Overly bitter foods are not necessarily appreciated by the American palate, but foods such as spinach, broccoli, asparagus, and eggplant have an element of bitterness to them.

SALTINESS

Moderately salty foods prepared with good-quality salt pair well with a wide range of wines, and salt—along with acidity in food—can be described as a food component that tends to "soften" many styles of wine. In particular, salt in food tends to decrease the perception of bitterness, both in the food and in an accompanying wine, as can be seen in the salt used to season a grilled steak "taming" the tannic bitterness of a young red wine. Additionally, the cooling, refreshing acidity of wines such as Sauvignon Blanc and Champagne pairs well with moderately salty foods, and the combination of salt and acidity can lend a pleasant accent to the flavors of both the wine and the food. Salty foods also pair well with sweet wines, as seen in the classic pairing of sweet wines with salty blue cheeses.

INTENSITY

In many successful wine and food pairings, neither one overpowers the other in intensity. Many refer to this as matching the intensity of the wine to the food. In most cases, it is best to pair a light dish (such as steamed chicken and spinach) with a lighter wine (such as an Argentine Torrontés or an Albariño from Spain). Heavier dishes, such as grilled steak or oven-baked pork chops, will likewise tend to pair better with heavier wines. This is one reason that the "red wine with red meat" guideline (as old-fashioned as it may be), works a good deal of the time—although a heavy-bodied white wine could be made to work as well.

In the case of very rich food, such as blue cheese, roasted meats, or rich desserts, it may also work to contrast the heaviness of the food with a lighter wine. In this case, the wine serves as a refreshing break from the heaviness of the food and acts as a palate cleanser. For instance, a rich dessert, such as apricot cheesecake, can pair delightfully with a similarly rich and heavy dessert wine such as Sauternes. However, it could also make a successful pairing, albeit in a different way, with a light dessert wine such as Moscato d'Asti.

FLAVORS

Much attention has been paid to matching and contrasting flavors in wine and food. For example, it can be argued that matching flavors in the food and the wines—such as the grapefruit flavors in a South African Sauvignon Blanc paired with a grapefruit and butter lettuce salad—makes for an appealing combination. Likewise, many would recommend a pairing based on contrasting yet complementary flavors, such as the matchup of the meaty, smoky flavors of grilled pork with the cherry-berry flavors of an Oregon Pinot Noir. This is, however, one area of food and wine pairing where it is difficult to generalize, as the effect of a certain flavor combination is very difficult to predict. Thankfully, most flavor interactions are pleasant, and as long as a wine pairing is predicted to be successful based on taste components, the flavors will most likely be harmonious as well.

SPICY FOODS

Foods that are hot—in terms of heat from spice (such as cayenne, ginger, or cloves) or chili pepper-type heat—require some additional care when pairing with wine. Spicy flavors in wine do not typically enhance the spicy flavors in food – instead, they make the level of alcohol seem elevated and only serve to accentuate spiciness. Rather, with spicy cuisine, reach for a softer wine with a touch of residual sugar. Examples include off-dry styles of Gewürztraminer, Riesling, or Chenin Blanc (such as a demi-sec Vouvray).

Figure 8.6: Preparation and seasoning is an important part of the food and wine pairing equation

CONSIDER THE FOOD'S PREPARATION

Many food items—particularly chicken, pork, and some fish—are rather neutral in flavor on their own, and the methods used in preparation will have a significant impact on the appropriate wine selection. For instance, consider a boneless, skinless chicken breast that has been poached or steamed. Most likely, this will produce a dish that is light in flavor and body, creating an appropriate pairing for a light-bodied wine. However, if that same chicken breast is prepared by roasting, grilling, or sautéing—the preparation method itself would likely add flavor intensity to a dish that will turn out to be medium-bodied or even heavy, and a better match for a medium- to full-bodied wine.

Sauces can add the same type of diversity to an otherwise basic dish—whether a light vegetable puree or vinaigrette, or a weightier sauce based on butter or cream. In many cases, the seasoning and cooking methods used in the preparation of a dish do more to add tastes, flavors, and textures to a dish than does the base ingredient on its own, so much so that one of the more insightful guidelines of food and wine pairing is "don't pair just to the protein—pair to the preparation."

PUTTING IT ALL TOGETHER

When helping your guests choose a wine for a particular dish or meal, keep in mind that guidelines such as these are by no means a "rule book." The most important thing is always to read your guests carefully and be flexible—ideas, experiences, and personal preferences can vary dramatically. Practice is also very important, and you should take every opportunity to taste wine and food together in order to find combinations that work for you, so as to be able to describe and recommend them to your guests and customers.

BEER

CHAPTER NINE

Beer has been brewed for over 10,000 years—since the cultivation of grain began—and is the most consumed type of alcoholic beverage worldwide. It can be defined as a fermented product achieved from steeping a grain in water and often including a flavoring or bittering agent. Throughout history, different ingredients have been used to this end, such as millet, sorghum, rice, and herbs; however, today the vast majority of beer styles are brewed with barley, water, yeast, and hops. Other grains may be used as well, particularly wheat, rice, and corn, for stylistic or economic reasons.

Historically, beer spread throughout the world as the ruling and imperialistic empires began to take a foothold in areas and regions that were too cold for wine production, yet were well suited for the cultivation of barley and other grains. The church and their monasteries experimented with, documented, and made substantial discoveries in the production of beer much like they did with wine and other agricultural products at this time.

Throughout the Industrial Revolution, the quality, technique, and availability of beer all continued to improve. However, during the 20th century, several world wars, widespread temperance movements, and global consolidations set the industry back in terms of the diversity and authenticity of its products, favoring instead the rise of mega-businesses and the homogenization of flavor.

In the last thirty years, there has been a revival of the beer industry in terms of a return to traditional styles, an interest in unique and intense flavors, and a public that is embracing innovative producers worldwide.

In this chapter, we'll cover the history of beer production from ancient and medieval times through the boom in the craft beer movement of the last thirty years. Special attention will be paid to ingredients

and production methods, as well as the diverse styles of beer available. Finally, we will cover the aspects of beer appreciation, including sensory evaluation, service, storage, and beer and food pairing.

THE ANCIENT ORIGINS OF BEER

The exact origins of beer brewing are not fully known, but it is thought that many ancient civilizations developed independent methods of creating alcohol from the grains they cultivated, such as rice across Asia and millet and sorghum in Africa. More specifically, it is believed that the first beer production could be placed in early Mesopotamia, sometime around 9000 BCE. This assumption is based on the pattern of crops known to have been planted between the Tigris and Euphrates Rivers at this time.

The first hard evidence of beer production is believed to be the residues of a grain-based ferment on pottery, found in China dating from around 7000 BCE. We also know, via written records, that the Sumerians were brewing different types of beer by approximately 3000 BCE. One such Sumerian document explains the process of baking bread and then soaking the loaves in earthenware pots of water in order to achieve fermentation.

At about this same time (3000 BCE), it was apparent that the Egyptians were using barley as their main grain and had implemented a primitive form of malting. While brewing started in the home, by 500 BCE large-scale beer-making operations had been set up in many parts of the world to supply large populations, such as laborers and armies, with beer.

Oxidation was always a problem in ancient brewing, and as such all sort of spices and herbal mixtures—which included juniper, ginger, and saffron—were used to delay oxidation and to disguise potential off-flavors. Hops were also used by apothecaries in ancient medicines and known for their anti-oxidant and antiseptic properties and, as such, made their way into the beer-production process during medieval times. By the time beer production ceased in Egypt due to religious influences, the knowledge and appreciation of beer had made its way to Europe and continued to flourish, particularly in those areas where the climate proved too cool for wine grape production but where grains could thrive.

Figure 9.1: The Orval Monastery (and brewery) in Belgium

During Medieval times in Europe, alcoholic beverages proved to be safer than water or milk, and beer became the drink of choice in the areas—particularly in the north—where wine was not readily available. With the fall of the Roman Empire in the 5th century, monasteries took over much of the role of supplying beer (and wine) to their own communities as well as to pilgrims and travelers passing through. This is witnessed by the remains of complex malting and brewing operations—complete with the cultivation of most of the required ingredients—on monastic lands. As of the 1300s, hops were the most common beer-flavoring agent used in continental Europe, and one hundred years later they were used in England as well.

In addition to monastic brewing, beer continued to be brewed in the home. As the more successful home brewers gained recognition, they would attract visitors to their homes. These neighborhood gathering spots became main social centers, eventually taking on the term "Public House" and playing an important and ongoing role in history and society.

In the 1500s, the monasteries in Bavaria began to ferment their brews in their cool, underground cellars in order to prevent bacterial spoilage. At the same time, this practice attracted certain strains of yeast that could function better at lower temperatures. This new style of beer production became known as lagering.

THE GERMAN BEER PURITY LAWS
A landmark in the history of beer came about in 1516, when the *Reinheitsgebot*, now known as the German Beer Purity Laws, was first proclaimed. In these laws, the Bavarian Duke Wilhelm IV stated that beer must be brewed with only barley, hops, and water. The law set the price of beer and created the penalty—confiscation—for the production of impure beer. Besides ensuring the safety of beer, the purpose of the law was to ensure the availability of affordable bread by preventing price competition for grains, and allowing the bakers access to a steady supply of wheat and rye.

Since the original proclamation of the Reinheitsgebot, there have been relatively few revisions in the law. For instance, it is now accepted that the original law is specific to bottom fermented beers, allowing wheat and rye for top-fermenters. Outside of Bavaria, German brewers were allowed to add other ingredients such as sugarcane to their beer until 1906. However, when Bavaria became a part of the Second German Empire, the rest of the Empire was required to follow the law as well. Despite some changes in the politics, the Reinheitsgebot can be considered the world's oldest consumer protection legislation, all thanks to beer!

THE MODERN HISTORY OF BEER
The 1700s and 1800s saw substantial innovations in roasting grain, which was no longer done exclusively over an open flame, but often through indirect heat, thus introducing paler malts. In 1842, a clear, golden, lager style was invented by Josef Groll in the town of Plzen, Southern Bohemia (in the present-day Czech Republic). This style of beer, known as pilsner, was a great success and remains popular to this day. Pilsner is named after the town where it was first produced, and Groll's original brew—the world's first blond lager (known as Pilsner Urquell)—is still produced there today. A number of factors contributed to the invention of pilsner,

including the low protein malt, the soft water source, and the availability of glass bottles.

Figure 9.2: Pilsner Urquell—the world's first pilsner beer

The industrial revolution brought its own modernizations to beer production and transportation. The steam engine made the world smaller and allowed for the transport of ingredients and the final product, as well as consumers (people). Advancements in science—particularly Louis Pasteur's discovery of the mechanisms of yeast and fermentation in the 1860s—improved all stages of beer production, from grain cultivation to transportation and storage.

Beer arrived in the American colonies along with the first European settlers. One of their primary concerns as they approached the New World was that they arrived with enough beer to serve as a starter for a new brew—after all; beer was safer to drink than water. As a matter of fact, an often-repeated story tells that the original landing spot of the Pilgrims aboard the Mayflower—Plymouth Rock—was chosen despite the fact that the ship was originally heading for the Virginia colony 600 miles away. As the story goes, after being at sea for two months, Plymouth Harbor was the first land they spotted, and by that time they were in danger of running out of beer—and so ashore they went. Hops arrived in America in the 1700s, and later generations would discover that they grew exceptionally well in the climate of Washington State and Oregon.

The Industrial Revolution brought a series of technological improvements in refrigeration and pasteurization, as well as the arrival of the railroads; all of these developments allowed large breweries to thrive. In 1880, there were 2,830 breweries in operation in the United States. This number declined to 1,500 by the year 1910, as larger breweries began to gain power in the market and smaller breweries closed.

In the late 1800s, the temperance movement trying to "battle the evils of drunkenness" had made its way to the United States, culminating in the passage of the 18th amendment to the US Constitution and effectively ushering in Prohibition. Prohibition in the United States lasted from 1920 until its repeal in 1933. Some of the larger breweries in the United States survived through Prohibition by selling malt syrup for home brewing, legal "near beer" (which had only 0.5% abv), or other agricultural products such as milk and cheese.

Several decades later, during the grain shortages of World War II, breweries turned to adjuncts, such as corn and rice, to allow large-scale beer production to continue. These circumstances helped give rise to a particularly American style of beer. This light, crisp style of beer is still enjoyed in America today, and adjuncts are still used to maintain this style in many top-selling commercial beers.

After Prohibition and two World Wars, forty breweries dominated the entire American beer industry—each of which tended to brew the same style of beer. This was reflective of a global trend that saw many larger breweries all around the world either out-competing the local businesses or outright buying them up. In the post-war United States, this homogenization of beer offerings could be further understood as a reflection of the overall food culture of the 60s and 70s and the American predilection (at the time) for bland, convenience, and processed foods. However, in the mid-1970s there was a revolution brewing.

THE AMERICAN CRAFT BREW MOVEMENT
In the 1970s, beginning in California, a growing interest in all aspects of food—healthy eating, local food, fine dining, and food-as-entertainment—along with an increase in the number of Americans traveling to Europe—created a demand for more diversity in the selection of beers available in America. This in turn gave rise to some of the early American micro-breweries.

In San Francisco, Fritz Maytag, heir to the very successful washing machine company, marked a turning point with his purchase of Anchor Brewery in 1965. He began by reviving old and lost styles of beer. The most famous style was the Steam beer of the 1800s, which he produced and trademarked as "Anchor Steam" in 1981. Following suit, the first post-Prohibition micro-brewery in Sonoma (California) was set up by Jack McAuliffe in 1976. Called New Albion, the brewery only lasted for six years, but during that time it inspired other California breweries, such as the Mendocino Brewing Company, to gain a foothold.

By 1977, a fledgling (and now famous) beer critic named Michael James Jackson first published his book "The World Guide to Beer," providing Americans with intriguing information regarding the treasures of the greater beer-producing world. These developments combined to offer a huge impetus to the craft beer movement. Soon thereafter, in 1978, President Jimmy Carter signed a law allowing home brewing and thus created a new breed of amateur brewers, many of whom followed their dreams and turned commercial. Other changes in legislation, particularly at the local level, expanded the possibility of commercial brewery-restaurants as well as micro-breweries (defined as a brewery with production of fewer than 15,000 barrels per year). These businesses soon spread from California to Oregon and Washington, and then exploded across the country.

In the beginning, the signature style of the growing league of micro-breweries was the American pale ale. This choice was primarily due to ease and the economy of production as opposed to the expense of the wide-scale refrigeration required to produce lagers. However, micro-breweries are often known for their creativity and, as such, many small, cash-strapped breweries concentrated on ale production while at the same time showing great creativity in style and flavor.

With time, American pale ales became further defined by utilizing the more aggressive and aromatic Cascade hops grown on the West Coast. The epitome of this style of American Pale ale is considered to be Sierra Nevada Pale Ale, produced since 1979 in Chico, California. A bit further up the West Coast, in Yakima, Washington, Grant's Brewery Pub—founded by Bert Grant—became

Figure 9.3: Sierra Nevada Pale Ale

the first post-prohibition brewpub as well as one of the first American producers of a "hoppier" style of ale known as India pale ale (IPA). Grant, an expert in hops, was not worried about loading his beers up with the sharp Cascade variety of hops, despite the fact that this would have offended the original English (and early American) beer brewers. IPAs quickly transformed into an iconic American style of beer, and craft breweries continue to rally around it.

In the short history of American craft breweries, there are many other prominent breweries that added to the history and culture of American beer. Some of these are discussed below:
- The Boston Beer Company: The Boston Beer Company was one of the first breweries to gain popularity on the East Coast. Its flagship product is Samuel Adams Boston Lager. The owner, Jim Koch, has several ancestors who were avid brewers.
- Yuengling: Located in Pottsville, Pennsylvania, Yuengling Brewery has been declared the country's oldest continuously operating brewery. Yuengling was founded in 1829 and continued

to operate through Prohibition by brewing "near-beer" and producing dairy products.

- Brooklyn Brewery: Brooklyn Brewery, established in 1987, was created in homage to the tradition of the forty-eight pre-prohibition brewers—many of them immigrants from Germany, Belgium, and Ireland—who operated in Brooklyn. (During the 19th century, Brooklyn was a center of beer culture, and produced upwards of ten percent of America's beer, using mostly New York State-grown hops and grains.)
- Celis Brewery: Pierre Celis is credited with single handedly reviving the Belgian Wit (wheat) beer movement, having first revived the style in his Belgian home town of Hoegaarden in 1966, and later by bringing it to the United States at his namesake Celis Brewery located in Austin, Texas (in 1992). The Celis Brewery was sold to MillerCoors in 1995, and dissolved several years later. However, in 2012, Pierre's daughter, Christine Celis, purchased the rights to the name "Celis Brewery." Some of the original brewing equipment, including its massive copper kettle, has also been restored to the family and Belgian-style beers are being brewed once again under the Celis brand name.

Today, the continued growth of craft and micro-brews is staggering. According to the Brewer's Association, 2015 figures for the craft beer industry show that there are currently over 4,200 breweries in the United States—a far cry from the forty breweries that were operating post-Prohibition. The number of beer-producing companies has been steadily increasing since 2010, in the past five years there has been an average growth of 155 brew pubs and 400 micro-breweries per year. Some experts predict that the industry will begin to slow, and while growth dipped from 2014 to 2015, it was still growing and the craft industry is continuing to boom.

RAW INGREDIENTS FOR BEER PRODUCTION

There are, for the most part, recognized formulas for each classic style of beer, and the raw ingredients used for making beer have an obvious impact on the flavor, texture, and quality of the final product.

Even subtle variations in the ingredients or procedures used in the production process can make a huge difference in the resulting beer—this is what gives rise to the hundreds of unique styles of beer available on the market.

The most common raw ingredients used in beer production are discussed below:

Water: Like many beverages, beer is mostly water—as much as 90% to 95%. The quality and mineral content of the water affects the final flavor of the beer and influences the style of beer that will be made in a certain region. Additionally, the hardness of the water—mainly affected by calcium and magnesium content—will affect the enzymes activated during brewing as well as other trace minerals required by the yeast for a healthy fermentation.

Figure 9.4: Barley in the field

Historically, certain beers developed in particular locations largely because of the type of water available. Examples of this are the stouts originally developed in Ireland, porters originating in London, and the crisp lagers of Plzen. At present, as water is able to be treated in order to maximize the desirable minerals and minimize those that negatively affect the brewing process, virtually any style of beer can be made anywhere in the world.

Malted Grain: Barley is the most common grain to be used as the basis for beer production, although some specialty beers may use wheat, rye, or other grains (sometimes in limited amounts). Similar to wheat, barley grows as a grass, with the seed head harvested as a grain. In fact, the three main types of barley are named after how many rows of seed—2, 4, or 6 rows—grow at the top of the central stem.

To prepare barley for beer production, the individual barleycorns (or seeds) are typically malted. This will begin the process of converting their starch into sugars, which will in turn be converted in alcohol during the fermentation process. Barley that has gone through the malting process is referred to as *malt* or *malts*.

The three steps in the malting process are steeping, germination, and kilning, as discussed below:
- Steeping: The first step in malting is to steep the barley in water. The barley is then drained and held at a constant temperature for about five days.
- Germination: The increased moisture content in the steeped seeds causes them to germinate, or sprout, and develop enzymes that help nourish the growing plant.
- Kilning: Once the barley is germinated, it is dried in a kiln to stop the growth of the sprouts. The enzymes that were activated during germination then complete the conversion of starch to sugars during the mashing process.

Kilning greatly influences the color and flavor of the final beer, depending on the length, temperature, and moisture involved in the process. Light or pale malts will turn into a beer with a correspondingly light color and flavor. Light malts make up most of the malt content of any beer recipe, as heavy kilning kills the enzymes necessary for sugar conversion. Dark or "specialty" malts are most often used in small amounts to lend flavors such as chocolate, coffee, caramel or burnt toast to the finished brew.

Figure 9.5: Malted barley in various levels of caramelization

Malting is often done before the barley arrives at the brewery. The brewer may order the different malts based on the type of beer to be made. There is considerable attention paid to the proportions of malts included in the grain bill, which is usually composed of a base grain plus any specialty malts that will contribute to specific characteristics such as mouth feel, color, or head retention.

Hops: Hops have been used for centuries in beer making as a preservative and as an important source of bitterness and aroma. Before hops became the main bittering and preserving agent, all sorts of spices, herbs, and resins were used.

The hop plant is a vine (actually, the more technical term is a "bine," which climbs up a support in a helix shape, as opposed to a vine that uses tendrils to grab the support). The flower from the female plant is harvested, usually in late summer, looking something like a soft green pinecone. The base of the petals, inside the cone, contains the resins and essential oils that give beer its bitterness and aroma. The hop bine can grow up to 16 feet (5 m) tall, and is harvested by cutting the entire plant, with the flowers being separated during processing.

There are many different varieties of hops, each with its own aroma and bitterness profile. Common aroma descriptors for hops include fruity, citrusy, spicy, floral, piney, earthy, and herbaceous. The variety and amount of hops used in beer making, as well as the point at which they are added during the process, determines their flavor effect in the beer. The longer the hops boil, the more bitter components are extracted and the more volatile aromatic compounds are evaporated. Therefore, hops are usually added at several different stages of the boil as well as after the boil—a process known as "dry-hopping." The final beer's bitterness is measured on the scale of International Bitterness Units (IBUs). Using this scale, a beer above fifty IBUs would be considered very "hoppy."

Hops are most frequently processed into pellets to help prevent spoilage and for ease of handling. Hops can also be used in natural cone form or as extracts. Germany, the Czech Republic, and Washington State are the world's major growers of hops for use in beer making.

Figure 9.6: Hops on the vine (bine)

Yeast: There are two basic species of cultivated yeast used in brewing, bottom-fermenting or lager yeast (*Saccharomyces pastorianus* or *uvarum*) and top-fermenting or ale yeast (*Saccharomyces cerivisiae*). These yeasts are chosen according to the desired flavor profile of the beer. The top fermenting ale yeasts usually undergo fermentation much quicker and result in a beer with fruitier aromas and flavors. The lager yeasts ferment longer and slower while maintaining crisp, clean flavors.

Wild yeast can also be used, and is often used in certain Belgian beer styles. The most famous examples might be *Brettanomyces lambicus* from the Zenne Valley in Belgium, used in producing Lambic-style beers. Today, there are many craft breweries experimenting with the use of several strains of Brettanomyces (as well as *lactobacillus* and *pediococcus* bacteria) in the production of farmhouse and sour styles of beer.

Adjuncts: Adjuncts are fermentable ingredients that may be used for stylistic or economic reasons. Corn and rice are widely used by commercial breweries and are the two most commonly used adjuncts in the United States. Other additions—often used

by craft brewers—include oats, rye, fruit juice or extract, honey, and molasses. Though technically not adjuncts, spices also may be added to beer, such as the coriander and Curacao orange peel used in Belgian Wit beers, as well as a myriad of more experimental flavorings such as hemp, ginger, and chili peppers.

THE BEER MAKING PROCESS

The production of beer is a complex process dependent on steps such as mashing, brewing and conditioning. Each step yields a crucial raw material or condition for quality beer making. The most important of these steps are discussed below:

Milling: The grain to be used for a particular recipe is fed into a mill, which cracks the grains so that the starches within can be exposed to water in the mashing stage. The milled grains are called *grist*.

Mashing: The grist, along with hot water, is fed into a container called a *mash tun*. This creates a sort of slurry referred to as the *mash*. During this stage, the combination of heat, moisture, and time causes the enzymes in the grains to convert the starches to sugars. Because these enzymes function at different temperatures, the brewer might choose a multi-stage mash where temperatures are increased in stages in order to optimize the particular enzymes' activity. Alternatively, the brewer may choose to use an average temperature where all the enzymes will activate at the same time. Variations in temperature and duration will result in differing levels of sweetness, body, and alcohol in the final product. The result of mashing is a mass of spent grain and sweet liquid called *wort* (pronounced "wert").

Lautering and sparging: During lautering and sparging, the wort is separated from the spent grain. To begin the process, the wort is transferred to the *lauter tun*, where blades circulate it through the grain bed multiple times. The grain bed acts as a natural filter, allowing clarified wort to drain through holes in the bottom of the tun. Sparging is a process in which water is sprayed over the grain bed to draw out the last of the sweet wort.

Brewing, kettling, or boiling: These are three terms for the actual process of brewing, during which the wort is boiled in a kettle for sixty or ninety minutes. The boil yields a number of results:

- It sterilizes the wort, making it less susceptible to bacterial action
- It concentrates the wort and further caramelizes the sugars
- It further clarifies the wort, causing proteins to coagulate and settle to the bottom of the liquid as *trub* (pronounced "troob") or residue
- It boils off undesirable flavors that can come from the malt or the hops
- It draws the bitterness compounds from the hops, in the form of alpha acids

Figure 9.7: Copper Brew Kettle

Hops, in the form of cones, pellets, or extracts, are first added during the boil. Hops added at the beginning of the boil impart bitterness to the liquid; those added at the end impart aroma.

Chilling: The end product of the boil is a high-temperature mixture of sweet wort, hop solids, and trub. The hop solids and trub are separated from the wort by means of a whirlpool, in which centrifugal force separates the solids from the liquid. Next, the wort is chilled by being pumped through a cold-water heat exchanger. Finally, the wort is injected with oxygen in order to create an environment conducive to yeast growth and fermentation.

Fermentation: To begin the process of fermentation, the wort is transferred to a temperature-controlled fermentation tank and yeast is added according to the type of beer being made. Fermentation is typically done in stainless steel tanks, although oak casks may be used.

- Top-fermenting yeasts (and most wild yeasts) tend to rise to the top of the tank, work better at higher temperatures, and ferment the wort faster. These yeasts produce fruity, ale-type beers.
- Bottom-fermenting yeasts remain suspended beneath the surface of the liquid and take much longer to ferment. Bottom-fermenting yeasts work at colder temperatures and produce lager-type beers.

Total fermentation time is dependent upon the style of beer being made and the fermentation temperature, and can vary greatly, from a few days for simple ales, to over a month for lagers.

Conditioning: Conditioning is the process of maturing a beer in order to allow its flavors to meld and mellow. After fermentation, the yeast sediment settles to the bottom of the fermentation tank and the beer is pumped off into conditioning tanks, where it rests for anywhere from a few days to several months. The yeast may also be removed by mechanical means, or with the use of filtering agents. While conditioning is typically done in stainless steel tanks, there is a growing trend to age more full-bodied beers in oak casks—such as oak barrels previously used to store wine or whiskey.

Lagering: Lagering is a process of cold aging, such as was done historically in the caves of Bavaria. Lagering, which takes a few weeks, matures the flavors of the beer and allows any still-active yeast to slowly continue their work. Ale-type beers do not require this extended cold-aging period.

Carbonation: The carbon dioxide that remains dissolved in beer during fermentation is not enough to allow it to form a sufficient head when poured. Carbonation can be added to beer in one of the following ways:

- Force carbonation is done after filtration, when the beer is held under pressure in a tank with a device at the bottom that disperses tiny bubbles of CO_2 into the liquid, allowing the gas to dissolve into the beer. The beer is then bottled under pressure, capturing the dissolved CO_2. This, or a similar process of injecting CO_2 into the beer on the way to the packaging tanks, is used for the vast majority of beers.
- Natural carbonation is a traditional and more time-consuming alternative. Natural carbonation is created via a second fermentation in the bottle or cask that traps the carbonation inside. Beers that have been naturally carbonated are referred to as bottle-conditioned or cask-conditioned. Bottle-conditioned beer may enjoy an extended shelf life, as the yeast will consume any oxygen that seeps into bottled beer.

Finishing: Most beers are filtered after carbonation, then packaged and released to market.

DISCUSSING BEER STYLE

There are two major families of beer: ales (which use top-fermenting yeasts), and lagers (which use bottom-fermenting yeasts). These two families of beer are distinct in character due to differences in the length and temperature of fermentation as well as resulting conditioning processes. Both styles have the ability to produce both light-colored and light-bodied beers as well as dark, full-bodied beers (as discussed below). Beers made with wild yeasts may fall into either major style, although they are usually top-fermenting.

There are some general terms that may be used in reference to beer style, for example:
- Helles: Helles is the German term for "light" and refers to light beers such as "Munich Helles"
- Dunkel: Dunkel is the German term for "dark" and refers to dark beers such as "Dunkelweisse"
- Doppel: Doppel is the German term for "double," and refers to a beer with higher levels of alcohol and malt, as in "Doppelbock"
- Imperial: The term *imperial* refers to a beer with a relatively high alcohol content, full-body, and high hop content (for balance), as in "Imperial IPA" or "Imperial Stout"

THE FAMILY OF ALES

The ale family of beers is far larger in its range of styles than the lager group (although lagers actually dominate in terms of the volume of beer sold). Ales are especially popular with micro-breweries, partly due to the need for less refrigeration. This family includes many familiar styles of beer, including brown ale, extra special bitter (ESB), India pale ale (IPA), Trappist ale, and Belgian ales. Some of the better-known ales are discussed below:

India Pale Ale: India pale ale, or IPA, is a type of ale made with pale malt. IPA was originally developed for export to India during British colonization in the late 1700s. Its higher alcohol and heavier-hopped style prevented it from spoiling during the long, hot voyage to India. Aromatic hops that were packed into the barrels distinguished this export style from regular pale ales. Today, IPAs are still slightly strong, rather bitter, and highly aromatic.

Porters and Stouts: Porters and stouts are barley beers and are very dark in color, often with a robust, roasted flavor. Some stouts may be slightly sweet. Well-known variations include oatmeal, milk or cream (so named because they contain milk sugar [lactose]), coffee, and imperial stouts.

Wheat Beers: Wheat beers are made with a grain bill of up to 50% malted wheat in addition to malted barley. These beers are light, fruity and refreshing. Well-known styles include wit (from Belgium, also brewed with orange peel and coriander), weisse, and hefeweizen.

Lambic: Lambic is a type of Belgian Ale. Lambic is brewed with about 30% wheat that is allowed to spontaneously ferment using only ambient wild yeasts. These yeasts, native to the Zenne Valley of Belgium, yield a soft, smooth beer with slightly sour, toasty notes. Some styles of Lambic spend up to three years in oak barrels developing the sour qualities produced by lactic acid bacteria and the barnyard flavors produced via the yeast strain *Brettanomyces*. A blend of young and old lambics is termed a *gueuze* and can retain some residual sugar.

Figure 9.8: Belgian Lambic

Fruit Lambic: Fruit lambics are made with fruit added to the fermented beer, which in turn causes a second fermentation. Flavors include sour cherry (kriek), raspberry (framboise), peach (pêche) and currant (cassis).

Saison: Saison, meaning "season," is a farmhouse pale ale originating in Wallonia (a French-speaking region of Belgium). Traditionally, saison was brewed in the cooler, less active months, and stored for drinking in the summer months by seasonal workers. Modern saison is generally highly carbonated, fruity, and palate cleansing, and are sometimes flavored with spices.

Abbey Beers: Abbey Beers developed over the centuries in monasteries, primarily in Belgium. This heavy, sometimes sweet, beer may have been used as a substitute for bread during Lenten fasts. The most famous of the Abbey Beers is Trappist Beer (discussed below). While there is no definition of style, most abbeys brew the popular styles *Dubbel* and *Tripel*. There are a few theories as to how these got their names, one refers to an arcane rating of quality linked to double and triple the amount of malt in the mash and *XX* or *XXX* were written on the cask. Another theory concerns the number of times water was passed through the mash resulting in high alcohol beers. Nowadays, Tripels are higher alcohol (8%-10%) yet a paler blond in color, while the Dubbels are typically a darker brown, though the color comes from candied sugar not roasted grain, with more malt character but lower alcohol (6%-8%).

Trappist Beer: This particular style of beer may only be produced by Trappist breweries. The Trappists are a monastic branch of a Roman Catholic religious order known as the Cistercians. There are currently only eleven designated monasteries in the world currently permitted to brew these beers and sell them as an Authentic Trappist Product. The use of the name "Trappist" requires that the product meet some very exacting standards, the most important of which is that it must be brewed within the walls of a Trappist monastery (by the monks themselves or under their supervision). Other standards dictate that the brewery must be a secondary venture within a working monastery given to the monastic way of life, and that all proceeds benefit the monastery itself or a qualified charity. Authentic Trappist Beers include the following:

- Achel (Belgium)
- Chimay (Belgium)
- La Trappe (Belgium)
- Orval (Belgium)
- Rochefort (Belgium)
- Westvleteren (Belgium)
- Westmalle (Belgium)
- Stift Engelszell (Austria)
- Zundert (Netherlands)
- Spencer (United States [Massachusetts])
- Tre Fontane (Italy)

Mild, Bitters, and Extra Special Bitters: These beers are classic English ales that show a malty profile, with progressively more hop content, but nothing nearing the American pale ales. These beers are often cask conditioned, and served at cellar temperature

Brown Ales: These ales are, as the name suggests, darker in color although they may also appear to be quite amber. These ales are appreciated for their pronounced nutty character.

Scottish Ales: Scottish ales are generally less bitter and less "malty" than English beers. The Wee Heavy style is the darkest and strongest of these, and meant to be served in smaller (wee) portions.

Irish Red Ale: This style of reddish-amber ale gets its color from the roasted malt, and tends to be slightly sweet, lightly hopped, and dry on the finish.

German Ales: While most German beer is lager, there are a few notable exceptions. Produced in Cologne, Kölsch is light, delicate, and quite similar in flavor to a Pilsner (although a bit softer and more aromatic). Altbier, from Düsseldorf, means "old" (referring to the production method) and is deep bronze in color with a pronounced maltiness.

Barley Wine: This style of beer is based on (but not stylistically identical to) a fermented grain beverage produced in ancient Greece known as *krithinos oinos* (barley wine). In the 1870s, Bass Brewery created the first modern barley wine and marketed it in the United Kingdom as "Bass No. 1 Ale." The Anchor Steam Brewing Company introduced the style to the United States in 1976 with its "Old Foghorn Barleywine" (spelled as such so as not to use the word "wine," which would likely violate labeling standards). While there is no single agreed-upon style, barley wine typically is a very malty brew with alcohol levels as high as 8% to 12% by volume—as high as that of some wines.

Bière Brut: Also known as bière de Champagne, this relatively new style of bottle-conditioned ale goes through a disgorgement process to remove the yeast sediment (as is done in Champagne). The style tends to be fruity, estery, and spicy with a fine "bubbly" texture akin to sparkling wine.

Winter Warmer: Winter warmer, very dark and high alcohol, is considered a seasonal winter favorite due to the "warming" effect of the alcohol. Some versions are brewed with spices such as clove, nutmeg, and cinnamon.

THE FAMILY OF LAGERS

Lager-type beers are relatively few in number, but rank very high in popularity. Lager-type beers include Munich styles, Märzen, Oktoberfest, bock beers, and pilsner. Most of the top-selling, commercial American beers are bottom-fermenting pilsners. Well-known lagers include the following:

Pilsner: Pilsner, the style origin of much of today's commercial American beer, developed in Plzen (Pilsen)—located in today's Czech Republic—around 1842. Pilsner is a particularly light, bright lager with an aromatic hoppiness. Today there are many imitators of true Pilsner—which simply means "from Pilsen"—but the original remains Pilsner Urquell.

Figure 9.9: A bottle of Shiner Bock (note the picture of the goat)

Bock: Bock is a strong, dark lager thought to have originated around the town of Einbeck, Germany. There are those that believe the name *bock* was derived from the shortening of the name of Einbeck, while others believe it is due to an Old World belief that the beer was only to be brewed during the sign of Capricorn (the goat)—"bock" being the German word for "billy goat." This mythology led to the goat being somewhat associated with bock beers, as may be seen on many labels, which feature a picture of a goat as something of a visual pun. It is also common for the name of bock beers to include references to religious festivals such as "Easter Bock" and "Christmas Bock" as the beer was meant to be consumed leading up to the festivals. Other specific styles of bock include the following:

- Meibock/Hellesbock: a light, hoppier style meant to be consumed in May

- Doppelbock: a darker style with higher levels of alcohol
- Eisbock (ice bock): a unique bock that has part of the water frozen off and discarded during the production process, resulting in higher alcohol and flavor; can be almost syrupy

Märzen: Historically, beer was not typically brewed during the summer months, and Märzen (March beer) was often the last beer brewed of the year. This style of beer is deep amber in color, quite malty in flavor, and a bit high in alcohol—which would give it the preservative effect necessary to allow it to last in the cellars over the summer. Traditionally, the last of the Märzen was consumed during the Oktoberfest festival. These days, Oktoberfest beers tend to be a little lighter in color and alcohol, but retain the malty character shown by the original Märzen.

Vienna Lager: Vienna lager developed in the Austrian city of Vienna, very similar to and concurrently with Marzën. Both of these beers, developed in the early 1840s, were among the first Central European beers to utilize the paler malts that were becoming available due to innovations in the malting process. The Vienna version tends to be a bit drier and hoppier.

Rauchbier: Also known as "smoked beer," rauchbier gets its smoky character from the drying of the malts over an open fire of beech wood.

Schwarzbier: Schwarzbier is also known as "black" beer, and is characterized by its very heavily roasted malts and "burnt" flavor profile.

Steam Beer: Also known as California Common, steam beer originated in California during the gold rush of the late 1800s. This lager-style beer was brewed at higher temperatures, which were typically used due to the lack of refrigeration available in the expanding west. During the brewing process, the beer would build up a great deal of pressure in the cask and later let out "steam" when opened. The Anchor Brewing Company trademarked the name "steam beer" in the 1970s and is the only producer allowed to use this term; other companies producing this style of beer may bottle it under the "California Common" label.

THE STORAGE OF BEER

In general, beer comes in casks (more commonly referred to as kegs), bottles, and cans. Casks are used for cask-conditioned beers and look like metal barrels. However, the market is increasingly open to alternative and environmentally friendly packaging, such as reusable growlers and mini-kegs.

Kegs are small reusable barrels–typically 15.5 gallons in the United States, but defined differently around the world and available in a range of sizes. An advantage to the use of kegs is that there is no oxygen contact in the container, as the beer is pushed out via CO_2 (or Nitrogen). This allows keg beer to stay fresh for several weeks after being tapped. Kegs also provide craft brewers the opportunity to distribute limited-release brews; this can provide a competitive advantage to specialty beer bars where competition for tap real estate is fierce. In addition, many avid consumers have set up home systems for keg beer dispensing.

Figure 9.10: Kegs are convenient, cost-effective, and reusable

Bottles are the most common consumer packaging for beer, and come in many sizes and shapes, usually with a crown cap (metal cap) but sometimes with a cork and cage—similar to sparkling wine. Brown bottles are used to prevent UV light from affecting the beer (see flaws), while green and clear bottles are used for marketing reasons and do little to protect the beer from light.

Up until a few years ago, cans were used primarily at the economy end of the market. However, in recent years there has been over 20% growth in the use of cans by craft brews; this is due to several factors surrounding supply and logistics. The can, just like the bottle, does not lend any flavor to the product, but proponents of canning cite the following advantages:

- Cans are environmentally friendly due to lighter weight and ease-of-recycling
- Cans may reduce shipping costs
- Cans keep out all UV light, potentially further preserving freshness
- Cans are very portable and may be easily disposed
- Cans are often allowed in places where glass is prohibited (such as camping sites and pool areas)
- Cans provide an increased canvas for marketing, as 100% of the package can be used for graphic design (as opposed to being confined to labels)

While most beers are meant to be consumed as close to release as possible, there is a growing trend, particularly in the craft beer world, to cellar-age certain brews deemed to be age-worthy. Such beers may include certain full-bodied IPAs, Abbey Strong Ales, or Barley wines (among others). In such a case, the brewery might indicate a certain batch number or special name allowing beer collectors to identify the origin of the aged beer. Alternatively, some beers may indicate a "bottled on" date or an in-house code on the label that might either indicate the aging time of the beer. (Note that this is different from a "best before" date that would indicate a beer intended for immediate consumption.) When aging is desired, beer should be stored at cellar temperature (55°F to 60°F [13°C to 15°C]). Unlike wine, beer should most often be stored upright in order to limit time in contact with either the cap or the lower-grade cork (which is often used in the beer industry).

THE SERVICE OF BEER

Serving beer often involves far more than just popping the cap off a bottle, and may require the selection of a proper glass, a specific serving temperature, the maintenance of the tap lines, and capturing the perfect foam at the top of the glass.

As with wine, a wide range of different glass shapes is available, all of them meant to optimize the experience of drinking specific styles of beer. These specialty glasses are meant to allow an ideal head to form on the beer or to accentuate a particular aspect of the beer, such as a particularly aromatic or effervescent component. Many Belgian beers specify a goblet type glass with a flared lip intended to boost aromatic complexities, while many German and Czech glasses are narrow and tall, accentuating the crisp hop character. Additionally, there is a growing trend to use wine glassware for serving beer: white wine glasses for pilsner and crisp styles, and red wine glasses for more robust styles of beer.

Many beer makers issue their own branded glasses in unique shapes and sizes for use in restaurants and bars. However, the most important factor in beer service is that the glass be clean and polished to remove any particles or residues that may interfere with the delicate formation of the head. This is referred to as "beer clean." Any trace of oils or soap will ruin a beer's head retention.

The foam head on a beer is important because it captures the beer's aromas, allows for a silkier texture, and prolongs the sensory experience for the taster. The ideal foam leaves a lace-like residue on the glass often referred to as "Brussels (or Belgian) lace." This residue indicates quality and freshness in the beer and requires a very clean glass.

In the case of draft beers, it is vitally important that the lines from cask to tap be cleaned on a regular basis. This will most likely be done by a representative of the brewery, the distributor, or another professional contractor. Clean beer lines help to avoid bacterial buildup, which, if left unabated, will affect the flavor of the beer as well as a particle buildup that can create an excessive amount of foam.

Ideal Serving Temperature: The ideal serving temperature of beer varies, based on style. The perfect serving temperature will maximize the beer's aroma and mouth feel. Lower temperatures will emphasize the bitter component of the beer as well as its dry, crisp, and refreshing characteristics. As the beer warms, the aromatics, maltiness, body, and overall flavor is better appreciated.

Figure 9.11: A wide range of glass shapes are used to serve beer

In general, lagers should be served colder than ales, and it is better to err on the cold side and warm the beer in the hands if necessary. In addition, beer should never be served with ice, nor should beer glasses be frosted—this practice can dilute the drink and keep the head from forming properly.

While individual preferences and service standards may vary (particularly between countries), three separate temperature zones are recommended, as shown below:
- Cold: no lower than 41°F (5°C); recommended for draft and bottled lager and other lighter styles of beer
- Chilled: no lower than 46°F (8°C); recommended for wheat beers, draft ales, lighter bottled ales, and most craft beers
- Room (cellar) temperature: around 53°F (12°C); recommended for heavier, richly flavored beers such as some Belgian ales, brown ales, stouts, and barley wine

The Proper Pour: The proper pouring technique, applicable for most beers—bottle or tap, will create an ideal head of about two fingers in height. Start with the glass at a 45° angle and aim for the beer to hit about halfway down the inside of the glass. When you've poured half the beer, continuously bring the glass to the upright position and finish pouring.

If the beer is bottle conditioned and contains yeast sediment, this is usually not poured into the glass.

However, in the case where the yeasty note is desired—such as certain styles of hefeweizen—the bottle may be agitated about ¾ of the way through and the rest poured to intentionally include the yeast. Alternatively, after the beer is decanted, the yeast may be served "on the side" in a small glass (such as a shot glass) so the consumer can taste the quality of the yeast.

THE SENSORY EVALUATION OF BEER

The sensory evaluation of beer is quite similar to the process used for wine tasting. Typical steps include the following:

Sight: First, look at the beer in the glass and consider the color and clarity. The color should be consistent with what is expected for the style of beer being analyzed. Most light-colored beers will be crystal clear, but some may show a haze—particularly wheat beers or bottle-conditioned beers that may contain yeast sediment. Darker beers may be completely opaque. The foam head should also be considered during the visual inspection; it should be ample and persistent, or the beer may be stale.

Smell: Next, smell the beer. Its aromas may derive from the malt, from the hops, or from the yeast. Typical beer aromas include the following:
- Malt-derived: nutty, roasted, caramel, coffee, toast
- Hop-derived: floral, fruity, herbaceous, botanical, grassy, citrus, spicy, earthy, peppery
- Yeast-derived: bread, yeast, clove, banana, honey, cereal, biscuit

Palate: The next step involves actually tasting the beer and evaluating it in terms of taste components (typically sweet, acid, and bitter), flavors, and mouthfeel.
- The first stage of this process is to let the beer rest on your tongue and evaluate it for sweetness (which may or may not be present), acidity (which will be present at some level), and bitterness (which is likely to be present at some level, and may be quite high).

- Next, notice the body or mouthfeel of the beer: is it light-bodied, medium-bodied, or does it feel heavy?
- Notice the beer's flavors in terms of fruitiness, hoppiness, and maltiness. It is also important to keep in mind that flavors may be different or more numerous than the aromas that were noticed upon smelling the beer.
- Finally, note the level of carbonation—this will impact the beer's body as well as your perception of the other taste components.

When tasting beer, keep in mind that each of the elements you observe should be appropriate to the type of beer being tasted.

BEER FLIGHTS

When serving multiple courses of beer or planning flights of beer for a formal tasting, it is typically considered best to progress from lighter to more full-bodied beers, and from less to more hop character. Additionally, the sweetness in beer should progress from dry to sweet. This is a similar progression of food as it often appears in a multi-course meal, and also reflects the best practices of wine tasting. Here are a few examples and ideas for flights:
- Ale flight: Belgian witbier, American pale ale, Belgian dubbel, English stout
- Lager flight: Czech Pilsner, Oktoberfest, bock, doppelbock
- Unique Beer Flight: Kölsch, saison, steam beer, rauchbier, oatmeal stout

Figure 9.12: A flight of beer—perfect for a sensory evaluation exercise

BEER FLAWS

Beer is a complicated beverage and as such, there are many things that can go wrong in the production, storage, or serving processes. While there are dozens of potential flaws or faults that may be found in beer, it should be noted that, in some cases, a small amount of a particular compound (or taste, or aroma) is acceptable, while a higher concentration would be considered a fault. With this in mind, some of the more common beer flaws are discussed below:

Skunked: Skunked beer smells just like it sounds—a bit like skunk. This flaw is caused by ultraviolet light that reacts with compounds in the hops. If beer is improperly stored in a cooler that is too well lit, displayed in natural light, or stored near supermarket-style lighting, it may become skunked. Brown glass bottles help to block much of the light; however, green and clear glass bottles do little to prevent this problem. This is a main argument for the craft canning movement.

Wet paper or cardboard: Beer with an aroma of damp paper or old cardboard is likely to be oxidized or stale. If oxidized, the oxygen was most likely introduced during production. Other possible reasons for this flaw include poor storage conditions, heat and motion during shipping, or beer that is just too old.

Too sour or vinegary: Sour beer is often the result of a bacterial infection that occurred somewhere in the brewery. *Lactobacillus*, *pediococcus*, and *acetobacter* are often the causes of this fault. However, in small amounts, this character is sometimes acceptable in certain sour-style beers.

Haze: Haze in a beer that should otherwise be clear might be due to proteins or yeast cells that remain in the beer due to improper or incomplete filtration; haze may also be the result of bacterial infection.

Too fizzy/too flat: Incorrect levels of carbonation, as may occur either in the brewery or from improper storage, can be considered a fault. Flat beer—or one that is under-carbonated for the style—might feel weighty and lack freshness on the palate with an inability to retain a foam head. Overly carbonated beer may splash out of the container upon opening and will be somewhat uncontrollable and difficult to pour.

Excessive bitterness: Extreme bitterness or astringency may be caused by excessively high temperatures during the mash or sparge water. High temperatures will extract the bitter compounds from the grain.

Excessive butteriness: An overly buttery or butterscotch flavor comes from the presence of diacetyl. At low levels this flavor may be acceptable (or even positive), but in some styles of beer (such as clean lager styles) it is almost always considered a fault. Butteriness may be caused by improper aeration, unhealthy or curtailed fermentations, or bacterial infections.

Metallic: Metallic flavors may come from poor water quality, poor quality equipment, or the use of old, stale grain.

BEER AND FOOD PAIRING

Given the diversity of beer styles available—and the corresponding range of tastes, flavors, and aromas found in beer—it makes sense that the pairing of beer and food can be just as interesting as wine-and-food pairings. It is easy to find a list of "rules" for beer and food pairing, but (as is also seen in wine), these rules cannot (and do not) apply in all circumstances or for all preferences. As such, it may be best to stick to some simple guidelines based on the characteristics of the beer. Some of these guidelines are discussed below:

Bitterness: One of the first things to consider is the level of bitterness in a beer. Bitterness, coming from the hop character as well as the roasted grain used in darker beers, can easily overpower delicate food, but can be useful for cutting through fat and oil, just like acidity in wine. This explains how the crisp, hoppy, German and Czech beers go so well with Sausage. If there is a more pronounced bitter malt character, such as in ESBs or stouts, it might require a bit more sweetness in the food, such as may be provided by fruit, corn, or a sweet component in a sauce.

Sweetness: Sweetness in beer actually makes it very food-friendly. Beers that are slightly sweet pair well with spicy food and foods with chili pepper-type heat; the sweetness will tend to tone down the perception of the food's heat. Sweetness in food will make sweetness in a beverage less apparent, and can make dry beverages taste a bit off-balance or flat. As such, foods that have some level of sweetness to them—from slightly-sweet, fruit-infused entrees all the way up to desserts—pair well with beers that have a bit of sweetness to them as well.

Acidity: While it may seem counter-intuitive, acidity in food will make the acidity in the beer seem less apparent; thus high-acid beers, in general, pair well with high-acid foods. For this reason, sour beers—such as gueuze and farmhouse styles that have a pronounced tart character—would be the ideal style to pair with foods high in acidity, such as salads, or ceviche.

Carbonation: One component that sees a great deal of variation in beer is the level of carbonation. A highly carbonated beer will lift the hoppy bitter flavors, hide sweetness, and cleanse the palate. This makes high-carbonation beers very versatile in terms of food pairing—almost anything will work. In the case of beers with lower levels of carbonation, such as is common in many cask-conditioned English ales, the maltiness and sweetness of these beers will be accentuated, and should thus be the primary focus when pairing these beers with food.

Body: Body (sometimes referred to as "weight" or "mouthfeel") in beer is related to the alcohol content, from full-bodied Belgian triple and dubbel to the extremely light and delicate Kölsch or hefeweizen. Unfermentable sugars and starches from the grain will also contribute to body as we see with stouts and darker beers. These more full-bodied beers complement the richer flavors of meaty dishes, ribs, and roasts. Lighter-bodied beers are more suited to the delicate flavors of dishes such as simply prepared fish.

Figure 9.13: Beer can pair well with a range of food—from casual to fine dining

Once the general guidelines have been considered, it can be interesting to pair the more nuanced aromas or flavors in a beer to certain spices or flavors in food. Unlike taste components that have a predictable interaction, pairings based on flavors are subtle and hard to predict, so experimentation is in order. A great example would be pairing a beer with a highly aromatic hop profile to a chicken or pork dished flavored with sage, rosemary, and thyme, creating a flavor bridge between those herbs smelled in the beer and tasted in the food. Another example is fruit: when fruit is used to brew sour or wheat styles of beer, there is an excellent opportunity to match that to a pork or duck dish glazed with fruit, or to pair with a similarly-flavored dessert.

BEER AND HEALTH

As in all things, particularly those concerning alcohol, the best health-related advice for beer consumption is "always in moderation." A 12-ounce beer contains essentially no fat, and around 150 calories, although "light" beers might contain 60 to 110 calories and some of the dark, heavier beers may contain up to 200. While beer may not exactly be the nutritional equivalent of "liquid bread," beer does contain some of the same nutrients as its grain and hop components, such as B vitamins, riboflavin, niacin and zinc. A serving of beer may contain up to 92 mg of potassium, 14 mg of calcium, and 48 mg of phosphorus, as well as being a good source of soluble fiber and antioxidants.

SAKE

Sake—often referred to as *rice wine*—is a fermented beverage brewed from rice. Despite the popularized moniker, the sake-making process occurs in a *kura* (the Japanese word for "brewery"), in a manner more similar to beer making than wine production. It is also important to note that the term "sake" is the Japanese word for all types of alcoholic beverages, while in English the term refers solely to an alcoholic beverage produced via the fermentation of rice. The Japanese use the term *nihon-shu* for what English speakers refer to as premium sake.

The job title of the Japanese sake brewer is *tōji*. This is a highly respected job within Japanese society, and while today's tōji are typically university-trained or veteran brewery employees, the title was historically passed on from father to son.

HISTORY OF SAKE

While it may be produced anywhere in the world, the majority of sake is produced in Japan. Sake production began in Japan around the same time wet-rice cultivation was introduced to Japan from China, millennia ago. Early versions of sake were made primarily for personal consumption on a local level. In the seventh century, a brewing operation was set up within the Imperial Palace in Nara, which became one of the first early brewing centers. By the tenth century, sake was produced mainly in temples and often used for ceremonial purposes, and temples and palaces remained the leading source of sake production for the next 500 years.

In the mid-nineteenth century, new laws allowed anyone to set up a brewery, and the number of sake producers skyrocketed. At the beginning of the 20th century, the organization now known as the National Research Institute of Brewing was founded with the purpose of developing the alcoholic beverage industry in Japan, leading to many improvements in the sake production process and the overall quality of sake. During this time, the first national sake competition—now known as the Annual Japan Sake Awards—was held, which continues to this day to motivate quality.

Consumption reached its height in Japan in the early 1970s; however, the number of breweries and the volume of sake made have been in decline since then. This decline in consumption has, nevertheless, coincided with an increase in the amount of high-quality sake produced, and a growing interest in sake on an international level.

Today, there are over 1,200 sake breweries in Japan. Included in this number are about fifteen very large producers and about 200 mid-sized producers, with the rest being boutique (small) producers. As seen in many other parts of the beverage world, a younger generation of consumers in Japan and abroad are returning to this traditional beverage and propelling the industry to improve. New strains of rice and yeast are continuously being developed for use in sake, and there has been a renewed interest in sourcing local products and honoring the time-honored techniques of production.

RAW INGREDIENTS FOR SAKE PRODUCTION

Sake is brewed from four basic ingredients: water, rice, *koji* (a type of mold) and yeast. Certain styles of sake also contain brewer's alcohol (neutral spirits).

WATER

Sake itself is typically 80% water, and water is used in many stages of the sake-making process. As such, the quality of water used has a great influence on the quality and character of the finished product. Early sake brewing centers arose around the best sources of water, including mountain streams, springs, or underground rivers. Some of these sources are still used today, but there are also technological processes for altering the hardness or softness of water and for regulating the various minerals present in the water that can be essential or detrimental to certain stages of sake making.

In general, brewers look for a water profile that has potassium, magnesium, and phosphoric acid present, and a complete absence of iron and manganese. Corrections can only go so far, and most brewers still rely on high quality ground water, which is often unfiltered.

RICE

Of the hundreds of different varieties of rice grown in Japan, about one hundred are designated as sake rice. These varieties may be used on their own or in certain combinations for sake production. Each individual type of rice lends a different character to the final product, and certain brands and breweries are known for using certain rice varieties, leading to a recognizable "house style."

While not required by law, there is a growing trend to specify the type of rice used on sake labels. However, if a variety of rice is stated, it is required that the percentage of each variety used is listed as well. The top four varieties of premium sake rice are as follows:

- Yamada Nishiki: This variety of short grain rice is considered by many as the superior rice for use in high-quality sake; it is known to produce full-flavored, savory styles of sake.
- Gohyakumangoku: This is the second most used variety of sake rice; it tends to produce light-bodied sake with clean, pure flavors.
- Omachi: This type of rice produces sake with tight, complex, and herbal characteristics.
- Miyama Nishiki: This rice produces sake with light, clean flavors and a smooth texture.

One unique characteristic of sake rice is its physical composition. In sake rice, there is a central core of starch surrounded by an outer layer containing the proteins, amino acids and other substances. This outer layer, if left intact, could give rise to impure flavors in the sake. Because of this, sake rice is milled in order to remove these outer layers in preparation for brewing. Different styles of sake are designated, in part, by the maximum percentage of the rice grain that remains after polishing. The more the outer layer of the grain is removed, the purer the resulting sake.

KOJI

Koji, technically the combination of steamed rice and a mold (*Aspergillus oryzae*) referred to as *koji-kin*, is the pride of the sake breweries and what differentiates sake production from that of beer and wine. To produce koji-kin, the powdered mold is introduced to a portion (about 20% to 30%) of the total amount of the steamed rice to be used in a batch. This leads to the creation of enzymes that break apart the starch in the rice to create fermentable sugars.

The koji is one of the most important variables in defining a house style, and its cultivation is an incredibly complex process. For low-grade sake, breweries can use an automated process to develop the koji. However, for premium grades, this is still done mostly by hand. The process requires a special koji-making room and begins by dividing the steamed and cooled rice into small trays. The trays are then rearranged as frequently as every few hours. This ensures that the circulation of moisture in the koji-making room stays consistent. The humidity is a very important factor in this process and can determine whether the koji mold stays on the surface of the rice or works its way in between the grains, vastly changing the style of the final sake.

Figure 10.1: Koji-making room

YEAST

As it does for beer, the type of yeast used in the brewing process affects the aromas of the sake. Many new strains of sake yeast are being developed with different performance and aroma features, and the type of yeast used is now often listed on the sake bottle. Typically, the yeast is propagated as a starter (moto) for a few weeks, after which it is combined with the koji and the rest of the steamed rice in a three-stage process. While there are a small yet growing number of brewers that use ambient yeast and spontaneous fermentations, most yeast starters are inoculated with purchased yeast selected for the specific characteristics that it will bring to the sake in terms of aroma, flavor, or consistency.

THE PRODUCTION OF SAKE

The principles at work in sake brewing—saccharification and fermentation—are quite similar to those used in the brewing of beer. However, the sake brewing process differs in that the majority of the saccharification of the rice occurs simultaneously with and in the same vat as the fermentation. This is known as "multiple parallel fermentation."

The entire sake-production process takes between twenty to forty days per batch before the sake is set aside for a short period of aging. The steps are as follows:

Rice milling/polishing: In this first step, a percentage of the outer layers of the rice grain are milled off in order to reach the "heart" of the grain. This pure, starchy part of the rice produces the finest sake, with more finely milled (polished) rice used for the best-quality sakes.

Traditionally, the milling process was accomplished using a type of mortar-and-pestle; however, today this step is done by machine. The milling machines are controlled via computerized settings that allow the brewer to choose the exact percentage of the outer layers of the grain to remove.

Each type of sake corresponds to a minimum percentage of grain remaining after milling, which is known as the *seimaibuai*. The seimaibuai can range from 35% to 75% of the original grain, with the higher-quality sakes considered to have more purity of flavor made from the more highly milled grains.

Washing and soaking: After the polishing is complete, the rice grains are rinsed and soaked in water. This soaking process continues until the grains have absorbed the proper amount of water for the steaming process. Often, rice used for low-grade sake will be left to soak overnight, whereas rice intended for use in premium sake will be closely monitored for the grain's water content. The amount of water soaked into the rice grains will impact the entire brewing process.

Steaming: To begin this step, the soaked rice is moved into a large vat. Today, this is most often done in stainless steel tanks of various shapes and sizes or—in the case of very large production—on a conveyor belt. Steam is then passed through the rice in order to alter the consistency of the grains. After steaming, the rice is cooled either on cloth mats or in a specialized machine.

Making the koji: To begin this step, a portion of the steamed rice is placed in a warm, humid room. The rice is then sprinkled with powdered koji mold, which begins to cultivate. The koji is carefully monitored and mixed for roughly thirty-six to sixty hours, with additional powdered koji added at least three more times. This cultivation of koji is perhaps the most important part of the brewing process, and slight changes in the process could have a significant impact on the flavor of the final sake. For this reason, handmade koji is considered superior to machine made.

Making the yeast starter (*moto*): The yeast responsible for fermentation is cultured from a mixture of koji rice, steamed white rice, water and yeast (often from a selected strain). The moto develops for about two weeks before it is moved into a larger container to begin the fermentation process. Traditionally, native yeasts were used, but now there are a number of selected yeasts favored for certain flavors and reliable fermentation.

Mashing and Fermentation: To begin this step, the moto (yeast starter) is combined with steamed rice, koji, and water in a large container. This is done in three stages over approximately four days. This timing helps to maintain the proper ratio of yeast to sugar. Fermentation, which is occurring alongside saccharification, takes from eighteen to forty-five days. At this point in the process, the fermenting mash is known as the *moromi*. During fermentation, the temperature and other variables of the moromi are monitored carefully. When fermentation is complete, the alcohol content is typically 17% to 20% alcohol by volume. For some styles of sake, a small amount of brewer's alcohol is added at the end of the fermentation process. This is not done for all types of sake, and is an important factor in style, as will be discussed later in this chapter.

Pressing: In this stage, the cloudy lees (expired yeast) and any other solids are separated away from the clear sake. Traditionally, this was accomplished by placing the moromi into large cotton bags and placing the bags in a wooden press. However, modern breweries typically pump the entire moromi through an accordion-type press. A third and very labor-intense method involves putting the moromi in suspended bags allowing the sake to drip through with no physical pressure; this produces a style of sake known as *shizuku*.

Filtration: In some cases, after the clear sake has settled it may be charcoal-filtered. The use and degree of filtering is another element that determines the style of the sake, and much care must be taken to strike the perfect balance between clarity and flavor.

Pasteurization: This step, intended to improve stability, involves momentarily heating the sake to 150°F (65ºC). Most sake is pasteurized twice— once before ageing in the brewery and again before packaging and shipping. However, some styles of sake are only pasteurized at one of these stages, and some styles—known as *namazake*—are not pasteurized at all. This is an element of style that varies from brewery to brewery.

Aging: Most quality sake is aged for three to six months (or longer) in the brewery to allow its elements to harmonize. Batch blending is sometimes implemented for consistency, and pure water is usually added to reduce the overall level of alcohol to about 16%.

Bottling: Bottling the sake is the final step. This is typically done by machines that fill and seal the cap on each bottle. Some styles of sake are pasteurized at this stage. After the bottles are sealed (and cooled, if pasteurized), they are labeled and prepared for distribution.

Figure 10.2: Sake brewery in Fushimi

TYPES OF SAKE

Quality sakes are divided into categories based on two parameters: the percent of the rice grain that remains after milling (the lower, the better), and whether or not distilled spirits are added. In any style of sake, the term *junmai* indicates that no alcohol has been added.

JUNMAI DIAGINJO
Junmai daiginjo, considered to be one of the highest-quality sakes available, is produced from rice that has been milled so that it retains 50% or less of its original mass—this means that at least 50% of the grain is removed. Some breweries leave as little as 35% of the original grain. Junmai diginjo is considered by most to be the purest, most complex, and fragrant style of sake available.
- Daiginjo: Daiginjo (where the word junmai is not present in the name) is also made from rice that has been milled to remove at least 50% of its original mass; however, in this product, a small amount of brewer's alcohol is added during fermentation. (Junmai daiginjo is daiginjo-grade sake to which no alcohol was added.) Many sake aficionados believe that the addition of brewer's alcohol adds to the aromatic intensity of the sake.

JUNMAI GINJO

Junmai ginjo is made from rice milled so that it retains 60% (or less) of its original mass (meaning that at least 40% of the grain is removed). Junmai ginjo is complex and delicate, and considered to be the second-tier of quality sake.

- Ginjo: Ginjo sake is also made from rice milled to 60% (or less) of its original mass, and has had a small amount of alcohol added during fermentation.

JUNMAI

Junmai sake is made from rice milled to 70% (or less) of its original mass (at least 30% of the grain is removed). It is made from only yeast starter, steamed rice, koji rice and water; no alcohol is added to this style. The word *junmai* is used in conjunction with other types of sake to indicate that no brewer's alcohol was added at any stage of production. Junmai-style sake typically has a fuller flavor and richer texture than non-junmai sake.

HONJOZO

Honjozo sake, like junmai, is made from rice milled to 70% (or less) of its original mass. Honjozo sake has a small amount of brewer's alcohol added during fermentation. Honjozo is usually lighter in style and more aromatic than junmai.

Table 10-1: Styles of Quality Sake

Maximum Percentage of Rice Grain Remaining	Pure Rice Sake	Fortified Sake (with the addition of distilled spirit)
50%	Junmai Daiginjo	Daiginjo
60%	Junmai Ginjo	Ginjo
70%	Junmai	Honjozo

Table 10-2: Sake Terminology

Genshu Sake	Undiluted sake; typically bottled at 19% to 20% alcohol by volume (abv)
Jizake	Artisanal sake from a small, independent brewery (an unregulated term)
Koshu	Aged sake; while the term is not legally defined, it is widely considered that the best examples are aged for three years at the brewery
Namachozo	Sake that has been pasteurized once, before bottling
Namazake	Unpasteurized sake; considered by some to have a heightened flavor
Namazume	Sake that has been pasteurized once, before cellaring
Nigori sake	Unfiltered sake
Shiboritate	Recently-pressed sake
Shizuku	Sake that has been separated from the solids and the lees via being suspended in in cotton bags and allowed to drip out without a physical pressing

FUTSUU-SHU

One final sake style is futsuu-shu, which refers to bulk, mass-produced sake that does not qualify for one of the quality categories discussed above. This style of sake often has a large amount of alcohol added in order to increase yields, and is often served warm.

SAKE TERMINOLOGY

When discussing types of sake, there are other factors to be considered, such as whether the sake was aged, filtered, or pasteurized. Table 10-2 defines some of the terms related to these factors, as they apply to sake.

THE TASTE COMPONENTS OF SAKE

The basic taste components of sake can be analyzed and measured, and while not required, this information is sometimes indicated on the label. This information includes the following:

- Sweetness: Sake may be dry or sweet. The sweetness level of sake may be indicated by a number on the "sake value meter" (nihonshudo). This scale runs from about -3 (negative 3) to +12, with the lower numbers indicating sweetness, and the positive numbers indicating dryness. (This is often simplified to "the higher, the drier.") The number on the scale relates to the sake's specific gravity (its density as compared to water). Most sake today falls around the +4 (off-dry to dry) value.

- Acidity: Sake is much less acidic than beer and wine and uses a specific, rather arcane, scale to measure its acidity. The scale (which should not be confused with the pH scale) has a range of 0.9 to 2.0 and measures the amount of alkaline solution needed to neutralize the sake. In this scale, the higher numbers equal higher levels of acidity. The average acidity for sake is usually between 1.2-1.4; however, there are exceptions.

Figure 10.3: The kiki-choko (traditional sake tasting cup)

SERVING SAKE

Although some sake is aged before release, in general it is not considered to improve in the bottle as a fine wine can, and most sake is best consumed within a few months of purchase.

Unopened sake should be refrigerated or stored in a cool, dark place. Unpasteurized sake (namazake) must be refrigerated at all times in order to maintain its freshness.

Like wine, sake begins to oxidize once it is opened and, as such, sake is best consumed immediately after opening. An opened container of sake may be stored in the refrigerator for a day or two after opening, but, as with wine, this sake may not be served at its prime.

Quality sake shows best when served chilled or at room temperature, as heating sake masks its delicate flavors. Despite the once-popular practice of serving sake warm, only the lower grades of sake—such as futsuu-shu (which may actually benefit from this masking of flavors)—should be served warm.

Some sake enthusiasts think that a wine or sherry glass is the best vessel from which to appreciate sake; however, this is not a common practice in Japan. Beyond the commonplace, tiny ceramic cups and narrow topped carafes, the tasting cup used by most sake professionals is known as the kiki-choko. This cup is made of white porcelain with bright blue, concentric circles inside (on the bottom of the tumbler). The blue concentric circles allow for better visual appreciation, and the larger-size bowl (about 6 ounces/177 ml) allows for better appreciation of the aromatics.

CIDER AND PERRY

Traditional cider is a lightly alcoholic beverage (usually less than 7% abv) produced from apples that have been crushed and pressed, with the resultant juice fermented. It is often called "hard cider" in the United States to distinguish it from unfiltered apple juice. Cider production is centered in the UK, which has the highest consumption, but many other countries and regions—including the United States—produce it as well. Many of the apple varieties used are grown specifically for cider making and are inedible, but some proportion of standard apples may also be used. Cider styles vary from dry to sweet, from cloudy to clear (depending on the level of filtration used), and from light to dark in color. Most are lightly carbonated.

Perry, or *poiré* in French, is traditionally made in much the same way as apple cider. In general, perry tastes sweeter than apple cider, and it is also typically lightly carbonated. The pears used are not an edible variety, but are ideal for perry making.

Both cider and perry are experiencing a renaissance that is running parallel to the other craft beverage industries.

THE ORIGINS OF CIDER AND PERRY

Historians are divided as to the origins of cider and perry. Many assume that as it is simply fermented from fruit juice, ancient civilizations may have been able to produce a type of rudimentary cider or perry. However, others believe they came about much later due to the fact that a press was an essential piece of equipment to extract the juice from an apple or a pear.

Regardless of the earliest examples, it is clear that the Romans—who used both lever and screw-presses for olive oils—produced some kind of cider. The Romans also did much to spread the cultivation of the specific varieties of apple and pear trees used, as well as the technology required to make cider on par with wine and beer—as a piece of the Roman Empire's culture.

By the time the Roman Empire was nearing collapse in the 5th century, fermented beverages from apples and pears were very common in Europe, in the zones considered unsuitable for viticulture (such as areas around present-day England, Normandy and Brittany in France, and Northern Spain).

As Europe fell into the Dark Ages, the monasteries of the Catholic Church continued to cultivate apples and pears, but they frequently took a back seat to grapes and grains. However, in certain areas of Northern Spain (in present-day Basque Country and Asturias), cider or *sidra* continued as a strong part of the culture. This area is still considered one of the oldest-apple growing areas of Europe and a center for cider production and consumption.

During the expansion to the New World, each of the prominent cider-producing countries brought the beverage to their colonies: England to the United States, France to Quebec, and Spain to South America. The apple quickly became one of the most beloved fruits of the newly-formed United States. Despite this popularity, the American cider industry was all but obliterated with the temperance movement and Prohibition, and it took until the early 2000s for the cider industry to experience an uptick. Cider is still a very small player in the US beverage market, in 2012 its consumption was only 0.3% of that of beer and flavored malt beverages.

THE BASE MATERIALS: APPLES AND PEARS

Despite the vast diversity of raw materials—which at one time included upwards of 10,000 varieties of apples and 5,000 varieties of pears—apples and pears can be placed into three broad categories: dessert (or eating), cooking (or culinary), and cider. The categories are based, for the most part, on the levels and balance of acidity, sweetness, and tannin, as well as the nature of the pulp. Dessert varieties have a low tannin level, cooking varieties are more acidic and will cook down to a puree, and cider apples tend to be higher in acidity, tannin, and sweetness in addition to having a fibrous interior that allows for easier pressing. These differences are similar to those found between wine grapes and table grapes, as wine grapes with their thick skins and plentiful seeds do not make good-tasting grapes for eating.

Work performed in 1903 at the Long Ashton Research Station in Herefordshire, England, further divided cider apples into categories that are still considered the most applicable reference point for the industry. Cider apples are labeled as "sharp" with acid levels above 0.45% (4.5 g/L) and "bitter" with tannin levels above 0.2%. Table 11-1, below, details these traits and provides the name of some common varieties within each category.

Table 11-1: Categories of Cider Apples

Category	Acid*	Tannin	Varieties
Sharp	> 0.45%	< 0.2%	Newtown Pippin, Spitzenburg, Ashmead's Kernel, Hewe's Crab, Granny Smith
Bittersharp	> 0.45%	> 0.2%	Kingston Black, Foxwhelp, Redstreak, Stroke Red, Mettais, Porter's Perfection
Bittersweet	← 0.45%	→ 0.2%	Dabinett, Yarlington Mill, Tremlett's Bitter, Chisel Jersey, Frequin Rouge, Bedan, Michelin
Sweet	← 0.45%	← 0.2%	Calville Blanc d'Hiver, Sweet Coppin, Roxbury Russet, Fuji, Gala

*Note: Acid is expressed in terms of malic acid

The overwhelming majority of ciders are blends of various different varieties. However, there are a few varieties, such as Dabinett and Kingston Black, which can produce excellent single-variety ciders. It should be noted that due to a lack of cider apples in the US, dessert varieties are often used in the blend.

Pears destined for perry usually have a bit more sugar than cider apples, but are characterized in a similar way in terms of acidity and tannin: medium sharp, bittersharp, bittersweet and sweet. Similar to cider apples, bittersharp pear varieties are deemed almost inedible but very desirable for perry. The cultivation of pears is more challenging in comparison to apples. The pear tree is more selective of its microclimate and offers a much smaller window to harvest the fruit once it has achieved ripeness but before it starts to rot. This results in more single-variety bottlings.

Like cider apples, perry pears take on a wide variety of names, in Gloucestershire alone there are over 100 different varieties known by over 200 different names. The most widely used variety is the Blakeney Red, which is medium sharp. Other examples of commonly used pears include the Barnet and the Red Pear (both sweet pears) and Barland (a bittersharp).

THE PRODUCTION OF CIDER AND PERRY

While much of what is labeled cider on retail shelves around the world is produced from a mixture of apple concentrate, sweeteners, and other additives, the production of traditional cider and perry is quite similar to the process used in wine production. These products may be referred to as *artisan* or *farmhouse* ciders (or perrys). The steps in the traditional cider- and perry-production process are discussed below.

Harvest: The process beings with the harvest, which occurs in the fall. In the Northern Hemisphere, the apple and pear harvest will generally begin in late September and end in early December; the exact date within this window is determined by the variety.

Figure 11.1: Various cider and dessert apples

Sweating: As apples continue to respire, mature, and ripen after they are picked, they are allowed to "sweat" for a short period of time before juicing to allow the apples to release excess water content and convert additional starches to sugars. This process, which is basically a storage period, may last anywhere from a few days to several weeks or even months. During this time, the apples will be stored in a well-ventilated, cool environment, and are expected to lose up to 10 percent of their water content while gaining 6 to 8 percent in sugar content. Pears may also undergo a period of sweating before being processed for use in perry production, but the process is usually only allowed to proceed for a few days, with the goal of getting the fruit to optimal ripeness before they start to deteriorate.

Milling: When the fruit is ready to be processed, it may or may not be washed with cold water, sorted to remove rotten fruit, or combined with other varieties to create a blend. Following this, the fruit is ground to create a pulp—a process known as *scratting*. Historically, this step was done by hand or

via a stone mill. Small batches of fruit may still be pulped by hand (using a blender, food mill, or even the bucket-and-pole method), but on a larger scale this job is typically accomplished via some sort of mechanical scratter or food mill designed to break large quantities of apples or pears into a pulp.

Some traditional producers employ a period of maceration between milling and pressing that may last anywhere from eight to forty-eight hours. This step may be undertaken in order to produce a cider with a darker color profile, or to soften the impact of the tannins through a short period of oxidation. This practice can yield variable results, but when done correctly it can yield ciders of tremendous depth and character.

Pressing: Traditionally, the pulp was separated from the juice by placing the pulp into a permeable container—often made from cloth—and placing the container between wooden slats (either in a vertical fashion or a horizontal accordion arrangement), or in a horizontal tank. Once the pulp and the barriers were in place, some sort of force would be applied via human power, wooden screws, and/or a lever of sorts. These days, the same principle applies, but a mechanical press is more likely to be used.

Fermentation: Fermentation may be accomplished via natural or commercial yeasts. Natural yeast fermentation occurs at low temperatures and can take anywhere from several weeks to several months. Alternatively, a specific commercial yeast strain may be chosen in order to encourage a faster or shorter fermentation time, or to impart specific characteristics to the final cider or perry.

Aging: Some ciders are considered "ready to drink" as soon as fermentation is complete. Others may undergo a short period of aging in order to allow flavors to marry, to allow the spent yeast (lees) to settle, and for the product to stabilize. A variety of containers, including oak barrels and stainless steel, may be used for this step. If oak is used, older barrels are typically preferred so as not to introduce any overly strong barrel-related flavors to the cider.

Carbonation: Cider may be still or sparkling. Many sparkling versions are force-carbonated via an addition of carbon dioxide just before packaging.

While somewhat of a rarity in the cider industry, natural methods of creating carbon dioxide (similar to those used in bottle-conditioned beer) may also be used.

Packaging: Before being packaged, some versions of cider may be filtered, pasteurized, or dosed with sulfur dioxide. Cider is packed in a variety of formats, including bottles, barrels, cans, kegs, and even bag-in-a-box.

Keeved Cider: *Keeving* is a unique method of artisan-style cider production. The process involves allowing the pulp to macerate long enough to allow the pectin in the pulp to gel and form a "net" of sorts that rises to the top of the tank, carrying proteins, nitrogen, and nutrients along with it. The nutrient-poor juice is then drawn off the middle of the tank and natural-yeast fermentation begins. Due to the lack of nutrients, the fermentation will halt prematurely, creating a naturally sweet product. This style of cider is sometimes bottled before the fermentation is complete, creating a naturally (lightly) sparkling cider. Keeved cider typically has between three and five percent alcohol by volume.

Note: It should be noted that some brands of commercial cider are produced using apple concentrate, water, and added sugar. This style of product, which is often promoted as an alternative to beer, accounts for a portion of the cider that is consumed in the United States.

Figure 11.2: Pears for perry await the harvest

LEADING CIDER- AND PERRY-PRODUCING REGIONS OF THE WORLD

Cider and perry are produced in many parts of the world, and many regions have developed their own versions of cider-and perry-related traditions. Some of the leading regions of cider and perry production are described in the section that follows.

THE UNITED KINGDOM

Britain is the world leader when it comes to cider, producing and consuming almost half of all the cider in the world on an annual basis. The most acclaimed products are considered to be those from the *West Country*—a somewhat loosely-defined area situated in the far southwest of England (about 130 miles [209 km] west of London, and between Bristol and Birmingham).

Three counties in this area—Herefordshire, Gloucestershire, and Worcestershire—have achieved protected geographic indication (PGI) status for both perry and cider. Other West Country regions, including Somerset, Dorset, Devon, and Cornwall counties, also produce outstanding ciders despite not having yet achieved PGI status.

Overall, there has been a significant cider renaissance in Britain in the past few decades, which included the formation of the Herefordshire Cider Route to promote cider tourism, and the *Campaign for Real Ale* (CAMRA) which helps market and organize events surrounding traditional cider and perry (as well as some styles of beer).

Overall, it can be observed that English cider tends to be dryer, more often still (non-sparkling) or bottle-conditioned, and a bit more alcoholic than its French and Spanish counterparts. A unique, quintessentially English style of cider is the *scrumpy*, considered to be one of the most natural and un-manipulated examples of artisan cider. Scrumpy is often cloudy, never filtered, quite acidic, and characterized by strong biological (sometimes referred to as *funky*) flavors.

Another important part of the English cider tradition is the festival of *Wassail*, whose name is derived from an Anglo-Saxon toast meaning "be well." Traditionally held on the third Monday of January, a Wassail ceremony from days past would find the community marching through the orchards accompanied by the raucous noise of banging pots and pans and firing rifles. The concept behind the custom was to "awaken the trees from their winter slumber" and drive away evil spirits. The modern-day Wassail ceremony, which varies greatly from place to place, may include such elements as a bonfire, folk dancers, the election of a Wassail queen, and most definitely includes the consumption of cider.

IRELAND
Ireland is a large consumer of cider as well, and might be the largest cider consumer worldwide on a per-capita basis. Much of Ireland has a mild climate ideal for the cultivation of cider apples and, as such, the country has both a long history and a modern revival of artisan cider production. The great majority of the cider consumed in Ireland is made by Magners, a huge (and now, nearly worldwide) brand that merged with Bulmers (the other large cider brand in Ireland) some time ago.

SPAIN
Spain is considered to have the longest continuous cider (*sidra*) culture in Europe. Spain's cider production is centered in the regions of Asturias and Basque Country, located in the northern part of the country. The climate, cooled by ocean breezes and with decidedly more rainfall—an annual average of 68 inches (173 cm)—than much of the rest of Spain, makes for the ideal growing conditions for apples.

Asturias makes 80% of Spanish cider, produced by more than a hundred small producers. *Sidra de Asturias* was awarded denominación de origen (DO) status in 2003. According to the DO guidelines, the cider must be made exclusively with cider apples of specified varieties (within a designated geographical region) using traditional production methods, and under strict quality controls.

Figure 11.3: The "trasgu" (mythological gnome) announcing Sidra de Asturias

While Spanish cider is produced with essentially the same techniques of that in England, the character is very distinct. Traditionally, Spanish cider in both the Basque country and Asturias is completely fermented to dryness using native yeasts, unfiltered, and either still (non-sparkling) or very lightly carbonated. This very dry and highly acidic style comes from a dominance of sharp apples (often more than 50% of the blend) as well as some acetic acid produced during the wild ferments. Spanish cider often contains some strong "biological" flavors (such as barnyard and leather) that, in a different context, might be thought of as flaws.

Another style of Spanish cider, termed the "new expression" (*nueva expressión*), is also dry, but filtered in order to produce a clear appearance. Finally, the sparkling version (*achampanada*) goes through a natural secondary fermentation either in the bottles (traditional method) or in the tank (charmat method).

Most artisanal Spanish ciders benefit from aeration just before drinking; this helps to bring out the inherent complexities of the beverage as well as release some dissolved gas. This has given rise to a few colorful traditions, such as serving cider via a "long pour" with the bottle raised high above the server's head, while the glass is held at arm's reach below. This is termed *escanciar la sidra*, or "throwing the cider."

The first cider of the season is ready to be consumed in January, and ushers in the beginning of the *txotx* (pronounced *choach*) season. At this time of year, the cider is served directly from large chestnut wood casks (called *kupelas*). Another tradition of txotx season, known as "breaking the cider," entails allowing the cider to "shoot" from the valve of the barrel in a very thin stream while thirsty bar patrons take turns filling their glasses while holding them at arm's length. Once the weather turns warm in April, the cider that remains is bottled to be enjoyed throughout the rest of the year.

FRANCE

The cider and poiré industries of France are centered around Normandy and Brittany in the north, as well as the French Basque Country to the far south along the border with Spain. Cider and perry are considered to be local delicacies in these areas, and France has three AOC-designated regions (two for cider and one for perry).

The region of Normandy, well-known for Calvados (the area's famous apple-based spirit), produces a range of apple- and pear-based products including cider and perry and has one appellation d'origine controlee (AOC) for cider and one for perry. The Cidre Pays d'Auge AOC overlaps the Calvados Pays d'Auge AOC and specifies fifty varieties of apples that may be used (out of the 700-plus grown in the region), as well as a minimum alcohol content of 6% abv. Cidre Pays d'Auge AOC is always produced in a slightly sparkling style, with a second fermentation done in the bottle and a minimum of 3 atmospheres of pressure (atm) in the finished product.

The Domfrontais region, located in the south of the Calvados-producing area, is particularly well suited to the cultivation of pears due to its deep clay

Figure 11.4: American hard cider

and limestone soils. Here, perry is produced under the Poiré Domfront AOC. The preferred variety of pear in this area is known as Plant de Blanc. Plant de Blanc pears typically comprise at least 40% of any blend, and may only be harvested if the fruit has naturally fallen to the ground. Of the thirty varieties of pears grown in the region, only ten are allowed to be used in Poiré Domfront AOC. Poiré Domfront AOC is slightly sparkling due to a second fermentation in the bottle, and must have a minimum alcohol content of 5.5% abv.

The department of Finistère (located in the extreme west of France, bordering the English Channel) is home to the Cornouaille AOC, approved for a slightly sweet apple cider produced from a range of apple varieties. Cornouaille ciders are made naturally sparkling via a second fermentation in the bottle.

In France, both cider and poiré are often packaged in bottles reminiscent of sparkling wine and under cork, a style that is endearingly termed *cidre bouché* (literally, "cider with a cork"). French versions of cider and perry typically contain a small amount of residual sugar in order to balance the tannin content. The bottle-fermented sparkling versions may or may not be riddled to remove the spent yeast cells. Overall, cider from France is considered to be clearer, sweeter, and more effervescent than its Spanish and English counterparts.

THE UNITED STATES

Early American settlers took great pride in cultivating the apple tree, as evidenced by the story of the folk hero and nurseryman Johnny Appleseed (John Chapman, 1774 – 1845). Some of the oldest apple orchards in the states are located in the more temperate areas of New England, such as Vermont, upstate New York, Massachusetts, and New Hampshire. The spread of various types of apple seeds gave rise to myriads of new, purely American varieties, such as the Newton Pippin, that were then grafted and propagated. By the mid-1800s there were over 1,000 varieties of apples growing in the United States, most of which were used for cider.

The popularity of American cider declined with the rise of industrialism, as the population migrated towards city life, and was further thwarted by Prohibition. This coincided with a drastic decline in the cultivation of cider apples. These days, the majority of the apples and pears in the United States are grown in the Pacific Northwest, and most of these are for eating; however, small pockets of apple production may still be found in many parts of the country.

Leading areas for American cider production include New England, the Blue Ridge Mountains of Virginia, the Great Lakes area, and pockets of the Pacific Northwest. The most recent statistics from the Alcohol and Tobacco Tax and Trade Bureau (TTB), which regulates cider, show that Vermont produces the most cider at about 5.3 million gallons, with New York second at 4.4 million, and California and Tennessee both at about 2.9 million gallons.

The craft cider movement is growing in the United States, but is considerably behind the renaissance sweeping craft beer and local wine. There is, however, a noticeable interest in reviving heirloom cider varieties, whole fruit processing, and artisan cider production. Some American cider producers are making ciders inspired by the Old World, while others are proving to be more experimental and creating hopped versions of cider, wine barrel-aged ciders, or combining honey and fruit to produce *cyser*, sometimes referred to as "apple mead" and best described as a cross between cider and mead.

CANADA

Like the United States, cider production in Canada is seeing a slow but certain growth trend, as evidenced by a 55% increase in sales from 2005 to 2009. Apples and pears are cultivated in the more temperate regions of the country, including British Columbia, Southern Ontario (the Great Lakes area), Quebec, and Nova Scotia.

Of these, the leading area for cider is Quebec, renowned for the ethereal *cidre de glace*, or ice cider. This relatively new style of cider was first commercially produced in 1994. Cidre de glace requires that the apples be harvested while naturally frozen (and shriveled) in the orchard. These ultra-ripe, frozen apples are pulped and pressed, which creates an intensely sweet juice. This super-concentrated juice is then fermented, resulting in a sweet cider with an alcohol content that ranges from 7% to 13% by volume. Quebec grows a good deal of "sharp" cider apples, which provide an ideal base for ice cider.

GERMANY AND AUSTRIA

While Germany is much more renowned for wine and beer, there is considerable production of cider as well. Cider here goes by many names, including *Apfelwein* (literally, "apple wine"), *Most* (from the Latin for "squeezed fruit") or *Viez* (from the Latin for "substitute" meaning Germans would substitute cider for wine in difficult years). Sachsenhausen, a district in the city of Frankfurt located on the south bank of the River Main, is known as the "apple wine district," and is considered the epicenter of German cider production with over sixty cellars still in business. German cider is traditionally served in a fat, grey, stoneware jug called a *Bembel*, and tends to be sweeter and contain less tannin than its other European counterparts. There is also notable production in Austria, particularly in the district of *Mostviertel* in Lower Austria (*Niederösterreich*), which is named after their cider production.

ARGENTINA

Argentina is the fifth largest cider-consuming country in the world, and is a very large producer as well. The main apple and pear growing regions are centered in the Río Negro province in Patagonia, as well as the Mendoza province in the western section of the country. Argentina is home to more than a dozen cider houses; these enterprises process a portion (approximately 15%) of the apple harvest into cider, while a good deal of the remainder is made into concentrate to be exported to North America and Europe. In Argentina, cider is heavily associated with the Christmas holiday season, with close to 80% of all consumption occurring during October, November, and December.

THE SENSORY EVALUATION OF CIDER AND PERRY

The steps in the sensory evaluation of cider are similar to those in wine tasting, and include analyzing a product by sight, by smell, and on the palate. Cider should typically be served chilled, but for sensory evaluation a higher cellar temperature is acceptable if not preferred.

Sight: The visual appearance of cider and perry will vary a great deal based on the type, style, and method of production for an individual product. Some will be highly filtered and seem brilliantly clear, others will appear slightly cloudy. Color as well will reflect the production method, and may range from quite pale to light yellow, medium-yellow, medium-gold, or even amber.

Smell: Cider may contain a wide range of aromas, starting with the scent of fruit, which may range from the expected aromas of apples and pears to citrus fruit, stone fruit such as peaches and apricots, and even berries. It should be kept in mind, however, that not all ciders or perrys will smell

overwhelmingly of apples or pears; much like fine wine does not smell overwhelmingly of grapes. Herbal and spice-related aromas are also common, and may be expressed as cinnamon, clove, pepper, lavender, or herbs de Provence. Many ciders have some floral notes, such as rose, geranium, or orange blossom. Some ciders, particularly aged versions, may smell of honey or butterscotch. Traditional ciders, particularly those fermented with ambient yeast, may also exhibit some biological or "funky" aromas such as acetic acid, balsamic notes, or "barnyard."

Palate: Cider can be thought of as a balancing act between acidity, tannin, and sweetness.

- Acidity: Like wine, cider is highly acidic and falls in the pH range of 3.0- 3.8. The main acid in cider is malic acid, followed by trace amounts of citric acid and perhaps lactic acid; perry tends to be higher in citric acid. A cider that is lacking in acidity will feel flabby on the palate and have a very short finish.
- Tannin: The tannin in cider and perry is extracted from the skins and seeds as well as the flesh of the fruit; therefore it is possible to perceive tannin even in products that have not undergone any extended skin contact. Bitter apples, in particular, are highly prized for their high tannin content.
- Sweetness: Residual sugar may be expected in some cider or perry products and if present, will have the effect of balancing a high acidity as well as high tannin content. Cider can be further categorized by sweetness levels as dry (less than 0.9% RS), medium (0.9% to 4%) and sweet (more than 4%), or in French, sec, demi-sec, and doux. However, it should be recalled that the level of sweetness may be perceived to a lesser degree if the acidity and tannin levels are high.

These three components—acid, tannin, and sugar—combine to create the body or mouthfeel of the product. In general, cider and perry will be lighter in mouthfeel than beer, and be more akin to a light- to medium-bodied wine. Carbonation may vary from non-existent (still), to slightly fizzy (often described as pétillant), or fully sparkling.

Figure 11.5: A cider pouring race in Asturias

THE SERVICE OF CIDER AND PERRY

Glassware for serving cider varies by region, or in some cases, the producer's preference, and may resemble a curvy pint glass, a Belgian beer goblet, or a flute. In Spain, *sidra* is poured from on high ("thrown") into an informal tumbler-style glass. In other parts of the world, there is a growing trend to serve cider and perry out of a white wine glass such as might be used for Riesling or Sauvignon Blanc.

Most cider is consumed very young, fresh, and is not meant for aging; however, some well-structured ciders are made in such a way (typically with high levels of tannin and acidity) as to be able to improve with time in the bottle. With proper aging, this style of cider may undergo some of the same transformations as wine, losing the fresh fruit character and taking on more spice- and earth-like notes.

With its low levels of alcohol and natural high acidity, cider is a natural pairing partner for many foods. Many of the foods that seem to pair naturally with apples or pears—such as pork and chicken—may also pair well with cider. Cider also enhances a wide range of cheeses, as seen in the natural pairing of Cidre Pays d'Auge AOP with the local Camembert, in which the acidity of the cider cuts through the fat content of the cheese, and a slight herbaceous note is bridged. Cider with a degree of sweetness makes a wonderful complement to Asian food, whether spicy or not. In addition to all the pairing possibilities, cider can be used as an ingredient for cooking, often in lieu of stock or water, and makes an outstanding ingredient for use in cocktails as well.

THE PRODUCTION OF DISTILLED SPIRITS

Spirits are defined as beverages in which the alcohol content of a fermented liquid has been concentrated by the process of distillation, resulting in a high-alcohol beverage. As with other alcoholic beverages, spirits contain ethanol, which is commonly known as ethyl alcohol.

BASE INGREDIENTS

Distilled spirits may be produced using a variety of different base ingredients. Like wine, spirits are frequently produced from grapes or other fruits. Spirits may also be produced from other natural sugar-based materials such as honey, sugarcane, or molasses, or from starchy materials such as rice, potatoes, or grains.

FERMENTATION

Generally when using a base material of grapes or fruit, the fermentation process results in a "wine" ranging from 8% to 14% alcohol. Starchy grains that have undergone an enzymatic conversion ferment into a "beer" with roughly 5% to 10% alcohol. The balance of each liquid (86%–95%) is made up of water. However, the liquid will also contain acids, aldehydes, esters, and other compounds that were created during the fermentation process. These compounds, known as *congeners*, are important in spirit production as they add distinct aromas and flavors to the finished product.

DISTILLATION

Once the initial ferment—now referred to as wine, distiller's beer, or wash—has been obtained, the distillation process can begin. This stage of the production process concentrates the alcohol to a desired degree and, in some cases, separates it almost completely from the water and the other dissolved components.

Distillation is a complex process. However, the process is based on one simple fact. Water has a higher *boiling point* than ethyl alcohol; therefore, the alcohol in a solution will "boil off" before the water even begins to boil. The boiling point of pure water is 212°F (100°C), while that of pure ethyl alcohol is 173°F (78°C).

As heat is applied to a solution of water and ethyl alcohol, the temperature of the heated liquid slowly rises. When the temperature reaches a point where the alcohol is above 173°F (78°C), the alcohol (along with some water) will transform from the liquid state into a gas. This is known as *vaporization*.

The vaporized alcohol and water are then captured in a closed vessel and cooled. As they cool, the vapors will return to liquid form; the resulting liquid will thus have a higher concentration of alcohol than the original alcohol-water mixture.

TYPES OF STILLS

Distillation takes place in an apparatus called a *still*, which heats a fermented liquid and allows the alcoholic distillate to be vaporized and collected. The main types of stills are discussed below:

The Pot Still: The pot still, which was developed from the original alembic stills used in the 13th and 14th centuries, consists of an enclosed vessel in which the liquid is heated. Alcohol vapor rises through a narrow neck at the top, called the swan's neck, then through a tube that passes through cold water, which condenses the vapor inside the tube into liquid alcohol.

The basic principles of pot still distillation include the following:

- Pot stills can distill only small batches of spirits at a time, and the first distillation yields only about 20% alcohol. As such, pot stills work in what is known as the batch process.
- The spirits must be redistilled to reach the desired alcohol level. After two or three distillations, a typical level of alcohol is 55% to 70%.
- Pot stills are preferred for artisanal quality spirits as they allow more of the flavoring agents (congeners) from the original liquid to remain in the distillate. This makes for a more rustic and flavorful spirit.

Figure 12.1: Traditional pot still distillation used in the production of brandy (northeastern Greece)

The Column Still: Not surprisingly, after centuries of pot still use, people began to search for a more efficient method of distillation. In 1826, Robert Stein, a member of a famous Scotch whisky-distilling family, invented the column still. It was later perfected by Aeneas Coffey, whose patent replaced Stein's.

This type of still, also known as a patent or Coffey still, allows a continuous stream of liquid to be distilled to a set strength in a single distillation. The basic principles of column still distillation include the following:

- Column stills are faster—often requiring a single, cyclical distillation—and are, therefore, less labor-intensive than pot stills.
- Column stills produce spirits with higher levels of alcohol and fewer congeners than spirits produced via a pot still.

The Multiple-Column Still: When a very pure-strength spirit is desired, along with significant efficiency, the basic column still can be further adapted by adding more columns. This type of still is called a multiple column still or a continuous still.

The Hybrid Still: Given that each type of still has its advantages and disadvantages, there are some producers of premium spirits who prefer to use the traditional pot still. However, as previously mentioned, these stills are typically limited to outputting an alcoholic concentration of about 70% alcohol by volume. Although further batch distillations could possibly produce the alcoholic purity desired in a higher-proof spirit, this procedure is time-consuming, very energy-inefficient, and expensive.

Accordingly, a hybrid still (sometimes called a pot-and-column still) may be used to achieve the desired results. This type of still is basically designed as a column still sitting on top of a heated pot still so that the initial distillate is transferred from the pot still to the column for distillation to a higher concentration. There are many shapes, sizes, and configurations of hybrid stills in use.

Figure 12.2: Column still distillation used in the production of rum

The points of separation between the head and heart and between the heart and tail are referred to as *cut points*. Specific cut points vary based on the type of spirit being produced and the level of congeners desired by the distiller. The distiller has learned from experience at what temperatures and alcohol levels these congeners can be concentrated or reduced. As such, he or she can control the amount that is left in the final product.

PROOF

The term proof has been adopted to accurately describe the strength of alcoholic beverages. In the United States, a 100 proof spirit is one containing 50% alcohol by volume at a temperature of 60°F (15.5°C).

It is generally a requirement to list the amount of alcohol in a spirit on the product's label in terms of the percentage of alcohol by volume. For distilled spirits, the proof measurement is now commonly placed after the alcohol by volume measurement, such as 40% abv (or, simply, 40% alcohol) and 80 proof (or 80°).

CUT POINTS

Regardless of the type of still used, distillation is repeated or cycled until the desired level of alcohol and purity is reached. Using either type of still, the product of distillation has three parts: the head, the heart, and the tail.
- The heart, or middle portion of the distillate, is the only potable portion.
- The heads and the tails contain toxic alcohols such as methanol and may be redistilled in another batch in the case of the pot still, or added back into circulation in the case of the column still.

POST-DISTILLATION PROCEDURES

Regardless of the type of still used for distillation and the raw materials used for the initial fermentation, all newly distilled spirits, known as *new make spirits*, are colorless, or water-white. They possess a sharp, biting aroma and taste, which will mellow if the spirit is given time to mature.

At this point, some spirits are ready to be finished by being reduced in strength and bottled, at which point they are ready for consumption. However, it is common for many types of spirits to be treated with a variety of post-distillation processes before being bottled. Such post-distillation treatments include filtration, coloration, barrel aging, and blending.

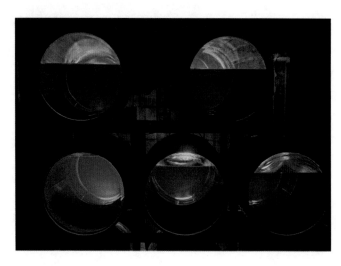

Figure 12.3: Whiskey at different stages in the aging process (Jameson Distillery)

Filtration: A spirit may be filtered to remove impurities, color, or both. Filtration most commonly involves the use of activated charcoal, which absorbs the harsher characteristics of the spirit. In the process of filtration, care must be taken to avoid filtering out desirable components that contribute to body and flavor along with those components that are unwanted.

Barrel Aging: Many spirits, particularly those known as "brown spirits" (such as many forms of brandy and whiskey) have been matured in oak barrels. Oak aging of spirits can last anywhere from several months to several decades, allowing the spirit to evolve over time. The specific chemistry involved in the maturation of spirits in oak is quite complicated; however, the following processes may all take place:

- Extraction: Depending on the type of wood and the level of toast, aromas and flavors may be extracted from the barrel and into the spirit. This extraction will occur more readily if the interior wood surface of an oak barrel is often either toasted or charred. The aromas and flavors extracted from oak include a range of seemingly sweet aromas and flavors—such as cedar, chocolate, butterscotch, maple, and caramel. Some spirits are matured in barrels previously used to mature other kinds of beverages, such as Sherry, in which case the barrel may impart various other flavors to the newly distilled spirit.

- Evaporation: Because of the permeable nature of oak, some of the liquid in the barrel will evaporate through the pores in the wood. Depending on the temperature and humidity where the barrels are stored, there is an approximate 3% loss of liquid annually. This can be much higher in warmer climates. This loss is sometimes called the "angel's share," as the components in the spirit leave the barrel and travel skyward.
- Oxidation: The semi-porous nature of oak allows oxygen to seep through the wood and enter the barrel. The oxygen dissolves in the spirit and causes a desirable oxidation of the spirit's components. Over time, additional esters are formed, and aldehydes and acids increase.
- Concentration: As mentioned above, evaporation of the alcohol and water reduces the total volume of spirit remaining in the barrel. Thus, the unchanged, original components of the spirit are concentrated over time in the barrel, along with the newly extracted and oxidized constituents.
- Filtration: When the inside of the barrel is charred, a layer of charcoal is produced. This charcoal acts as a means by which to filter the spirit.
- Coloration: The charring process somewhat degrades the tannins in the wood, which may give the spirit a reddish color that deepens as it ages in the barrel. In addition, the spirit's color may turn brown with exposure to oxygen via the process of oxidation. The longer a spirit ages, the more color it takes on. Spirits that are aged for only a brief period will be much lighter in natural color than those aged for several years.

At the end of the oak-aging process, the colorless, harsh new-make spirit has been converted into a tawny-hued, mellower, sweeter-tasting, and more multifaceted flavorful spirit.

Blending: In some cases, the finished spirit will be taken from a single batch or cask. However, in many cases, the completed spirit will be a combination of many different spirits or batches blended from among casks, ages, or even distilleries.

Some blended spirits contain many dozens of different component spirits. The job of the master blender is extremely important, as the blending process helps to maintain the house style of a particular spirit and allows the producer to create complexity and balance in the final product.

BOTTLING

Most spirits when taken off the still have an alcohol concentration of 58% to 96.5% by volume, which is generally reduced prior to bottling. To reduce the alcohol concentration after filtration or aging, high-quality, often demineralized, water or a mixture of water and spirit, is added to the spirit. For certain types of spirits, this process must be done very carefully and slowly to avoid a negative impact on the final product. Some spirits that have been matured for a long period of time will lose alcohol strength naturally via evaporation, and will thus need little to no dilution before bottling. Most spirits are bottled at 37% to 43% alcohol by volume.

CHAPTER THIRTEEN DISTILLED SPIRITS

DISTILLED SPIRITS

As discussed in the previous chapter, spirits are defined as beverages in which the alcohol content has been concentrated by the process of distillation. Early spirits were used for medicine, and were usually rough and bitter. Flavorings of honey, seeds, grasses, or fruit made alcohol-based medicines more palatable. This use of flavorings to make spirits palatable is the origin of today's liqueurs and flavored spirits such as gin.

The main categories of spirits include vodka, gin, rum, tequila, brandy, and whisky (whiskey). Sweetened, flavored spirits are typically referred to as liqueurs; spirits flavored with bittering agents are often referred to as bitters or amari.

This chapter will take a close look at each of these categories of spirits, discussing base materials, typical methods of production, and traditional regions of production. It will also discuss typical methods of service, including some of the best-known cocktails made using each spirit.

VODKA

Vodka is a clear, unaged spirit that is often considered to be completely neutral—without distinct characteristics, flavor, color, or aroma. In fact, this is how US standards define vodka produced in the United States. This is, however, somewhat mistaken in that vodka produced in the United States often has traces of flavor from both the ethyl alcohol present and the type of water used in its production. Moreover, vodka produced in the European Union is often made in ways that allow its raw materials to express themselves. For this reason, many imported vodkas have subtle flavors, textures and aromas.

THE ORIGINS OF VODKA

The origins of vodka are difficult to pinpoint. Depending on which sources you consult, the first documented production was either in eighth century Poland or ninth century Russia. If one places the origin in Russia, then it makes sense that the typical archaic description of ardent spirits, "water of life," was eventually reduced to simply *voda*, the Russian word for water. Over the years, it stands to reason, the term acquired an additional letter, *k*, and the spirit became known as vodka, as it has been named since the fourteenth century.

An alternate theory refers to the Polish word *wódka*, the earliest known mention of which can be found dating to 1405 in the Akta Grotskie court documents of the Palatine of Sandomierz, Poland. It is used there in reference to a medicinal drink.

Whichever version one believes, it is well documented that by the 1500s, vodka began to be used as a beverage as well as a chemist's distillate for medicines and perfumes throughout the regions known today as Eastern Europe and Russia.

Vodka was introduced to the United States commercially in 1934, and, in the 1970s and 1980s, became the number one selling spirit in the United States. It is popular for its relative neutrality, which makes it versatile in mixed drinks. Today, vodkas are produced in the United States, Russia, Ukraine, Poland, Sweden, Finland, the Netherlands, England, France, and many other countries.

THE PRODUCTION OF VODKA

Vodka is unique in that, unlike most of the other spirit types, it has no required source of ingredients or required geographic area of production. Moreover, it is neutral in style as a result of having been distilled to a very high proof and, quite often, consequently filtered, as well as being generally unaged. Therefore, its production generally ends without the benefit of time in casks or other vessels that may impart flavors.

Throughout history, vodka was typically produced using the most plentiful and least expensive materials, which were often potatoes and various grains—primarily corn. These days, the majority of vodkas are produced from mixed grains, and many high-quality versions are produced using potatoes. Additionally, some brands of vodka are produced using grapes, sugarcane, or sugar beets.

Fermentation is typically conducted quickly in order to minimize congeners. Many producers use ionized, softened, or demineralized water to further reduce unwanted flavors.

Vodka is often distilled in an energy-efficient column still at proofs over 190. This still boils off almost all congeners to an indistinguishable level, giving vodka its "neutral spirit" designation. It should be noted, however, that neither US nor EU standards require a specific distillation method. Many types of vodka are made in pot and single-column stills, and some are even produced using multiple alembic distillations.

Vodka is often processed after distillation to further neutralize its character. However, contrary to popular belief, vodka is not required to be filtered or further processed after distillation—even in the case of American vodka, which is expected to be "without distinctive character, aroma, taste, or color." The standard allows for this to be accomplished via the manner in which the spirit is "distilled, or so treated after distillation."

Figure 13.1: Vodka on the bottling line

Vodka is bottled in a variety of alcoholic strengths, from as low as 37.5% alcohol by volume (the European minimum standard) or 40% alcohol by volume (the United States' minimum standard). It may be bottled at levels of alcohol ranging up to 50% by volume or higher, if desired, for a particular marketing purpose. While vodka is typically not aged before bottling, aging is permitted. Some specialty vodka products—both traditional and modern—are aged.

FLAVORED VODKA

Flavored vodkas are available in all kinds of flavors these days, including typical fruit flavors such as lemon and green apple, sweet-sounding flavors such as whipped cream and vanilla, and even those a bit harder to categorize such as salted caramel, espresso, and smoked salmon. While flavors such as these might be considered to be a modern trend, flavored vodka can actually trace its origins back to some of the earliest vodkas produced in Eastern Europe, particularly in the vodka strongholds of Russia and Poland.

Infusions and mixtures of herbs, grasses, spices, leaves, honey, and flowers were initially used to disguise the unpleasant tastes of primitive vodka; however, eventually these flavored spirits became popular for their own sake, leading to the long-standing tradition of Russian and Polish flavored vodkas. Some of these include the following:

- Pertsovka is a Russian term for vodka flavored with red chili pepper, with a resulting distinctive hot spiciness. Traditionally, the flavor would have also included honey.
- Zubrówka is Polish vodka flavored with bison grass. Often, the vodka would be tinged yellow in the process. The result is floral and somewhat herbal and sweet.
- Starka, traditionally from Poland and Lithuania, is vodka that is aged in oak casks and often flavored with spices and herbs.

TASTING AND SERVING VODKA

Vodka is considered by many to be the ultimate base for mixed drinks and cocktails. Popular cocktails based on vodka include the Cosmopolitan, the Bloody Mary, the Black Russian, and the Screwdriver. High-quality vodkas are also enjoyed

Table 13-1: Common Vodka Brands and Their Sources

Brand	Country of Origin	Typical Base Ingredient
Absolut	Sweden	Wheat
Belvedere	Poland	Rye
Cîroc	France	Grapes
Finlandia	Finland	Barley
Grey Goose	France	Wheat
Ketel One	Netherlands	Wheat
Luksusowa	Poland	Potato
Skyy	USA	Grain
Smirnoff	USA	Grain
Stolichnaya	Russia	Grain
Tito's	USA	Corn
Wyborowa	Poland	Rye

straight up or on the rocks. Vodka is most often enjoyed chilled, so while tasting a sample at room temperature is certainly an option, vodka is likely to show at its best when well chilled.

GIN

Gin is essentially a clear, neutral spirit flavored with juniper berries. While juniper must be the dominant flavor, other botanicals—including a range of herbs, spices, roots, flowers, seeds, and leaves—may also be used in the production of gin. Gin has its origins in Holland, Germany, and England, but today it can be produced anywhere in the world.

THE ORIGINS OF GIN

The Dutch physician Franciscus Sylvius is often credited with the invention of gin in the mid-seventeenth century; however, juniper-infused spirits were produced long before Dr. Sylvius was even born. The first mention of gin (then known as *genever*) in writing dates all the way back to a thirteenth-century encyclopedia, *Der Naturen Bloeme*, written in Bruges. The term *genever* was based on the Dutch word for juniper and over the years became shortened to *gin*.

Nevertheless, Doctor Sylvius, a professor of medicine at Holland's University of Leyden, can at the very least be acknowledged for popularizing a medicinal tonic made with neutral spirits and the oil of the juniper berry. The juniper berry was believed to cure all sorts of ailments afflicting the bladder, kidneys, and circulatory system. Soon, "gin tonic" became a popular cure.

Gin became popular in England during the 1689–1702 reign of King William III of England (known as William III of Orange), who lowered the excise taxes and other restrictions on distilled spirits produced within England. This incentive led English distillers to make their own versions of gin using inexpensive corn spirits blended with juniper berries and other flavorings, and soon gin was easily available to the masses.

This ease of access led to a period between 1720 and 1751 known as the "gin craze" when the per capita consumption of distilled spirits almost tripled. This accessible, inexpensive drinking culture became popular with the working-class poor and was blamed for a myriad of social problems.

In response to the public disorder brought on by the gin craze and the general drunkenness of parts of the population, the British government eventually passed several Gin Acts. These new laws required a license in order to legally sell gin and also instituted taxation of the product; as a result, easy access to gin slowed. The "gin joints" were eventually licensed and expanded their range to include beer and wine, becoming the precursors to the modern-day pub or bar.

Gin remained popular with the British population, and England's empire helped spread the taste for gin to all continents. In America, gin was featured in many pre-Prohibition cocktails, including the "original" Martini. Today, gin is produced in a number of different styles, in a variety of different locations, and manages somehow to be both classic and modern in terms of taste and style.

Figure 13.2: Juniper Berries

THE PRODUCTION OF GIN

The standards of the United States and the European Union both allow for gin to be produced using two different procedures; these processes in turn create two categories of gin known as distilled gin and compound gin.

Distilled gin is considered to be the highest-quality product and is produced by direct distillation or re-distillation. To produce gin using direct distillation (also known as original distillation), a fermented mash is placed into a special still that contains a mesh tray and a basket or perforated rack known as a gin *head*. The gin head is filled with juniper berries and other botanicals, according to the distiller's formula. As the mash is distilled, the alcoholic vapors pass through the gin head and take on the flavors of the botanicals.

The re-distillation method is similar to original distillation; however, the mash is distilled into a neutral spirit before being flavored during a second distillation.

Compound gin is produced by combining neutral spirits with botanicals or botanical flavorings during the flavoring stage, without the use of a still. Compound gin may be produced via "cold compounding" in which juniper berries and botanicals are soaked (or macerated) for a period of time with neutral spirits. Alternatively, compound gin may be produced using the essential oils method, which entails combining a neutral spirit with a recipe of essential oils. After either of these procedures, the mixture is allowed to rest for a period of time, after which it is filtered and, if unaged, reduced to bottling strength and bottled.

LEADING STYLES OF GIN

Leading styles of gin include the following:

London Dry Gin: London dry gin is perhaps the best known style of gin—light, dry, and crisp. It originated in London but may be produced anywhere in the world, and is the predominant style of gin made in the United States. The European Union defines London dry gin as having less than 0.1 gram of sugar per liter. As London dry gin is defined as a type of distilled gin, all of its flavoring must be created via original distillation or re-distillation, with no flavoring or other additives (besides water) added post-re-distillation.

Old Tom Gin: The slightly sweet Old Tom Gin was one of the predominant styles of gin in the mid-1800s; it was popular in both England and America with the growing cocktail culture. Old Tom gin fell into obscurity for a while after the rise in popularity of London dry gin. However, the Old Tom style gin is enjoying a resurgence in popularity and is now appreciated as a sipping drink as well as for use in craft cocktails.

Plymouth Gin: At the time the London dry gin style became popular, distillers in other English cities developed their own styles of gin as well. Plymouth gin, produced at the Black Friar's Distillery in Plymouth since 1793, is the only one of these historic gins still produced today. Plymouth Gin tastes slightly less dry than the London dry style, and has a smoother juniper flavor.

Genever: The original Dutch gin was called *genever*, the Dutch word for juniper. Genever gin is made using flavorful malted grains, and thus has a less obvious juniper flavor than other types of gin. Genever is highly flavored and often earthy. It can be slightly sweet or light and dry, and some examples may be aged. It is considered to be its own spirits category. Genever was awarded a Protected Geographical Indication (PGI) by the European Union in 2008. According to these standards, production is limited to the Netherlands, Belgium, two departments in France, and some areas in Germany.

TASTING AND SERVING GIN

Gin is one of the more uniquely flavored spirits and, therefore, tends to maintain its character more than some spirits when used in a cocktail or mixed drink. Gin blends well with juices, sodas, soda water, and, of course, tonic. Popular mixed drinks and cocktails made with gin include the classic dry Martini, the Gin and Tonic, the Tom Collins, the Pink Lady, and the Singapore Sling.

Table 13-2: Common Brands of Gin

Brand	Country of Origin
Beefeater	England
Bombay Sapphire	England
Gilbey's	USA
Ginebra San Miguel	
Philippines	
Gordon's	England
Hayman's Old Tom	England
Hendrick's	Scotland
Plymouth Gin	England
Tanqueray	England/Scotland

BRANDY

Brandy is a class of spirits distilled from fruit. More specifically, brandy is produced from grape wine, the pomace left after winemaking, or the fermented juice of other fruits. Cognac and armagnac, arguably the most famous of all brandies, are distilled from grape wine and produced in specified regions of France. Grape-based brandy is also made in many places around the world, and most wine-producing regions have their own brandy traditions. Brandy is also made from apples and pears, such as the French apple-and-pear brandy calvados and the historic American product known as applejack. Brandy is also produced around the world from cherries, plums, apricots, berries, and other fruits. In the European Union, spirits distilled from fruit other than grapes are technically classified as "fruit spirits" rather than brandy; however, in this guide, the term *brandy* will be, at times, used to refer to all fruit-based spirits, as is commonly done in many parts of the world.

THE ORIGINS OF BRANDY

Brandy has been produced in simple forms since the early days of distillation. It is said that in the 16th century, during prosperous maritime trade between the French and the Dutch, a Dutch trader suggested distillation as a way to "condense" wine for shipping with the intention of diluting the wine again when it reached its destination.

As the first shipments of "concentrated wine" arrived in Holland, it was discovered that the concentrate had a unique, pleasing flavor of its own. It became apparent that after being shipped in wooden casks, the product was better than the original wine. The Dutch called the new product *brandewijn* ("burnt wine"), and eventually the term was anglicized to form the present-day word, *brandy*.

GRAPE BRANDY

Grape brandies are produced in most countries that produce wine, and many are not regionally specific. They may be made in pot stills or continuous stills according to regulations and traditions that vary with the country of production. The United States, South Africa, Australia, Germany, and France are among the world's leading producers of both fine and commercial-style brandy.

Other styles of grape-based brandy—including cognac, armagnac, and brandy de Jerez—are region-specific and highly regulated as to base materials, method of production, and aging requirements. These brandies are discussed in the sections that follow.

Cognac: Brandies from the Cognac region in southwestern France (just north of the Bordeaux wine region) are among the best known and most highly regarded brandies in the world. The Cognac region was awarded appellation d'origine contrôlée (AOC) protection for its spirits in 1936, making it one of the first regions in France to receive the AOC designation.

The Cognac AOC is divided into six *crus*—officially recognized districts that may be used on labels to indicate geographic origin. If the name of a cru appears on a label of cognac, then 100% of the grapes must have been grown in the named region. In order from most prestigious to least renowned,

The Cognac Region

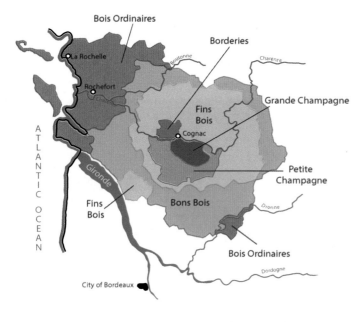

Copyright: The Society of Wine Educators 2015

Figure 13.3: Map of the Cognac Region

the crus are *Grande Champagne*, Petite Champagne, *Borderies*, *Fins Bois, Bons Bois*, and *Bois Ordinaire*s. The term Fine Champagne may be used to indicate a cognac produced with a combination of grapes from the Grande Champagne and Petite Champagne areas, with at least 50% of them grown within Grande Champagne.

Cognac is produced from white grape varieties, with Ugni Blanc (locally known as Saint-Émilion, and known as Trebbiano in Italy) the leading variety. Other permitted grape varieties include Folle Blanche, Colombard, Montils, Sémillon, and Folignan, Jurançon Blanc, Meslier-Saint-François, and Sélect. In reality, Ugni Blanc is the sole grape variety used in most versions of cognac, as it is prized in the area for its disease resistance and neutral flavors.

Distillation takes place in a traditional alembic or pot still, known as a *Charentais* still in this region. Cognac distillation is a two-stage process known as *à repasse*. The still must be made of copper, directly heated, and limited in size. The first stage of

distillation, known as the *première chauffe*, produces a distillate with an alcohol volume of 28–32% known as *brouillis*. When enough brouillis is collected, the product is sent through the second stage of the distillation.

To perform the second-stage distillation, known as the *bonne chauffe*, the brouillis is returned to the boiler for a second heating. The heart of the run, coming off as a clear distillate at about 60% alcohol by volume, will be matured into cognac.

Cognac is matured in oak for a minimum of two years, but some versions are aged for much longer. The leading brands of Cognac include Hennessey, Martell, Rémy Martin, and Courvoisier.

Armagnac: Armagnac is a French grape-based brandy produced in the department of Gers, located southeast of Bordeaux in the heart of the Gascony region. The Armagnac region received appellation d'origine contrôlée (AOC) protection in 1936.

The Armagnac region is divided into three sub-regions. These are, in order from the most prestigious to the least renowned, the Bas-Armagnac (the most westerly area), Ténarèze (the central growing area), and the Haut-Armagnac (the most easterly). The Bas-Armagnac produces the richest and most elegant spirits.

The four main grape varieties used in the production of armagnac include Ugni Blanc (sometimes known in the US as Saint-Émilion), Baco Blanc, Folle Blanche, and Colombard. Of these, Ugni Blanc is the most widely planted, accounting for almost 60% of the vines. Six other varieties are allowed and are planted throughout the region in small amounts. These include Clairette de Gascogne (Blanc Dame), Meslier Saint-François, Plant de Graisse, Jurancon Blanc, Mauzac Blanc, and Mauzac Rosé.

Armagnac is generally distilled using only a single distillation via an armagnac still, which is an early, small-scale version of a column still. (Double distillation using a pot still is also permitted but is used only by a few distillers.)

The Armagnac Region

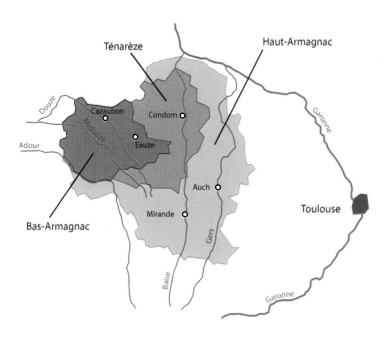

Copyright: The Society of Wine Educators 2015

Figure 13.4: Map of the Armagnac Region

After distillation, young armagnac may be aged for three months in inert containers and released as a clear spirit labeled as "blanche" armagnac. However, most armagnac is aged, and those not using the "blanche" designation must be aged for at least one year in oak barrels. Most armagnac is, however, aged for much longer.

Brandy de Jerez: Spain produces a unique, highly regarded brandy known as *brandy de Jerez*. Despite its name and origination in Jerez, most of the grapes sourced for the production of this brandy come from the region of La Mancha. The grapes used are 95% Airén, a white grape variety that does well in the hot, dry climate of central Spain.

Brandy de Jerez has Denominación de Origen (DO) status and must be aged within the "Sherry Triangle," defined by the towns of Jerez de la Frontera, Sanlúcar de Barrameda, and El Puerto de Santa María.

Brandy de Jerez is unique in that it is aged using the solera system that was originally developed for the aging of the famous wines of the region. The barrels used for aging the brandy must have previously held sherry for at least three years. Brandy de Jerez must be aged in the solera for at least six months, but many styles are aged for much longer. The use of the solera method, which promotes oxidation, coupled with the warm climate in which the barrels are matured, adds to the rich, sweet, and softer style of these brandies.

POMACE BRANDY

While still technically a grape brandy, pomace brandy is made from the grape skins, seeds, and stems left over after wine production. To produce pomace brandy, the skins, pulp, and seeds are lightly pressed or steamed to release the remaining juice, to which water may be added before the mixture is fermented and distilled. The pomace must be kept fresh to avoid spoilage or oxidation, if one is to produce a high-quality product.

Most pomace brandy is bottled unaged, however, aging is allowed. Pomace brandies are produced throughout the winemaking world, although much is consumed locally. *Marc* (produced in France) and *grappa* (produced in Italy) are two types of pomace brandy that are distributed internationally.

Figure 13.5: Bottles of grappa at the Poli Museo della Grappa (Bassano del Grappa, Italy)

APPLE BRANDY

Calvados is an apple-based fruit spirit (brandy) produced in the French area of Lower Normandy (Basse-Normandie). The climate there is a bit too cold for the successful farming of grapes, but the region is home to vast apple and pear orchards, as well as a thriving cider and fruit spirits industry.

Calvados is distilled from cider made from specially grown and selected apples. Some versions use pears in addition to apples. All fruit used in the production of calvados must be grown within the delineated Calvados region. There are currently three separate appellation d'origine (AOC) designations for calvados. They are as follows:

- **Calvados AOC:** Calvados AOC is considered to be "basic" calvados and may be produced anywhere within the designated region. Calvados AOC requires a minimum of two years of aging in oak barrels. This type of calvados makes up over 70% of the total production.
- **Calvados Pays d'Auge AOC:** Considered to be the highest quality, the production area for Calvados Pays d'Auge is limited to the east end of the département of Calvados and a few adjoining districts. This style of calvados must be produced using pot still distillation and requires a minimum of two years of aging in oak.
- **Calvados Domfrontais AOC:** Calvados Domfrontais requires the use of a minimum of 30% pear cider, reflecting the long tradition of pear orchards in the area. Many versions of Calvados Domfrontais actually use between 70% and 80% pears in their production. This style of calvados is distilled in a continuous reflux column still and must be aged in oak for a minimum of three years.

Applejack, a type of brandy made from apple cider, was one of the most popular beverages in colonial America. Applejack was historically made by a traditional method known as *freeze distillation* (congelation), which involved leaving apple cider outside to freeze and chipping off chunks of ice in order to concentrate the alcohol content. The term *applejack* derives from the term *jacking*, meaning "freeze distillation."

In 1780, soon after the American Revolution, the new nation's first distillery permit—US License #1—was granted to Laird's Distillery of Scobeyville, New Jersey— a producer of apple brandy. Laird's had been producing its proprietary applejack since the late 1600s and supplied brandy to George Washington's troops during the Revolutionary War. AppleJack is still produced by Laird's Distillery, albeit using modern distillation methods. The distillery is now located in Virginia near the source of Laird's apples, but the historic New Jersey site is still maintained for use in maturing and bottling the spirits. Demand for apple brandy declined in the 1960s, but the spirit is seeing a renewed interest among mixologists and consumers. The classic cocktail made with applejack is the Jack Rose, a blend of applejack, lemon juice, and grenadine.

FRUIT BRANDY

Fruit brandies are produced in many parts of the world from plums, apricots, cherries, and berries. Most of these products are unaged in order to highlight the flavor of the base fruit. Many countries produce a fruit brandy that is typical of the region, such as the popular spirits discussed below:

- **Cherry Brandy:** Cherry brandy is believed to have originated in the Black Forest of Germany. It is traditionally made from the double distillation of the fermented juice of the black morello cherry. Known as *kirsch* or *kirschwasser* (German for "cherry water"), this style of cherry brandy is now made in Alsace, Switzerland, and the United States.
- **Apricot Brandy:** Hungary produces an apricot brandy known as *Barack Pálinka*. The term *pálinka* has been used historically to refer to a wide variety of fruit spirits produced throughout Central and Eastern Europe; however, since the 2008 passage of the Hungarian Pálinka Law, it can only be used for products produced in Hungary, and for apricot-based spirits produced in four specific regions of Austria. Another apricot brandy, known as *marillenschnaps* or *marillenbrand*, is produced in the Wachau region of Austria.
- **Plum Brandy:** Plum brandies are produced in many regions around the world. They are particularly popular in traditional forms throughout Central and Eastern Europe, where

they are known as *slivovitz*. Many brands of slivovitz are commercially produced and widely available in the United States. Slivovitz, which has many traditional spellings and many home countries, is produced in Serbia, Slovenia, Croatia, Bosnia and Herzegovina, the Czech Republic, Slovakia, Poland, Hungary, and Bulgaria, as well as in other countries.

- **Soft Fruit Brandy:** Soft fruits such as strawberries and raspberries are low in sugar compared to most fruits; therefore, they are not always fermented into wine to be distilled into brandy. Rather, they can be macerated in neutral alcohol to impart their flavor. The resulting liquid can then be distilled. France produces eaux-de-vie from raspberries, known as *framboise*, and from strawberries, known as *fraise*. Producers elsewhere, such as Bonny Doon and St. George's Spirits (both located in California), are producing artisanal brandies from soft fruits.

Figure 13.6: Fruit spirits such as kirsch are often an integral part of a local cuisine

TASTING AND SERVING BRANDY
For most consumers, the traditional way to serve brandy—as an unadorned after-dinner drink in a short-stemmed glass—is the best. This is undoubtedly the ideal choice for particularly fine aged cognac, armagnac, and the like. However, in many parts of Europe, it is common to serve a simpler brandy as a long drink with soda or fruit juice as an aperitif. Others prefer their brandy on ice. Classic cocktails based on brandy, such as the Sidecar, the Stinger, and the Brandy Alexander, are popular as well.

WHISKEY

Whiskey is a spirit produced from grains. Whiskey is produced throughout the world, and although the regulations for the production of whiskey vary from country to country, there is worldwide agreement that the distilling proof cannot be so high that the distillate loses its unique flavor. Most whiskeys are also required to be aged in oak, although there are a few products exempt from the requirement. Given these parameters, whiskey is generally considered to be a beverage whose main flavor profile is derived from its grain-based raw materials and the time it spends in oak.

A Note on Spelling: Different countries use different spellings of the word whiskey or whisky. Traditionally, Scotland, Japan, and Canada have used the spelling *whisky* (without the e), and Ireland and the United States use the spelling whiskey (with the e). While either spelling is considered correct in the United States, this Study Guide will use the version with the e when referring to whiskey in general, and the spelling without the e when referring to the products of Scotland, Japan, and Canada.

THE ORIGINS OF WHISKEY
It is generally believed that the Irish Celts were the first to produce a spirit from grains; it is believed that these early spirits were quite similar to the whiskeys presently made in Ireland. However, the first *written* evidence of a spirit produced from grain appears in the last decade of the fifteenth century in Scotland—a transfer of malt to be made into aqua vitae, by order of the king, is recorded in the Exchequer Rolls of Scotland.

The present-day name "whiskey" is attributable to either the Scottish Celtic words *uisge beatha* or the Irish Celtic term *uisge baugh* (pronounced *whis-geh-BAW*), both of which mean "water of life" or, as some scholars believe, "lively water."

WHISKEY INGREDIENTS
The quality of the raw materials—grain, water, and yeast—used to make whiskey has a great impact on the quality and flavor of the final spirit.
- Grain: The four primary grains used in the production of whiskey are barley, corn, rye, and

wheat. Of the four grains, barley is the most widely used (it is the best source of the enzymes that help to convert the grain's starch into a fermentable sugar). When barley is used in the production of whiskey, it undergoes a process of germination to release the enzymes that will aid in converting the starches in the grain to fermentable sugars. This procedure begins by steeping the grains in water to allow the grains to sprout, or germinate. When the ideal state of germination is reached, the growth is halted by heating the germinated grain in kilns. The specific "recipe," or list of grain ingredients that will be fermented for use in a particular spirit, is known as the mash bill or grain bill.

- Water: The first commercial whiskey distilleries, like those of beer, sake, rum, and other beverages, grew up around water sources that were considered ideal for the production of the spirit. The quality of the water—its hardness or softness and mineral content—contributes to each whiskey's style.
- Yeast: The specific strain of yeast used in whiskey production contributes its distinctive flavors and attributes, depending on which strain is selected for fermentation.

SCOTCH WHISKY

With its long history and commercial success, Scotland leads all countries in the number of distilleries producing whisky, with over 130 presently in operation. Scotch whisky has protected geographical indication (PGI) status in the European Union and is strictly defined according to a detailed set of laws known as the 2009 Scotch Whisky Regulations.

According to these standards, Scotch whisky must be produced from a mixture of water, malted barley, and other whole cereal grains. Fermentation and distillation (which may not exceed 94.8% alcohol by volume) must occur at the same location in Scotland. In addition, all Scotch whisky must be aged in oak casks in Scotland for a minimum of three years.

There are five distinct styles of Scotch whisky. As of 2011, one of the following must be stated on the label of Scotch whisky:

- **Single Malt Scotch Whisky:** Single malt Scotch whisky is generally considered to be a premium product. It is required to be distilled at a single distillery by batch distillation in a pot still, and it must be made solely with malted barley and no other grains.
- **Single Grain Scotch Whisky:** Single grain Scotch whisky is any Scotch whisky distilled at a single distillery and produced from other malted or unmalted grains (generally, wheat or corn) in addition to malted barley. (All Scotch must contain at least some malted barley.) "Single grain" does not mean that the whisky was made from a single type of grain; rather, the word single refers to the use of a single distillery. There are no specific requirements as to the type of distillation used in the production of single grain Scotch whisky; however, most are continuously distilled in order to produce a lighter style of whisky.
- **Blended Malt Scotch Whisky:** Blended malt Scotch whisky is a blend of two or more single malt Scotch whiskies that have been produced at more than one distillery.
- **Blended Grain Scotch Whisky:** Blended grain Scotch whisky is a blend of two or more single grain Scotch whiskies that have been produced at more than one distillery.
- **Blended Scotch Whisky:** Blended Scotch whisky is a blend of one or more single malt Scotch whiskies with one or more single grain Scotch whiskies. Blended Scotch whisky accounts for about 90% of the Scotch whisky consumed worldwide.

Scotch whisky is renowned for its unique flavor profile, which, aside from the blend, is partially derived from the aspects of its base materials (including the grain bill and the water), the fermentation process, the distillation process, and aging. Another unique characteristic of Scotch is the use of peat—a compacted, vegetative form of carbon—as a fuel during the kilning (heating) of the grain. The smoke from the burning peat is often allowed to come into contact with the grain through a peat box and permeate it with the aromas of smoke, seaweed, and tar, as well as what some describe as a slightly medicinal flavor. There is a common misconception that all Scotch whisky has a heavy peat flavor, but in reality most Scotches have only a mild peat influence, and the use of peat is optional.

The top-selling brands of Scotch whisky include Johnnie Walker, Glenfiddich, Ballantine's, Chivas Regal, Grant's, J&B, The Macallan, and Dewar's.

Figure 13.7: Wash still and spirit still at the Jameson Whiskey Heritage Center

IRISH WHISKEY

Irish whiskey, traditionally known as *Uisce Beatha Eireannach*, is protected by PGI status in the European Union and defined according to the Irish Whiskey Act of 1980 as well as a set of Technical Standards that were submitted to the EU in October of 2015. According to these standards, Irish whiskey must be distilled in Ireland from a mash of cereal grains (to an alcoholic strength of less than 94.8% alcohol by volume) and be aged in Ireland in wooden casks (not to exceed 700 liters [185 gallons] in capacity) for a minimum of three years.

These new standards also provide definitions for the following four types of Irish whiskey:

- **Irish Malt Whiskey:** Irish malt whiskey must be made from 100% malted barley, and must be distilled in pot stills. Irish malt whiskey is traditionally triple-distilled, although double distillation may be used.
- **Irish Grain Whiskey:** Irish grain whiskey is produced from a mash containing a maximum of 30% malted barley. The remainder is made up of unmalted cereal grains—typically maize, wheat, or barley. This type of whiskey is continuously distilled using column stills. Irish grain whiskey may have either a light or a full flavor profile, depending on the cut points and other techniques employed by the distiller. Irish grain whiskey is typically used in blends.

- **Irish Pot Still Whiskey:** Irish pot still whiskey is required to be produced using a mash containing a minimum of 30% malted barley and a minimum of 30% unmalted barley. The remainder of the mash may be malted or unmalted barley, and may include up to 5% other unmalted cereal grains (usually oats or rye). This type of whiskey must be batch distilled in pot stills. The traditional practice is triple distillation in large pot stills, although double distillation may also be employed. Irish pot still whiskey is a traditional product only produced by a few distilleries. Examples include Redbreast, Green Spot, and Jameson 15-Year-Old Pot Still Whiskey.
- **Blended Irish Whiskey:** Blended Irish whiskey is a blend of two or more different whiskey types, which must be made in accordance with the standards stated above, and which may include Irish malt whiskey, Irish grain whiskey, and/or Irish pot still whiskey. The whiskeys that make up the blend may also be chosen from different distilleries, ages, types of cask finish, and flavor profiles in order to achieve the desired flavor and consistency. Blended Irish whiskey tends to be smooth and mellow with a range of flavors, and a light, silky mouth feel.

As with Scotch, Irish blends are the most popular whiskeys in the category. Top-selling brands of Irish whiskey include Jameson, Tyrconnell, Black Bush, Bushmills, Paddy, and Tullamore D.E.W.

CANADIAN WHISKY

Early Canadian distillers began Canada's distillation industry in the 1790s. The conditions in the Eastern Canadian territories were perfect for growing rye and barley. As Canadian settlers extended their farms further west in the seventeenth and eighteenth centuries, corn and wheat became part of the grain blends used in distillation as well.

The laws regulating Canadian whisky, via the Food and Drug Regulations of Canada, specify that Canadian whisky must be made from a mash of cereal grains and fermented, aged, and distilled in Canada. Canadian whisky must be aged in small wooden containers for no less than three years. Popular brands of Canadian whisky include Canadian Club, Crown Royal, JP Wiser's, Collingwood, Masterson's and WhistlePig.

Most Canadian whiskies are marketed as blends and are comprised of a base grain whisky (typically made from corn) and a flavoring whisky. The flavoring whisky will typically contain high rye content or be produced in some other manner so as to provide a certain flavor profile to the finished blend. The law regarding blended Canadian whisky also allows for up to 9.09% added ingredients. These ingredients, added in order to produce a distinctive flavor profile, often include sherry, sweetener, caramel coloring, wine, or even non-Canadian whiskey or brandies.

Despite the popularity of blends, specialty distilleries producing unique whiskies can certainly be found in Canada. For instance, Glenora Distillery, located in Nova Scotia, bills itself as "North America's first single malt distillery" and produces a single malt Canadian whisky distilled from just water and malted barley. Other unique Canadian whiskies include Crown Royal's extra-rare whisky series, Hiram Walker's Lot 40 single copper pot still Canadian whisky, and Alberta Premium's thirty-year-old Canadian whisky.

Figure 13.8: Jim Beam Distillery in Clermont, Kentucky

AMERICAN WHISKEY

The story of whiskey in the United States dates to the late 1700s, with the founding of the original American colonies. During this period, Scottish, Irish, and German immigrants crossed the Atlantic to escape economic hardship and religious persecution, coming to America with the dream of farming their own property.

The vast territories of western Pennsylvania and Virginia were ideal locations for the production of whiskey. Rye grain grew exceedingly well in Pennsylvania's soil, while corn grew well in Virginia. These grains became widely cultivated, but as they were both perishable and expensive to transport, distilling them into whiskey became a profitable way to utilize the crops. Almost every farmer made whiskey, which was widely traded for other goods. Soon, a thriving market for whiskey had been established.

A wide range of whiskeys are made in the United States. Some of the leading products are discussed below:

Bourbon: While most often associated with Kentucky, bourbon may be produced anywhere in the United States. Bourbon is also unique to the US; a 1964 resolution of the Congress of the United States declared bourbon to be a "distinctive product of the United States."

Bourbon must be produced from a mash containing a minimum of 51% corn, must be distilled at less than 160 proof, and must be stored in charred, new oak barrels. While there is no legally mandated minimum aging requirement, it is typical for high-quality bourbon to be aged for two years or more. A few years of aging in new charred oak barrels gives the whiskey its typical vanilla, sweet toast, and caramel flavors.

Bourbon is currently being produced in California, Colorado, Kansas, Iowa, Missouri, New York, Ohio, Pennsylvania, Texas, and Virginia, among other states. However, 95% of all bourbon is produced in Kentucky, which is home to the Four Roses Distillery, Jim Beam, Maker's Mark, Wild Turkey, Buffalo Trace, and Woodford Reserve, as well as other established and craft distilleries.

Corn Whiskey: American corn whiskey is made from a mash of at least 80% corn. Corn whiskey follows all of the typical production standards for American whiskey, except that it is not typically aged. If it is aged, then it must be done in used or uncharred oak barrels. The high proportion of corn in the mash bill lends a smooth mouthfeel to the spirit and a slightly sweet corn note. Well-known producers of corn whiskey include Heaven Hill and Buffalo Trace.

Tennessee Whiskey: Tennessee whiskey is produced using the same parameters as basic bourbon whiskey. Tennessee whiskey may only be produced in the state of Tennessee, and must be produced using a charcoal filtering technique known as the *Lincoln County Proces*s. The Lincoln County Process uses sugar maple charcoal to remove some of the lighter congeners, giving the spirit a smooth texture and a full, robust flavor. Tennessee whiskey is often described as having maple syrup, vanilla, caramel, and smoke aromas. Producers of Tennessee whiskey include Jack Daniel's and George Dickel.

Straight Whiskey: There are six specific types of American whiskey—bourbon, rye, wheat, malt, rye malt, and corn—that may be labeled as *straight*. To be labeled as a straight whiskey, with the exception of corn, the spirit must have aged in charred new oak containers for at least two years. To be labeled as a straight, corn whiskey must still be aged for the specified period of time; however, the barrels must be used, or uncharred (if new). If a straight whiskey has been aged for four years or longer, then a statement of age is optional; however, if it has been aged less than four years, then the age (in years) must be stated on the label and if a blend, must reflect the youngest age.

Blended American Whiskeys: As in other parts of the world, blended whiskeys are widely produced and distributed in the US. An American blended whiskey contains a straight whiskey or a blend of straight whiskeys blended with light whiskey or neutral spirits. The various types of blended whiskey include blended bourbon, blended rye, and blended wheat whiskey, all of which must contain no less than 51% straight bourbon whiskey, straight rye whiskey, or straight wheat whiskey, respectively. Blended straight whiskey must be a blend of 100% straight whiskeys, while a product labeled simply as "blended whiskey" must be based on a minimum of 20% straight whiskeys blended with other whiskeys or neutral spirits.

TASTING AND SERVING WHISKEY

While whiskey is served in a variety of ways, most consumers prefer to take their whiskey neat, or with a single ice cube as an aperitif or after-dinner drink. Some people like to dilute their whiskey with a bit of water; for other people, this would be a travesty. Lighter, blended whiskeys are often enjoyed long, over ice, and with soda water, ginger ale, or cola. Classic whiskey-based cocktails, such as the Manhattan, the Rob Roy, the Old-Fashioned, and the Mint Julep, are popular as well.

RUM

Rum is a distilled spirit produced from sugarcane. Rum may be produced from sugarcane syrup, molasses (a by-product of sugar production), or from fresh sugarcane juice. The majority of the world's rum production occurs in the Caribbean and Latin America, with rum playing a large part in the culture of most islands of the West Indies. However, as there is no specified geographical region for the production of rum, it is produced in many different countries and locations throughout the world.

Figure 13.9: Sugarcane growing at Depaz Distillery on the island of Martinique

THE ORIGINS OF RUM

The history of rum is intimately connected to the sources of sugarcane, which was introduced into Europe after the seventh century, where it began to be grown in the warm climates of Spain, Portugal, and Northern Africa. Christopher Columbus brought sugarcane cuttings from the Canary Islands (off the coast of Africa) to the New World during his 1493 arrival in the West Indies. Sugarcane flourished in the climate of the Caribbean and soon, sugar was being shipped to Europe to supplement the sugar processed there from the sugar beet. European settlers in the West Indies soon found that the molasses residue from sugar production was easily fermented, so they began to distill the ferment, which led to the spirit we now know as rum.

THE PRODUCTION OF RUM

As a spirit category, rum has very few production requirements other than the required use of sugarcane as the base material. Sugarcane itself is a tall tropical perennial plant of the grass family *Gramineae*, specifically of the species *Saccharum officinarum*. There are different varieties of sugarcane grown in various parts of the world, most of which are actually hybrids developed from *Saccharum officinarum*.

Most rum is produced using molasses, which is the very viscous, concentrated substance that is left over after the sugar crystals have been evaporated or cooked away from the sugarcane juice. Molasses-based rums are sometimes referred to as industrial rum or *rhum industriel*. Other styles of rum, particularly those produced in the French Caribbean, are made from raw sugarcane juice. This style of rum is known as agricultural rum or *rhum agricole*. About 10% of all rum produced is made with sugarcane juice.

To begin the process of fermentation, the sugarcane juice or molasses is mixed with water and yeast is added. Fermentation may be accomplished with ambient (native) yeast or commercially-procured yeast, depending on the desired style of the finished rum.

When fermentation is complete, the resulting liquid is distilled. Distillation may occur in either a pot or a column still depending on the style of rum being produced. While there certainly are exceptions, the speedier column still is more commonly used for industrial rum while the pot still is often used for agricultural rum.

Rum is not required to be aged, and is often bottled soon after distillation is complete. However, as some styles of rum benefit from aging, it may be aged in oak or other containers for several months or years.

STYLES OF RUM

With few category-wide production requirements in place, rum is somewhat difficult to categorize. However, rum is produced in a range of colors, which are somewhat aligned with a particular style. Some of these styles are discussed below:

- **White Rum:** White rums are colorless and may be labeled as *clear, crystal, blanco, silver,* or *plata.* In terms of total volume of rum consumed worldwide, this color category is the most popular. White rum is usually a light style of rum that is unaged or lightly aged, made using column stills, and sometimes filtered to remove any color.
- **Amber/Gold:** Also known as *oro,* the gold color category denotes some aging, as the color presumably comes from the wooden barrel during the maturation process. In this case, this style of rum is expected to have some richness and complexity. However, as there is no universal, legal definition of aging, in order to use the term amber or gold, some distillers add caramel or molasses to white rum to give the impression of aging.
- **Dark:** Dark rums are presumably aged in charred oak barrels, some for as long as five to seven years or longer. A smooth, rich mouthfeel and aromas and flavors of sweet spices and dried fruits—such as raisin, fig, clove, and cinnamon—are common in aged rums, and many types of rum are produced in this style. These rums are sometimes labeled with the term *añejo*; however, as with gold rums, this term is not regulated and additives may, in some cases, be used to artificially darken the color of rum.
- **Flavored Rum:** Fruit-flavored rums, such as orange, coconut, lime, mango, and pineapple, are very popular, as are spiced rums flavored with vanilla, cinnamon, nutmeg, clove, and anise. Most flavored rums are slightly sweetened and produced using a base of unaged white rum.

Figure 13.10: Stills at the Habitation Clément Distillery on the island of Martinique

LEADING RUMS FROM AROUND THE WORLD

While a given region may produce many different styles of rum, many of the leading rum-producing regions of the world have rum styles or iconic rum brands for which they are particularly well known. Some of these are discussed below:

- **Jamaica:** Jamaica makes a wide variety of styles of rum, using a range of fermentation techniques, distillation styles, and aging processes. Rum production in Jamaica is unique in that a substance called *dunder* is the traditional yeast source for fermentation. Dunder is made from the highly acidic, yeast-rich foam "leftovers" left in the still after distillation is complete. The use of dunder encourages the creation of the highly aromatic compounds known as *esters*. Jamaica prides itself on its traditional, high-ester content pot still rums.

- **Martinique:** The French island of Martinique has been granted appellation d'origine contrôlée (AOC) status for rhum agricole—the only AOC for rum in existence. Martinique's AOC status means that the production of its rhum agricole is highly regulated, including the requirement that the spirit must be distilled to about 70% alcohol, a lesser degree than most molasses-based rum. This allows the rhum to retain a good deal of the sugarcane's original flavor.

- **Haiti:** French colonists brought sugarcane to St. Dominique (as Haiti was known at the time) in the 1600s. Not long after that, rum was being made in the area. Today, one of Haiti's most famous exports is the array of rum produced by the Societe du Rhum Barbancourt. This family business, which began on March 18, 1862, was founded by Dupré Barbancourt, a Frenchman from the cognac-producing region of Charente.

- **Brazil:** Cachaça is a type of Brazilian rum produced from sugarcane juice. It is by far the most popular distilled spirit among the 180 million citizens of Brazil, making it one of the most widely consumed spirits on the planet. Outside Brazil, cachaça is mainly known as the key ingredient in certain popular tropical drinks, namely the Caipirinha. (Note: In Brazil, Cachaça is often produced [at least partially] with corn syrup; however, these products do not meet the legal definition of "rum;" products for export to the United States or the EU labeled as "Brazilian rum" must be produced using 100% sugarcane-based products.)

- **Barbados:** Sugar plantations arrived in Barbados not long after the British colonized the island in 1627. Rum production was the natural by-product. Today, Barbados produces a wide variety of rum, mainly from molasses, specializing in rich, flavorful styles. Mount Gay, the world's oldest documented rum brand, was founded here in 1703.

- **Puerto Rico:** Puerto Rico produces a range of rum styles; however, the best-known style of Puerto Rican rum tends to be a light style of rum with delicate, clean, floral notes. Many Puerto Rican rums are based on the traditional Cuban style developed in 1862 by Bacardi. Bacardi Limited operates a large distillery in Cataño, Puerto Rico (as well as many others throughout the world).

TASTING AND SERVING RUM

As unaged rums can be a bit fiery when sipped straight, white rums are generally served long, mixed with soda or juice, or in cocktails. The Cuba Libre, Daiquiri, and Mojito are among the world's favorite rum-based drinks, as are many punches and tropical drinks. Aged rums mix nicely in drinks and cocktails, as well, but are often enjoyed as an after-dinner drink, to be sipped and savored on their own or over ice.

Table 13-3: Common Brands of Rum

Brand	Country of Origin
Appleton	Jamaica
Bacardi	Puerto Rico
Barbancourt	Haiti
Cruzan	US Virgin Islands
Gosling's	Bermuda
Havana Club	Cuba
Mount Gay	Barbados
Myer's	Jamaica
10 Cane	Trinidad
Zacapa	Guatemala

TEQUILA

Tequila is a type of spirit produced from the fermented sap of the blue agave plant. Unlike most other categories of spirits, tequila may only be made in its country of origin, Mexico. The center of tequila production is the small town of Tequila, located in the Mexican state of Jalisco. Tequila may be produced throughout the entire state of Jalisco, and in designated areas within the nearby states of Tamaulipas, Guanajuato, Nayarit, and Michoacán.

The international standard for tequila is described in the *Norma Oficial Mexicana* ("Official Standard of Mexico," often abbreviated as NOM). The NOM for tequila recognizes two distinct types of tequila—*tequila* and *100% agave tequila*. Tequila that is 100% agave must be produced with only the sugars (sap) of the blue agave plant. A product labeled simply as "tequila" must be produced using a minimum of 51% blue agave sap; the remainder is allowed to be any non-agave sugar and is typically molasses, cane sugar, or corn syrup. Non-100% agave tequilas are sometimes referred to as *mixto* tequilas.

THE ORIGINS OF TEQUILA

The agave (pronounced *ah-GAH-vay*) plant was used by the native inhabitants of Mexico for many practical purposes—such as food, medicine, binding cords, and building materials—long before it was discovered (circa 200 CE) that the juice of the agave plant could be fermented into an intoxicating beverage.

In the 1520s, upon their invasion of Mexico, Spanish conquistadors introduced the art of alcoholic distillation to the native population. The earliest experiments of making a distilled beverage using agave sap produced a spirit known as *mezcal wine* (alternately spelled "mescal"). Mezcal wine was produced all over central Mexico from the many varieties of agave native to the region.

By the eighteenth century, distillation was the main enterprise of the town of Tequila and its surrounding area. It was soon discovered that the specific variety of blue agave plant grown in the areas was the finest source of sap for distillation. In 1873, the blue agave-based "mezcal wine" from the region of Jalisco was officially renamed *tequila* in order to distinguish it from mezcal spirits produced in other parts of Mexico.

Figure 13.11: Agave fields in Jalisco

THE AGAVE PLANT

Most people mistake the agave plant for a cactus. While the two types of plants look similar and grow in the same type of climate, the agave is *not* a cactus. Rather, the agave belongs to the Agavoideae family of flowering plants and is classified as a succulent.

Over 130 different varieties of agave are known to exist. While many of them are used for industrial or agricultural purposes, only a few are suitable or desirable as a source for alcoholic beverages. The specific variety of agave used for tequila was classified by a botanist named Frédéric Albert Constantin Weber who, in 1902, gave the plant the botanical name *Agave tequilana Weber azul.*

For use in tequila, the flower stalk of the blue agave plant is removed before it has a chance to blossom, preventing the plants from reaching sexual maturity. This injurious process causes the center of the plant's stem to swell with juice, or *aguamiel* (literally, "honey water"). This swollen portion of the agave has two names: *piña*, as it resembles a pineapple, and *cabeza* ("head"), as it somewhat resembles the shape of a human head. It is this swollen portion of the plant that will be harvested and used in the production of tequila.

THE PRODUCTION OF TEQUILA

The production of tequila begins with the harvest. At harvest, the swollen stem of the blue agave plant is cut from its roots and rolled onto its side. From this position, the plant's leaves, known as *pencas*, are sliced off, leaving a relatively smooth piña to be hauled to the distillery. At this point, the piña may weigh up to 200 pounds.

Upon arrival at the distillery, the piñas are put in an oven or pressure cooker and baked for thirty-six to forty-eight hours in order to convert the starches to fermentable sugars. During this baking, they release a sugary liquid called *aguamiel*, which is collected and later added to the fermenting wort. After being cooled, the cooked piñas are shredded in a grinding machine to release the aguamiel remaining in the flesh. Some producers still use a traditional method of stone grinding the piñas in a pit using horse power.

Next, the aguamiel is diluted with water and yeast is added to start the fermentation. If the spirit being produced will not be 100% agave, liquid sugar is added to the aguamiel before the yeast. Fermentation typically takes from three to ten days. Once the alcohol is created, the fermented liquid is known as *mosto*. The alcohol content of the mosto can range from 4% to 8%.

As there are no regulatory limitations on the type of still used for the distillation of tequila, copper or stainless steel pot stills, single column stills, and even continuous distillation towers may be used. The vast majority of tequila producers use the pot still for two separate distillations, being careful to retain the congeners that will give the tequila its distinctive flavor.

As with other spirits, distillation results in a clear spirit. Some styles of tequila are unaged or aged very briefly and bottled as a clear spirit. Other styles may be aged in a combination of oak barrels or tanks for anywhere from a few months to several years.

AGING DESIGNATIONS FOR TEQUILA

Tequila is produced in several strictly regulated aging categories, as described below:

- **Blanco:** Also known as "plata," "white," or "silver," this style of tequila is water-white in the bottle. It can be bottled immediately after distillation, or it may be allowed to rest in stainless steel tanks for no longer than sixty days prior to bottling.
- **Reposado:** *Reposado* tequila is "rested" for two to twelve months in oak vats or barrels.
- **Añejo:** *Añejo* tequila must be matured in oak barrels for a minimum period of one year.
- **Extra-Añejo:** *Extra-Añejo* tequila must be aged in oak barrels for a minimum period of three years.

Another term that might appear on a tequila label is *oro* or *gold*. Somewhat confusingly, these two terms may mean something entirely different when applied to 100% agave tequila versus non-100% (mixto) tequila. When applied to 100% agave tequilas, the term indicates tequila produced via the blending of young tequilas with aged tequilas. Such products are rare, but they do allow for tequila to be labeled as oro (or gold) and still maintain the 100% agave status. It is actually far more common for gold tequila to be mixto tequila. In such cases, the tequila is considered to be joven abocado. The term joven abocado translates (roughly) to "young and mellowed." It should be noted that the only difference between this type of "gold" tequila and plata tequila is the caramel coloring.

Table 13-4: Common Brands of Tequila

Don Eduardo
Don Julio
Herradura
El Jimador
Jose Cuervo
Patrón
Sauza
El Tesoro

MEZCAL

Mezcal was, until quite recently, a traditional term referring to all agave spirits. However, in 1994, mezcal was awarded its own set of standards. As of 2016, these standards (as described in the *Norma Oficial Mexicana*) were updated such that the term *mezcal* can only refer to certain specific agave-based beverages produced within certain defined geographic areas.

While the Mexican state of Oaxaca is the traditional center and leading producer of mezcal, the NOM allows for the production of mezcal in a total of nine Mexican states. In addition to Oaxaca, approved production areas include the Mexican states of Guerrero, Durango, San Luis Potosí, Puebla, and Zacatecas; as well as portions of the states of Tamaulipas, and Michoacán—plus the town of San Luis de la Paz (located in the state of Guanajuato).

A range of agave plants are approved for use in the production of mezcal, and the rules also allow for the use of "other agave species" as long as they are not specified in the use of other NOM-regulated beverages within the same state. This means that a range of plants are used to produce mezcal, resulting in a selection of unique and artisanal beverages.

Figure 13.12: Prepared agave *cabezas*

LIQUEURS

A liqueur is a spirit that has been sweetened and flavored. This is a large and diverse category of spirits as liqueurs are produced in a range of styles and flavors, as well as in many different parts of the world.

Simply put, a liqueur is produced using a base spirit that is compounded or redistilled with fruits, fruit juices, spices, flowers, or other natural flavorings. Under United States law, liqueurs must have a sugar content of at least 2.5% (by weight of the finished product); however, most liqueurs are much sweeter. Liqueurs are consumed all over the world and, on many occasions, are appreciated as pre-meal aperitifs, post-meal digestifs, or as part of a recipe for a cocktail or mixed drink.

THE ORIGINS OF LIQUEURS

Beginning in the Middle Ages, liqueurs were created for use as medicinal remedies, love potions, and general cure-alls. This use of liqueurs, created using plants, herbs, and spices that were chosen for their health-giving properties, continued until the eighteenth century. However, by the beginning of the nineteenth century, medical science and chemistry had evolved, and liqueurs began to be appreciated for their flavors and sophistication in many parts of Europe.

Soon, France and Italy were the leading producers of liqueurs, while other countries specialized in certain types of products. Holland became known for orange-flavored liqueurs. Germany gained fame for its herbal products, notably caraway seed preparations. Denmark and Spain found fruit and spice combinations to be very profitable. Scotland and Ireland produced liqueurs using their whiskeys as a base for fruit and herbal concoctions.

The twentieth century brought a large and diverse assortment of liqueurs to the worldwide market, and this trend continues today.

TYPES OF LIQUEURS
Within the diverse universe of liqueurs, there are two main classes: generic and proprietary.
- Generic liqueurs include general flavor categories and may be branded but not trademarked. Thus, there are many similar products on the market.

- Proprietary liqueurs are the exclusive property of their creators and are made according to a unique recipe, even if the liqueur may fit into an existing flavor category.

For example, there are many generic products called coffee liqueur; however, both Kahlúa and Tia Maria are unique, proprietary versions of coffee liqueur.

Liqueurs may also be somewhat loosely categorized into broad types according to the source of their key flavor, such as fruit liqueurs, botanical liqueurs, liqueurs flavored with beans, nuts, and seeds, cream liqueurs and whiskey liqueurs.

Table 13-5 provides examples of both the generic and proprietary liqueurs within the various categories described above.

Table 13-5: Liqueurs by Category

Category	Flavor	Generic Example	Proprietary or Branded Examples
Fruit	Orange	Triple Sec	Cointreau Grand Marnier
	Melon	Melon Liqueur	Midori Melon
	Cherry	Maraschino Liqueur	Luxardo Maraschino Cherry Heering
	Raspberry	Raspberry Liqueur	Chambord
Botanical	Mint	Crème de Menthe	Bols Peppermint Liqueur
	Violet	Crème de Violette	Crème Yvette
	Elderflower	Elderflower Liqueur	St. Germain
	Ginger	Ginger Liqueur	Canton
Beans, Nuts, or Seeds	Hazelnut	Crème de Noisette	Frangelico
	Cacao	Crème de Cacao	Godiva Chocolate Liqueur
	Coffee	Coffee Liqueur	Kahlúa Tia Maria
Whiskey	Scotch Whisky	Whisky Liqueur	Drambuie
	Irish Whiskey	Irish Cream	Bailey's Irish Cream Irish Mist
	Bourbon	Bourbon Liqueur	Jeremiah Weed

BITTERED SPIRITS (AMARI)

The beverage world abounds with spirit amari (bittered spirits), which may be made in a variety of styles and flavors. The sweetened versions of bittered spirits may technically be classified as liqueurs. Others may be categorized as proprietary or specialty beverages that do not easily fit within the typical spirit classifications. Spirit amari are often flavored with a complex botanical blend; some even claim to contain more than a hundred ingredients as part of a secret formula.

Amari (the plural of *amaro*, the Italian word for *bitter*) are very popular in Italy, where they are commonly consumed neat or on the rocks, either before or after a meal as an aperitivo or digestivo, respectively. Amari produced in Italy are also the most likely versions of spirits amari to be distributed in the United States and other locales outside of Europe. Some of the more popular Italian versions include Fernet Branca, Campari, Averna, and Aperol.

France is also an avid producer of bittered spirits, and is home to Chartreuse and Bénédictine, among others. Many other European countries produce an iconic bitter, such as Hungary's Unicum and the Czech Republic's Becherovka. The top-selling bittered spirit in the world, Jägermeister, is made in Germany.

COCKTAIL BITTERS

Cocktail bitters are a flavoring agent that remain quite reminiscent of their historical style and use as health "potions" or rudimentary medicines. While always bitter, some may be bitter and sweet in equal measure, and all are made to proprietary formulas from roots, herbs, spices, flowers and other ingredients. Cocktail bitters are generally used, in very small portions such as a drop or two, as a flavoring agent in cocktails, mixed drinks, and non-alcoholic beverages. A drop of bitters can transform the flavor of a beverage, adding dimension, balance, and depth. Many classic cocktails, including the Manhattan, the Old Fashioned, and the Sazerac include a drop of cocktail bitters.

Some examples of traditional cocktail bitters include Angostura Bitters (produced in Trinidad), Fee Brothers, and Peychaud's Bitters (a must-have in the Sazerac recipe). Many contemporary brands are produced, such as Bittermens "Very Small Batch" bitters (which come in a range of flavors from hopped grapefruit to gingersnap), and Bitter Truth Bitters, produced in Germany (in flavors such as lemon, celery, and chocolate).

A career in hospitality often affords one many opportunities, such as the chance to travel the world and sample a wide range of cuisines. In addition, a hospitality professional's job often involves the ingestion of alcohol to some degree, including during training, sales, wine dinners, and trade tastings.

This can present a unique set of challenges in terms of health and safety for the individual as well as serious legal and liability issues for a business. This chapter looks at the best practices for the responsible service of alcohol, the steps to take to limit the liability of a business and its employees, and the current research on the risks and potential benefits of alcohol consumption.

Please note that nothing contained in this chapter or in the Study Guide as a whole constitutes medical advice. Such advice should only be obtained from a licensed medical professional.

RESPONSIBLE BEVERAGE ALCOHOL SERVICE

In many parts of the world, third-party liability and negligence laws affect anyone who serves beverage alcohol, whether in a food and beverage establishment, at a wine tasting event, or in one's own home. In the United States, there are a number of states that now require all servers of beverage alcohol to show proof of having successfully completed an acceptable, responsible, service-training program.

While some states require any public server of alcohol to have completed their own programs, most states recognize the validity of two programs that are offered throughout the United States and internationally: the National Restaurant Association's ServSafe Alcohol and TIPS (Training for Intervention ProcedureS). Regardless of local requirements, having such certification can reduce liability insurance premiums for any server or employer. In EU countries, laws tend to be even more stringent than the laws in the United States, and there is a concerted effort to counter alcohol abuse.

The Society of Wine Educators regards responsible beverage alcohol service to be a significant issue and encourages all persons involved in the hospitality industry to be properly trained and certified.

Although the food and beverage industry cannot be responsible for all of the problems associated with excessive alcohol consumption, professionals involved with beverage alcohol can ensure that their behavior promotes responsible consumption of alcoholic beverages by doing the following things:

- Checking identification as a matter of routine in every case in which there is doubt about a customer's age
- Recognizing the signs of intoxication and refraining from serving anyone who exhibits signs of intoxication
- Declining to serve any customer who appears to have consumed excess alcohol elsewhere
- Encouraging impaired customers to call for a cab or contact a friend to get a ride home, or offering to make the call oneself
- Persuading the customer to surrender the car keys when warranted
- Observing responsible and reasonable standards in serving and consuming alcohol so as to set a good example for fellow employees and friends

HARMFUL EFFECTS OF ALCOHOL

When ethanol, the main chemical in alcoholic beverages, is absorbed into the bloodstream, it enters the brain, where it induces feelings of pleasure. A moderate intake of ethanol at the appropriate time may be pleasurable; however, some of the effects of ethanol, particularly at higher doses, may be unwanted and have serious consequences.

The dangers of the abusive consumption of alcohol are well-known and publicized:

Intoxication: When alcohol is absorbed, it affects the brain's ability to further regulate its intake. This can lead to intoxication as the buildup of acetaldehyde in the bloodstream occurs. Acetaldehyde is a by-product of the metabolic process of ethanol in the liver and is more toxic than ethanol itself. When one becomes intoxicated, motor skills, speech, judgment, and the ability to drive become greatly impaired. In some cases, intoxication can lead a person to commit violent acts and exhibit socially inappropriate behavior.

Alcohol-Related Diseases: Consumption of alcohol can increase the risk of serious diseases such as cirrhosis, a potentially fatal liver condition. Additionally, studies have shown that 100 ml of ethanol a day (equivalent to just over a bottle of wine) may cause a condition known as fatty liver, in which fat accumulates within the cells of the liver. If alcohol consumption ceases, the condition can be reversed. Cirrhosis, however, cannot be reversed and may result from continued alcohol abuse. Alcohol consumption may also increase the risk of developing many types of cancer, especially cancers of the mouth, esophagus, stomach, and breast. Other risks include stroke, high blood pressure, and heart attack.

Alcohol Abuse: Individuals who abuse alcohol for extended periods of time often develop a tolerance. When this occurs, more and more alcohol is required to achieve past effects, and the likelihood of addiction greatly increases. Addiction can lead to severe problems with health, finances, relationships, and career. Prolonged, excessive drinking also contributes to several psychiatric conditions, such as depression.

Binge Drinking: In developed countries, alcohol ranks third among risks to health and is the largest cause of premature death in people between the ages of 15 and 29. This is largely because young adults may "save up" their drinking for one big night out a week, a practice known as binge drinking. Binge drinking may result in a rapid rise of alcohol in the bloodstream and also contribute to a host of alcohol-related incidents, such as motor vehicle accidents and fatal alcohol poisoning.

Figure 14-1: All things in moderation

BENEFITS OF MODERATE CONSUMPTION

There is strong evidence to support the claim that some degree of alcohol consumption may be beneficial to human health; however, there is no universally accepted "safe" level of consumption. The USDA recommends up to one drink per day for women and up to two drinks per day for men as a definition of moderate consumption. The definition of one drink is as follows:
- Wine (12% to 14% abv) – 5 ounces (148 ml)
- Beer (5% abv) – 12 ounces (355 ml)
- Spirits (40% abv) – 1.5 ounces (44 ml)

Studies have shown that the overall lowest mortality rates occur at this level of alcohol consumption, while the highest rates occur in heavy drinkers. Moderate alcohol intake has been shown to reduce the risk of dementia and Alzheimer's disease, osteoporosis, certain types of cancer, and stroke. Extensive studies indicate that moderate drinkers tend to have lower mortality rates than those who abstain or drink very rarely.

Perhaps one of the biggest potential benefits is the decreased risk of developing coronary heart disease. Studies have shown that in people who drink moderately, the risk is reduced by at least 20%. This is due to ethanol's clot- and plaque-reducing properties. However, this effect is only significant in people who are actually at risk of developing coronary heart disease.

Another important point to consider is that alcohol increases blood pressure, so a generalization cannot be made that a moderate amount of alcohol is beneficial for every individual. Furthermore, some individuals may be more prone to addictive behavior than others and should abstain from alcohol, as potential health risks far outweigh any possible benefits.

RESVERATROL

Wine drinkers tend to be better protected against coronary heart disease, dementia, Alzheimer's disease, stroke, osteoporosis, peptic ulcers, and many types of cancers than those who drink beer or spirits. Many studies attribute this to resveratrol, a potent phenolic compound present in grape skins and seeds, and therefore often present in significant levels in red wine. There are many phenolic compounds present in wine that are responsible for color and tannin content, and they are all powerful antioxidants that help to protect cells from free-radical damage.

However, it is resveratrol that has received the most attention for its anti-aging, disease-preventing, and cancer-fighting properties. It may even be an effective treatment in those with type 2 diabetes, helping the body to overcome insulin resistance. When weighing the potential health benefits associated with alcohol consumption, it is important to remember that these benefits occur only in certain doses and in certain individuals. There are many factors to consider, including gender, weight, medical history, and genetic makeup. More specifically, a healthy limit of alcohol for women is generally lower than that for men because women's bodies tend to metabolize ethanol more slowly. Additionally, some individuals are unable to tolerate even a moderate level of consumption due to the lack of a specific genetic enzyme needed to metabolize alcohol effectively.

THE DECISION TO IMBIBE

The decision to imbibe, and how much, should depend on one's specific situation. It would, of course, be ill-advised to consume alcohol to protect from one disease while putting oneself at greater risk for another. For example, alcohol has been shown to increase the risk of breast cancer in women. The risk may be lessened if the alcohol is red wine, consumed at a moderate level (1 to 1.5 glasses per day); however, at higher levels of consumption, this effect is nullified.

The greatest benefits of alcohol consumption to health have been shown to occur when alcohol is consumed with meals, preferably at the same time each day, and not in excess of the recommended servings. Consuming alcohol with food slows down its absorption, which is healthier for the liver, kidneys, heart, and nervous system.

173

CHAPTER FOURTEEN THE RESPONSIBLE USE OF BEVERAGE ALCOHOL

SOCIETY OF WINE EDUCATORS • BEVERAGE SPECIALIST CERTIFICATE

ADDITIONAL RESOURCES

GLOSSARY

Acid: The class of chemical compounds that produce a tart, sharp, or biting character in wine; see also lactic acid; malic acid; tartaric acid; citric acid; total acidity

Adjuncts: Non-essential, fermentable ingredients used in beer production for stylistic reasons, economic reasons, or for flavor

Agave: A genus of succulent plants in the amaryllis family

Aguamiel: Spanish. Honey water; the unfermented sap of the agave plant that is used to make an assortment of fermented and distilled beverages

Alcohol: The by-product of yeast and sugar; the intoxicating element of wine; see also ethanol

Ale: A top-fermented beer; the family of top-fermented beer styles

American Viticultural Area: An officially recognized wine region (appellation) in the United States

Americano: 1. A category of aromatized, fortified wines that may be flavored with wormwood or gentian; 2. A cocktail made with Campari, vermouth, and club soda

Añejo: Spanish. Aged; a classification with various meanings depending on the product to which it refers

Angel's Share: The portion of an aging spirit that is lost to evaporation during barrel maturation.

Anthocyanin: A type of pigment found in plants that gives grapes and wine a blue, purple, or red coloration

Appellation: A specific name, based on geography, under which a wine grower is authorized to identify and market wine, spirits, or other products; the area designated by such a name; see also Denomination of Origin; a geographical indication

Appellation d'origine contrôlée (AOC): French. The highest category of quality wine or wine region in France; a protected designation of origin (PDO)

Appellation d'origine protégée (AOP): French. Term used to designate the highest category of quality wine or wine region in France within the EU's overarching labeling protocol (equal to appellation d'origine contrôlée [AOC]); a protected designation of origin (PDO)

Arabica: A species of coffee considered to be high quality due to its acidity, flavor, and complexity

Armagnac: A French grape-based brandy produced within the delimited area in the department of Gers

Aroma: A sensory characteristic detectable by the olfactory senses of the nose

Aromatized wine: A wine-based beverage flavored with aromatic botanicals

Artemesia: A genus of herbs often used as a bittering or flavoring agent, a specific type of which is often referred to as "Wormwood"

Bereich: German. A regional or district appellation (plural Bereiche)

Bianco: Italian. White

Blanc: French. White

Blanc de blancs: French. 1. Literally, white from whites; 2. A white wine made entirely from white grapes, usually used to describe sparkling wines

Blanc de noirs: French. 1. Literally, white from blacks; 2. A white wine made entirely from red (black) grapes, usually used to describe sparkling wines

Blanco: Spanish. 1. White; 2. A label designation for rum and tequila indicating a spirit that is colorless and unaged; synonymous with plata or silver

Blush: Pink, typically referring to a rosé wine that is off-dry to sweet

Bodega: Spanish. 1. Winery. 2. Wine cellar. 3. Wine shop or market

Botrytis (*Botrytis cinerea*): Noble rot; a fungus that, under appropriate conditions, draws water out of grapes and thereby concentrates the sugar content (while simultaneously adding distinctive flavor elements)

Bottle-conditioned: A beer that has been produced using a second fermentation in the beer bottle in order to trap the resulting carbon dioxide

Brandy: A potable spirit produced from the distillation of wine or (in some cases) the fermented mash of fruit

Brewing: 1. The stage of beer production that involves the boiling of the wort; 2. The preparation of infused beverages such as coffee and tea

Brew pub: A public house or bar that both produces and serves beer

Brussels lace: The traces of foam left by beer (as it is consumed) on the interior of a glass

Caffeine: A central nervous system stimulant found naturally in the seeds, nuts, and leaves of some plants, including coffee beans and tea leaves

Caffeol: A fragrant oil found in coffee beans

Calvados: An apple brandy made in the delimited area within France's Normandy department

***Camellina sinensis*:** The tea plant; an evergreen plant indigenous to Asia

Carbonic maceration: An intracellular fermentation process that may occur in whole, unbroken grapes in the absence of oxygen and without the use of yeast

Chaptalization: Adding sugar to grape juice before fermentation to increase the alcohol content of the finished wine

Château: French. A wine estate, particularly in Bordeaux (plural châteaux)

Cider: A lightly alcoholic, fermented beverage produced from apples

Cinchona bark: The bark of an evergreen shrub, native to South American, sometimes used as a medicinal herb or a bittering agent

Clarification: The process of removing haze and particulate matter (from wine)

Cognac: A grape-based brandy produced within the delimited regions of the Charente and Charente-Maritime departments of France

Conditioning: The process of maturing a beer for a short time following the completion of fermentation

Congeners: Compounds produced during mashing, fermentation, distillation, and wood aging that contribute to the unique flavor profile of fermented and distilled products

Crema: The desirable layer of foam on the surface of espresso

Cupping: The formalized sensory evaluation of coffee

Cyser: A type of fermented beverage related to cider but produced from a combination of apples and honey; sometimes referred to as "apple mead"

Decanting: Moving wine from a bottle into another container (decanter) for the purposes of aeration and/or separating the wine from sediment

Denominação de origem controlada (DOC): Portuguese. The highest category of wine or wine region in Portugal; a protected designation of origin (PDO)

Denominación de origen (DO): Spanish. The second highest category of wine or wine region in Spain; a protected designation of origin (PDO)

Denominación de origen calificada (DOCa): Spanish. The highest category of wine or wine region in Spain; a protected designation of origin (PDO)

Denomination of origin: 1. The name of an officially recognized quality wine region; 2. The region itself; see also appellation; geographical indication

Denominazione di origine controllata (DOC): Italian. The second highest category of wine or wine region in Italy; a protected designation of origin (PDO)

Denominazione di origine controllata e garantita (DOCG): Italian. The highest category of wine or wine region in Italy; a protected designation of origin (PDO)

Distillation: The separation and concentration of the alcoholic content of a fermented liquid by a series of evaporation and condensation processes

Districtus Austriae Controllatus (DAC): The highest category of quality wine in Austria

Dry: Not sweet; lacking perceptible sugar

Enology: The science of wine and winemaking

Espresso: Strong, rich coffee brewed by forcing a small amount of nearly boiling water under pressure through finely ground coffee beans

Estate: Typically, a winery that owns and makes wine from the vineyards that surround it; may also be used for a distillery, farm, or other facility

Esters: Odiferous compounds that occur due to reactions between acids and alcohols and are thus responsible for many of the aromas detected in certain wines, beers, and spirits

Ethanol: The principal alcohol found in wine

Fermentation: A complex biochemical process by which yeast cells convert sugar to alcohol and other chemical compounds with carbon dioxide and heat as by-products; see also carbonic maceration; malolactic fermentation

Flavor: A sensory characteristic detectable as a combination of taste, aroma, and tactile sensations

Flight: A selection of products (such as wines or spirits) presented together for purposes such as sensory evaluation and comparison

Fortified wine: Wine to which distilled spirits have been added to raise the final alcohol level, generally to 15% or higher

Geographical indication: 1. The name of an officially recognized wine or spirits region; 2. The region itself; see also appellation; denomination of origin; protected geographical indication

Germination: The process by which a plant begins to grow from a seed, often part of the preparation of grain for use in the production of beer or whiskey

Gin: A distilled spirit that has been flavored with juniper berries

Green Coffee: Processed but unroasted coffee beans

Grist: Milled grains

Hectare: A metric unit of surface area, equal to 2.47 acres

Hops: A vine plant harvested for its resin and essential oils; the flowers of the hops plant are used to provide bitterness and aromas to many styles of beer

Indicazione geografica tipica (IGT): Italian. The higher category of basic wine in Italy, from a protected geographical indication (PGI)

Indigenous (varieties): Native to the area; not imported

International varieties: Grape varieties that have been widely transplanted to winegrowing areas in many parts of the world

Junmai: Japanese. Sake that has not had brewer's alcohol added during the production process

Keeving: An artisan-style cider production method that results in a lightly sweet, low-alcohol product

Kilning: The stage of grain preparation where heat is used for the purpose of drying (often germinated) grains, as used in the production of beer and/or whiskey

Koji: Japanese. A mold used in the production of sake

Kura: Japanese. 1. Brewery; 2. A sake-making facility

Labrusca (*Vitis labrusca*): A species of wine grape native to North America

Lager: A bottom-fermented beer; the family of bottom-fermented beer styles

Lagering: The process of the cool fermentation of beer, followed by maturation in cold storage

Lautering: In the context of beer production, the process of separating the wort from the spent grain

Lees: Sediment found in wine during and after fermentation, consisting primarily of dead yeast cells and grape solids

Legs: Streaks produced by viscous droplets of liquid that run slowly down the interior of a glass of wine after swirling; see also tears

Liqueur de tirage: French. A mixture of yeast and sugar added to a base wine to initiate a second fermentation and create a sparkling wine

Liqueurs: Sweetened, flavored spirits

Maceration: The soaking of grape skins and other solids in grape juice or newly made wine in order to extract color, tannin, and other phenolics from the skins and into the liquid; may occur before, during, and/or after fermentation

Malolactic fermentation: A biochemical process by which lactic bacteria convert malic acid to lactic acid, thereby reducing a wine's acidity and altering the flavor profile

Malted Barley: Barley that has been steeped in water and allowed to germinate in an effort to activate the enzymes in the barley to convert the starches to fermentable sugars

Malting: The process of steeping a grain in water and allowing it to germinate; the germination process activates enzymes that are used to convert the grain's starches into fermentable sugar

Mash: A slurry made by mixing grist with hot water in a container such as a mash tun; used in the production of beer and whiskey

Mash Bill: The grain recipe used to produce a specific whiskey

Mashing: The process of combining milled grain with water and heating this mixture; used in the context of the production of beer or whiskey

Mezcal: A distilled spirit produced similarly to tequila but made primarily in Oaxaca, Mexico, from a variety of agave subspecies

Molasses: A by-product of sugar production; a thick, black-colored sugary liquid that remains after all of the commercially salable sugar crystals have been removed.

Moromi: Japanese. The fermenting mash, as used in the production of sake

Moto: Japanese. A yeast starter used in the production of sake

Must: Unfermented grape juice, may also include skins, seeds, and stems

New Make: The spirit resulting from the distillation process, prior to any aging or maturation

New World: For wine and spirits purposes, all countries outside Europe, or the styles of product typical of those countries

Nihon-shu: Japanese. The proper Japanese term for the fermented rice beverage referred to in English-speaking areas as "sake"

Noble rot: A term used in France and elsewhere to refer to the beneficial form of botrytis; see also pourriture noble

NOM (Norma Oficial Mexicana): An official government standard that is regulated by a division in the Mexican government

Off-dry: Having a small amount of perceptible sugar

Off-odor: An unpleasant or atypical aroma in a wine

Off-premise: Away from the place of business; specifically, the segment of the wine industry that sells wine for consumption elsewhere, such as wine shops and supermarkets; cf. on-premise

Old World: For wine and spirits purposes, the countries of Europe, or the traditional product styles of those countries

On-premise: At the place of business; specifically, the segment of the wine industry that sells wine for consumption on-site, such as restaurants and wine bars; cf. off-premise

Organoleptic: Relating to the sensory qualities (such as taste, color, aroma, or texture) of a substance (such as a food or beverage)

Oxidation: Chemical changes that take place in the presence of oxygen

Oxidized: A wine that has undergone oxidation; such a wine may show discoloration as well as a stale, flat aroma and flavor

Perry: A lightly alcoholic, fermented beverage produced from pears

Pomace: The residue left after grapes are pressed, consisting of skins, seeds, stems, and other solids

Pomace Brandy: A spirit made from the grape solids (pulp, skins, seeds, and stems) left after fermentation and after pressing

Potable Spirit: A beverage fit or suitable for drinking

Pot Still: A type of still used in the distillation of spirits that require a batch process, whereby the liquid must be distilled twice in order to achieve the desired strength.

Pourriture noble: French. "Noble rot"; botrytis

Proof: An historical scale used to measure the alcohol content of a spirit; in the United States, the proof is two times the percent of alcohol by volume

Protected designation of origin (PDO): The legal category of officially recognized quality wine regions used throughout the European Union

Protected geographical indication (PGI): The legal category of officially recognized wine regions below the quality wine level used throughout the European Union

Pyrolysis: A heat-induced type of chemical decomposition of a substance such as the darkening of coffee beans during roasting

Quinquina: An aromatized wine flavored with cinchona bark

Recioto: Italian. A style of sweet wine made from dried grapes

Reposado: Spanish. Rested. A classification of tequila designating those products that have been aged at least two months but less than one year, usually in very large wooden vessels

Residual sugar: Sugar that remains (in a wine) after fermentation, usually measured in grams per liter (g/L) or percent

Resveratrol: A phenolic compound found in grapes that is believed to have beneficial health effects for humans

Rhum: French. Rum. Used to denote the difference between rum products of the French West Indies and those produced in all of the other islands and countries around the Caribbean Sea

Rhum Agricole: French. Agricultural rum. Rum made from fresh sugarcane juice, as opposed to molasses, from which rhum industriel is made. Martinique has an AOC for its rhum agricole

Robusta: A species of coffee known for its high yield and robust flavor

Rum: A spirit distilled from the fermented products of the sugarcane plant in the form of sugar, sugarcane juice, or molasses

Saccharomyces cerevisiae: The species of yeast most widely used in winemaking

Sake: Japanese. 1. In the Japanese language, a catch-all term for alcoholic beverages, 2. In English-speaking countries, a beverage produced from the fermentation of polished rice

Scratting: The process of grinding fruit into a pulp in preparation for the production of cider or other similar beverages

Scrumpy: A term used to describe certain artisanally-produced ciders such as those typical of the West Country of England

Sparging: A step in the production of beer where water is sprayed over the grain bed to draw out the wort

Sparkling wine: Wine that contains dissolved carbon dioxide under pressure so that it produces bubbles spontaneously when its bottle is opened

Spirit: A liquid containing ethanol (ethyl alcohol) and water that is the product of distillation

Steeping: Soaking by prolonged immersion; may be used in the context of preparing grains for fermentation or in the preparation of coffee or tea

Still: 1. Not sparkling; 2. A piece of equipment used for distillation

Sulfur dioxide: The most common form of sulfur in wine; a preservative

Sur lie: French. "On the lees," referring to wine that has had extended time in contact with dead yeast cells

Tannic: Containing high levels of tannin

Tannin: A phenolic compound found in grapes that gives wine a somewhat bitter taste and a distinctive mouth-drying feel

Taste: A sensory characteristic of a wine detectable by the taste buds of the tongue and mouth

Tears: Streaks produced by viscous droplets of liquid that run slowly down the interior of a glass of wine after swirling; see also legs

Tea liquor: A liquid made by steeping hot water together with tea leaves

Terroir: The all-inclusive physical environment of a vineyard or farm

Tisane: An infused beverage made from herbs, spices, or other botanicals; often called "tea" or considered a type of tea but containing ingredients other than tea leaves

Trub: The residue left over during the brewing of beer; coagulated proteins that settle to the bottom of the kettle during and after the brewing stage of beer

Varietal: Relating to a grape variety

Varietal wine: A wine made primarily with a single grape variety and named for a single grape variety

Variety: A named type of grapevine with recognizable characteristics; more or less synonymous with subspecies

Vermouth: An aromatized, often fortified wine that has been flavored with some version of the Artemesia herb

Vinifera (*Vitis vinifera*): The species of wine grape native to the Middle East and Europe that is used to produce most quality wine

Vinification: The process of winemaking

Vintage: 1. The year in which grapes were harvested; 2. A style of wine, generally used in reference to sparkling or fortified wine

Vodka: A somewhat neutral, often unaged spirit made from many base ingredients and in many parts of the world

Whiskey: A spirit distilled from a grain product; sometimes spelled whisky

Wormwood: A specific type of herb of the genus *Artemesia*, often used as a bittering or flavoring agent

Yeast: A living, single-celled organism used for many purposes, including the production of fermented beverages

BIBLIOGRAPHY AND SUPPLEMENTARY READING

The following works include sources used in the preparation of this guide and additional references that may be useful to candidates.

GENERAL

Dominé, André. *The World of Spirits and Cocktails: The Ultimate Bar Book. Cambridge*, UK: Tandem Verlag, 2011.

Dornenburg, Andrew and Karen Page. *What to Drink with What You Eat: The Definitive Guide to Pairing Food with Wine, Beer, Spirits, Coffee, Tea - Even Water - Based on Expert Advice from America's Best Sommeliers.* Boston: Bulfinch Press, 2006.

Gasnier, Vincent. *Drinks: Enjoying, Choosing, Storing, Serving, and Appreciating Wines, Beers, Cocktails, Spirits, Aperitifs, Liqueurs, and Ciders.* New York: DK Publishing, 2005.

Walton, Stuart, and Brian Glover. *The Ultimate Encyclopedia of Wine, Beer, Spirits & Liqueurs: The Definitive Reference Guide to Alcohol-Based Drinks.* London: Hermes House, 2011.

COFFEE AND TEA

Gaylard, Linda. *The Tea Book.* New York: Dorling Kindersley Publishing, 2015.

Heiss, Mary Lou, and Robert Heiss. *The Story of Tea: A Cultural History and Drinking Guide.* Berkeley: Ten Speed Press, 2007.

Hoffman, James. *The World Atlas of Coffee: From Beans to Brewing—Coffees Explored, Explained and Enjoyed.* London: Mitchell Beazley, 2014.

Kingston, Lani. *How to Make Coffee: The Science Behind the Bean.* East Sussex: Ivy Press, 2015.

Pendergrast, Mark. *Uncommon Grounds: The History of Coffee and How It Transformed Our World.* New York: Perseus Books, 2010.

Rao, Scott. *The Professional Barista's Handbook: An Expert Guide to Preparing Espresso, Coffee, and Tea.* Scott Rao: 2009.

Ulh, Joseph. *The Art and Craft of Tea: An Enthusiast's Guide to Selecting, Brewing, and Serving Exquisite Tea.* Beverly, Massachusetts: Quarry Books, 2015.

WINE

Bastianich, Joseph, and David Lynch. *Vino Italiano: The Regional Wines of Italy.* New York: Crown Publishing Group, 2005.

Clarke, Oz. *Bordeaux: The Wines, the Vineyards, the Winemakers, revised and updated.* New York: Sterling Epicure, 2015.

Goldstein, Evan. *Wines of South America: The Essential Guide.* Oakland: University of California Press, 2014.

Goode, Jamie. *The Science of Wine: From Vine to Glass*, 2nd ed. Berkeley: University of California Press, 2014.

Immer, Andrea. *Great Wine Made Simple: Straight Talk from a Master Sommelier.* New York: Broadway Books, 2005.

Johnson, Hugh, and Jancis Robinson. *The World Atlas of Wine*. 7th rev. ed. London: Mitchell Beazley, 2013.

Julyan, Brian. *Sales and Service for the Wine Professional*. 3rd ed. London: Cengage Learning, 2008.

Kolpan, Steven, Brian H. Smith, and Michael A. Weiss. *Exploring Wine*, 3rd ed. New York: John Wiley, 2010.

MacNeil, Karen. *The Wine Bible*, 2nd ed. New York: Workman, 2015.

McCarthy, Ed, and Mary Ewing-Mulligan. *Wine for Dummies*. 6th ed. Hoboken: John Wiley, 2015.

Robinson, Jancis. *How to Taste: A Guide to Enjoying Wine*. New York: Simon & Schuster, 2008.

Robinson, Jancis, Julia Harding, and José Vouillamoz. *Wine Grapes*. New York: Harper Collins Publishers, 2012.

Skelton, Stephen. *Viticulture: An Introduction to Commercial Grape Growing for Wine Production*. London: S.P. Skelton Ltd, 2009.

Zraly, Kevin. *The Windows on the World Complete Wine Course*, 30th Anniversary Edition. New York: Sterling Publishing, 2014.

BEER, SAKE, AND CIDER

Brown, Pete, and Bill Bradshaw. *World's Best Ciders: Taste, Tradition, and Terroir*. New York: Sterling Epicure, 2013.

Dekura, Hideo. *Sake: Discover the Culinary Pleasures of Sake's Long Relationship with Japanese Cuisine*. London: New Holland Publishers, 2015.

Gauntner, John. *The Sake Handbook: All the information you need to become a Sake Expert!* North Clarendon, VT: Turtle Publishing, 2002.

Hishinuma, Hayato, and Elliot Faber. *Sake: The History, Stories and Craft of Japan's Artisanal Breweries*. Gatehouse Publishing, 2015.

Huckelbridge, Dane. *The United States of Beer: A Freewheeling History of the All-American Drink*. New York: Harper Collins Publishers, 2016.

Jackson, Michael (editor). *Eyewitness Companions: Beer*. New York: DK Publications, 2007.

Jolicoeur, Claude. *The New Cider Maker's Handbook: A Comprehensive Guide for Craft Producers*. White River Junction, VT: Chelsea Green Publishing, 2013.

Markowski, Phil. *Farmhouse Ales: Culture and Craftsmanship in the Belgian Tradition*. Boulder, CO: Brewer's publications, 2004.

Oliver, Garrett. *The Brewmaster's Table: Discovering the Pleasures of Real Beer with Real Food*. New York: Harper Collins, 2003.

Watson, Ben. *Cider, Hard and Sweet: History, Traditions, and Making Your Own*. 3rd ed. Woodstock, VT: The Countryman Press, 2013.

Webb, Tim, and Stephen Beaumont. *The World Atlas of Beer, Revised & Expanded: The Essential Guide to the Beers of the World*. New York: Sterling Epicure, 2016.

SPIRITS

Broom, David. *Gin, the Manual*. London: Mitchell Beazley Publishers, 2015.

Broom, David. *Vodka: A Toast to the Purest of Spirits*. Chicago: Prion Publishing, 2015.

Brown, Jared and Anastasia Miller. *The Mixellany Guide to Vermouth and other Apéritifs*. New York: Harper Collins Publishers, 2011.

Curtis, Wayne. *And a Bottle of Rum: A History of the New World in Ten Cocktails*. New York: Random House, 2007.

Dominé, André. *The World of Spirits and Cocktails: The Ultimate Bar Book*. Cambridge, UK: Tandem Verlag, 2011.

Faith, Nicholas. *Cognac: The Story of the World's Greatest Brandy*. Oxford, England: Infinite Ideas, Ltd. 2013.

Gasnier, Vincent. *Drinks: Enjoying, Choosing, Storing, Serving, and Appreciating Wines, Beers, Cocktails, Spirits, Aperitifs, Liqueurs, and Ciders*. New York: DK Publishing, 2005.

Morgenthaler, Jeffrey. *The Bar Book: Elements of Cocktail Technique*. San Francisco: Chronicle Books, 2014.

Risen, Clay. *American Whiskey, Bourbon, and Rye*. New York: Sterling Epicure Publishing, 2013.

Rogers, Adam. *Proof: The Science of Booze*. New York: Houghton Mifflin Harcourt, 2014.

Sanchez, Alberto. *Tequila*. New York: Smithsonian Books, 2004.

Stewart, Amy. *The Drunken Botanist: The Plants that Create the World's Great Drinks*. Chapel Hill: Algonquin Books, 2013.

Williams, Ian. *Tequila: A Global History*. London: Reaktion Books, Ltd. 2015.

ADDITIONAL RESOURCES APPENDIX B: BIBLIOGRAPHY AND SUPPLEMENTARY READING

Made in the USA
Columbia, SC
05 October 2020

22133304R00106